·WILLIAM· WARFIELD

My Music & My Life

William Warfield with **Alton Miller**

SAGAMORE PUBLISHING INC.
Champaign, Illinois

Production supervision and interior design: Susan M.Williams
Cover and photo insert design: Michelle R. Dressen
Marketing: Katherine K. Dressel
Editor: Sara Chilton
Proofreader: Phyllis L. Bannon

10   9   8   7   6   5   4   3   2   1

Library of Congress Catalog Card Number: 90-64225
ISBN: 0-915611-40-6

Sagamore Publishing Co., Inc.
P.O. Box 673
Champaign, IL 61824-0673

Printed in the United States of America

"Train up a child in the way he should go, and when he is old, he won't depart from it."   Proverbs 22:6

My parents truly believed in this verse, and their children were the recipients of that belief. I dedicate this book to them in grateful and loving memory.

W.W.

I dedicate these efforts to my family, with love.

A.M.

*'Twant me, 'twas the Lord. I always told him, "I trust
to you. I don't know where to go or what to do, but I
expect you to lead me," and he always did.*

—Harriet Tubman

CONTENTS

ACKNOWLEDGMENTS

The authors are grateful for the help and many courtesies provided by Clifton Johnson and his staff at the Amistad Research Center, located at Tulane University in New Orleans. Dr. Johnson, who founded Amistad, has built a large collection of original materials documenting the ethnic history of America, including the personal papers of William Warfield. The Amistad Center is open, without charge, to all serious students of American culture.

The publisher was also aided by Andrew Simons of the Amistad staff, who devoted countless hours to researching photographs for this book.

Much of the William Warfield story would have been lost were it not for the assiduous and loving stewardship of memorabilia by his manager, Larney Goodkind. Most of his materials are now safely archived at Amistad, but Larney is a living repository of many more recollections of his years as William Warfield's friend and partner. He was generous with his time, and his contribution to this project was essential.

This book owes its original inspiration to Peter Bannon of Sagamore Publishing, who worked hard to shepherd it through its initial development. And no author could hope for more tender care than that provided by Susan Williams and Kathy Dressel, Sagamore's professionals who ensured that the final product saw the light of day.

I owe a particular debt of gratitude to my wife, Cindy Bandle, who shared a lifetime of enthusiasm about William Warfield before she ever met him—throughout the months that I was engaged in this labor of love.

—Alton Miller

FOREWORD

The story of a life that has been as full, as rich, as colorful, as beneficent as that of William Warfield can be expected to be fascinating. The actual story of the real William Warfield is more. An intriguing account of the interaction of enormous talent, noble ambition, deep spirituality, and ceaseless industry, the story that is revealed to our ear—for it is the speaking voice of William Warfield that we hear—offers an exemplar of hope and possibility amid the increasingly jumbled passions of contemporary American life. For, as Warfield reminds us ever so gently, this is an American story in which the varied timbres of African-American life are echoed and ultimately reconciled without regret and without apology.

Warfield's life has been full. His career has lasted over four decades and has included success in all the areas to which a protean singer could aspire. His mastery of the concert stage was established with his first Town Hall recital and confirmed by countless appearances in all parts of the world. He is a consummate oratorio singer. He has appeared with great orchestras and great conductors, all of whom have applauded his musicianship. He has achieved a mythic identification with the baritone roles in *Porgy and Bess* and *Show Boat*. Television and film have recorded his triumphs as singer and actor. Critical opinion regards him as one of the great singer-actors of the century.

Warfield's life has been rich, not primarily in its decor and perquisites, but in the myriad associations he has had in the world of the arts. Fortunate in his teachers and collaborators, he has consorted with a wide range of creative people. He has himself found fulfillment as singer, actor, and teacher.

Warfield's beneficence is legendary. Always conscious of the favorable forces under which his own career has unfolded, he has been unsparing in his generosity to friends and colleagues, to students and admirers. One service that he does not mention in his story is his years as president of the National Association of Negro Musicians, an organization to which he brought his prestige and industry at a crucial moment in its history.

Warfield reflects in his thought and work a sense of the past, of the broad cultural history of African-Americans as well as of the special pioneers who preceded him in the concert field. His frequent and reverential mention of Roland Hayes, Marian Anderson, Paul Robeson, and Todd Duncan bear ample testimony to this aspect of his vision. His sense of the future is evidenced by the commitment he has demonstrated to the art of teaching and to the close bond he has established with a host of students who know him as "Uncle Bill."

Above all, Warfield has always accepted the challenges of the moment, confident of his preparation for them, and determined to surmount them both as artist and humanist.

The Warfield story is a valuable addition to our collective epic of artistic hope and possibility.

Richard A. Long
Atlanta, 1991

Chapter One

TOWN HALL

A review in *Variety*, "the Show Business weekly," June 22, 1949: "New Acts," reprinted just as it appeared:

WILLIAM WARFIELD
Songs, Piano
35 Mins.
Club Norman, Toronto

Former baritone lead with "Call Me Mister" and "Set My People Free," William Warfield is taking a flyer in night club work and scores with his solid drive and delivery. (The baritone will play Cal in Marc Blitzstein's musical version of "The Little Foxes" skedded for Broadway opening in late October.)

Singer and self-accompanist is currently clicking at the Club Norman, Toronto, where he was signed for two weeks and has now been inked for four, with possible subsequent holdover. A bet for the better niteries, Warfield immediately reveals his concert training background (he majored in music at the Eastman School) but his stint, when caught, also proved that he is versatile in tempo and mood changes from dramatic ballad to low-groove blues and skat. His work at the piano is also outstanding in wicked-harmony technique.

Opened with "Dusty Road" and immediately won audience with his basic talent and well-mannered cordiality. Fine routining in changed tempos received solid reaction for vocalistics that need no mike and were showmanly selected. Numbers included "So in Love," an Irish vs. American arrangement of "Molly Malone," "Big Fat Mamma" and "Outskirts of Town," etc. Warfield has vocal power, deep feeling, and fine shading and phrasing. He's a bet for any spot where the emphasis is on class.

McStay

In its glib showbiz style, the *Variety* review just about summed it up: a class act, a well-trained voice, a versatility that covered the waterfront, from Eastman's classrooms to smoky club rooms — and yet here I was, pushing thirty, living in a hotel room in NewYork City, building a career based on a week's gig in Youngstown, two weeks, maybe four, in Toronto, and a Broadway role if I was lucky. The *Variety* review was a rave, and I should have been pleased. I *was* pleased — and yet in those glowing, quotable words of praise I saw highlighted the dilemma of the career I was trying to build.

Or was I building a career? I couldn't even be sure of that. I was moving in a world where the definitions were indefinite, where the career ladder was missing a few rungs, where I couldn't even be sure who my role models should be.

There was Paul Robeson, of course: Since his earliest triumphs, going way back to his sensational Town Hall debut in 1926, every tall, solidly built black baritone was going to be compared to him. Robeson had performed on stage and in films, as well as in concert halls in the U.S. and abroad. Since his 1936 success in *Show Boat*, "Old Man River" had become a standard item in every black baritone's repertoire.

And there was Todd Duncan, another awesome baritone, who had created the first Porgy in Gershwin's *Porgy and Bess*, back in 1935. He was big on the concert stage, and he had also broken new ground for black classical singers by becoming the first black man to perform with a major opera, in *Pagliacci* and

Carmen with the New York City Opera. At the same time he had begun to develop his reputation as a teacher of music at Howard University, in Washington, D.C. — and he was somehow managing both careers together.

And then there were the two giants of the art, Roland Hayes and Marian Anderson. Hayes had, like me, been born to a family of Southern sharecroppers, and had gotten his start in the church choir. It was—and is—an inspiration to read how he had lifted his natural talent from Curryville, Georgia, to his debut at Boston's Symphony Hall. But it was just as important to remember that the debut didn't open any doors for him in the United States; like many of our artists of color, he had found it necessary to travel to Europe to study and perform before he was able to come back to his own country as a respected artist. Finally he had become renowned and showered with honors, including a string of honorary doctorates. He too was on his way to academe, on the music faculty of Boston University.

Marian Anderson had come under Roland Hayes's wing while she was still a teenager in Philadelphia giving church recitals. Her congregation collected contributions to allow her to study with the masters, and she won first prize in the New York Philharmonic competition in 1924. But her Town Hall debut didn't receive much press attention, and she too had discovered that she had to study and tour in Europe to be accepted in her own country. In Europe she had finally earned the recognition she deserved — Toscanini pronounced that "a voice such as this comes once in a hundred years" — and by the time she returned to America she was what today we call a superstar. In 1939— fifteen years before the civil rights movement gathered steam— she had caused a national sensation, when the Daughters of the American Revolution refused to let a black woman sing in their Constitution Hall. Through the intercession of the White House, she performed for 75,000 on the steps of the Lincoln Memorial, and Eleanor Roosevelt tore up her DAR card.

Paul Robeson, Todd Duncan, Roland Hayes, Marian Anderson. They were great artists who had achieved a life in art that I wanted to emulate. They were African-Americans, and had shared many of the experiences I had known, which helped me even more to identify with their accomplishments. But times were changing. Should they be my role models?

Now, in the summer of 1949, other black artists were

revolutionizing the world of mainstream popular music, which was just beginning to open up. To jazz musicians in New York that year, "The Street" was West 52nd between Fifth and Sixth Avenues, where singers like Billie Holiday, Ella Fitzgerald, and Sarah Vaughan had migrated from their Harlem haunts some time in the mid-'40s. Black and white worked easily together on The Street, and artists like Miles Davis were developing "cool jazz," a form of music that crossed not only racial but also cultural bounds. It was becoming clear that there was a whole new field of serious popular music growing up from black roots, for artists like Nat King Cole, Oscar Brown, Jr. — and William Warfield, if he wanted it.

And I did want it. I wanted it all. I wanted *Show Boat* and *Porgy*, as well as Brahms and Fauré. I wanted the spirituals along with the boogie-woogie, and grand opera too. I wanted the Hollywood film and I wanted the bistro gig, the international tour and the White House command performance. I wanted to teach music, to bring to a new generation the lessons of my life in art. I wanted to play a role in world culture — not just "Negro culture," not just "Western European culture." I shared the dream of every artist, regardless of his or her origins, to find my patch in that great tapestry of art. If West Helena, Arkansas, wasn't big enough for my sharecropper daddy, the East Coast cocktail lounge circuit wasn't big enough for my career. I wanted all the wonders of music, a taste of everything that the muses had to offer.

The *Variety* review confirmed what audiences were already telling me: I had a future in music. And I knew something they didn't: The pop sounds for which I was being praised were not the best part of my musical talent. As much as I enjoyed playing and singing those tunes, I was not born for nightclubs any more than my daddy was born to pick cotton. I was somehow going to spring from The Street to the concert stage.

But it was far from clear how I'd be able to make the leap. There were weeks when I was down to counting my pocket change, and it was hard to continue to entertain my high ambitions when I was worrying about next month's rent.

A debut at Town Hall, yes, that would be important. Though that was no guarantee of a career, as my precursors had proven, it was a critical first step, a showcase that could help launch a new talent. And then perhaps I should spend some time overseas, building a reputation. Or should I go back to Eastman for my master's degree, then get a teaching job and begin to build my base in academe? The choices would depend on whether I could show my stuff to the critics in a Town Hall recital.

The people I looked up to had all done it, each in his or her own way. They had proved it could be done, but none of that experience could be directly translated and applied. In the year of our Lord 1949, there was as yet no established curriculum for a black classical singer.

Yet, somehow, I had no doubt that things would fall my way. "Consider the lilies of the field," wrote St. Matthew, "how they grow; they toil not, neither do they spin," yet they managed to stay pretty well dressed. I couldn't quite follow the rest of that saintly advice though: "Take therefore no thought for the morrow: for the morrow shall take thought for the things of itself." I knew I had to have a plan. But somehow, somewhere, in my soul, I had been blessed with a conviction that things would work out for the best. Whichever way I turned, I believed that I would find the life that I was meant to live. Preparation plus opportunity equals luck — that was the equation. In that sense, one way or another, mine had always been a charmed life.

I had registered with the General Artists Corporation agency back when I first hit New York, and GAC kept me listed for club dates. I had also auditioned for Columbia Artists, an agency that worked with presenters in cities and on campuses across the country, booking concerts and recitals. And I had auditioned for the Sol Hurok organization, trying to get on the short list of singers handled by the great impresario. He paid his artists a retainer and managed every aspect of their careers; it would be not only prestigious but artistically nurturing to be under the protection and management of Sol Hurok.

General Artists had found me club dates in New York and in cities and towns as far afield as the Club Norman, a classy joint in Toronto where I had played several times and was developing a real following. And now I had been recognized as "versatile" by *Variety*. But I was still no closer to a career in classical music. Each way I turned, I ran into the circular logic of show business: An agent couldn't do much for me until I was "known," and I couldn't get "known" if I didn't have an agent working for me.

I used my free time wisely; when I wasn't working I was usually studying. As a World War II vet, I qualified for G.I. Bill scholarship aid, and put it to work under the auspices of the American Theatre Wing — vocal training with a European master, Yves Tinayre, and developing my classical repertoire with the pianist and teacher Otto Herz.

I even had an occasional opportunity to perform some of that literature. For instance, I was scheduled to sing Handel's *Messiah* with the Rochester Oratorio Society when I went home for the Christmas holidays at the end of the year.

But when I went, I knew I would be tempted once again to resume studies at the Eastman School of Music at the University of Rochester; I had an open invitation to complete my master's and then teach there. That was coming up in December — and who could say? Maybe this time I'd listen to parents and friends who wanted me to stay home, and give up the New York rat race.

In the meantime, though, my manager and friend Larney Goodkind was leaving no stone unturned to develop my career. He knew, better than most, that there was no clear path for me. He was forever promoting me for roles in the theater and encouraging my club dates, yet still reminding me that I had a gift for greater things. He knew music, and he believed in me. He and his wife, Karen, a literary agent, had a wide circle of friends whom they could enlist for help, once the main chance presented itself — the opportunity to perform in a traditional debut recital before the New York critics.

Larney and Karen had seen me through my recent disappointment. My big chance for a Town Hall debut had been the Naumburg Foundation's vocal competition, which every two years pitted new voices against one another. First prize was an all-expenses-paid recital at Town Hall. In 1947, my first full year in New York, I had gone all the way to the finals. That time I had given little attention to the other competitors, and concentrated on my own work.

When I failed to win first place that time around, I chalked it up to experience. I redoubled my efforts, and devoted myself in private classes and in solitary practice, to improve my voice and to add more of the classical literature to my repertoire. Over two years, while struggling to earn a living, I worked hard on my art; whenever I wasn't playing bebop or up-tempo spirituals in clubs to pay the bills, I was working on Schubert lieder.

Finally, in the spring of 1949, fully prepared and finely tuned, I brought myself to the Naumburg Competition once again, and once again made it easily to the finals. This time I was completely sure of myself. First, I knew how it worked and was comfortable with the mechanics of competition — not a small consideration for a performer, and often a stumbling block for one who has the art and even the stage presence but little experience before judges. Also, this time I paid attention to the other contestants, and I could see for myself that there was no one who would be likely to place higher. Finally, and most importantly, I knew myself to be at the peak of my powers, as ready as I would ever be. I went into the finals full of confidence.

So it was a severe disappointment when the winners were announced, and I had not taken the Town Hall prize. At a stroke, my best chance for a new career had been eliminated.

Reviews like the glowing report in *Variety* were reassuring, and I was optimistic that I could make a good living in pop music, if I were willing to settle for that. *Regina*, Marc Blitzstein's musical treatment of Lillian Hellman's *The Little Foxes*, opened and closed, and my role in it added a little more experience, another wrinkle to my brow, and another credit to my resume; maybe the stage would add some dimension to my art. My classes and coaching were going well. But I felt no closer to the career track I had been working toward.

I never lost my customary smile — not a brave smile but a grin of real enjoyment — and yet, hopeful as I was, I was always just a little disoriented. I knew that I was still working on the periphery of my real calling. I simply wasn't clear on how I was going to make a break into the center of the action.

That was the state I was in the night at the Club Norman in Toronto when I was invited to join Walter Carr at his table. I was walking past his table when he rose, stuck out his hand, and said, "Hello, my name is Walter Carr. Do you have a minute?"

I had seen him in the club before, always in the company of a younger woman who may have been his wife. She had complimented me in passing once or twice, and seemed sincere in her appreciation; he usually regarded me with something of a squint, not unkindly. He had been pointed out to me as a Canadian financier, a magnate among the leading local gentry, reputedly an accomplished huntsman when he wasn't making million-dollar deals in Canada and the U.S.

It was a week before Christmas. I had just done my last show of the Club Norman booking, and now I was hoping the good weather would hold up for my trip to Rochester first thing the next morning. Unwilling to turn down the chance to sing in the Oratorio Society's *Messiah*, I had agreed to the tight scheduling: I was due to sing it the very next day. This last show at the Norman had gone well, and it was clear to me that I had developed a loyal following at least as strong as the club's other regular headliner, Oscar Peterson.

I had done my usual mix, music that pleased the crowd as much as it pleased me. It included Cole Porter's "Night and Day," Duke Ellington material, and all the songs from Hammerstein's *South Pacific*; then I might drop into a skat tune, like "Straighten Up and Fly Right," and then change the pace with "The Toreador Song" from *Carmen*.

Though I was thinking about my *Messiah* the next day, and ruminating about the possibility of settling down and completing my studies, some part of me still was reconciling to the life of supper clubs like the Norman. It was in that mood that I came to the table of Mr. Walter Carr.

He wanted to buy me a brandy. I had finished my last set, so I took him up on it.

"Manya has a high opinion of you," he let me know, nodding toward his attractive companion. "She says you have a superbly trained voice." I smiled at the compliment, and she smiled back. "She tells me that this man is trained for more than the music we're hearing. Is that so?" I told him yes, I had graduated from the Eastman School of Music. I had been trained for a classical music career. Manya nodded as she listened; her ear hadn't been wrong.

"Then why are you working nightclubs?" His question was not belligerent, but it was more than polite curiosity. His tone somehow reminded me that my father, back when I was a kid, had forbidden me to play in a local club.

I told him I was doing club dates to pay the rent, but that I had been studying and rehearsing for the concert stage. I didn't know exactly how my classical music career would unfold, I told them, but I was sure it would, somehow.

"What would it take?" he wanted to know. "What does a career like yours involve?"

It was the old question, with no pat answer. There simply wasn't "a career like mine." I would have to invent it for myself. But one thing I knew for sure. "Everybody in this business wants a Town Hall debut," I said. "That's probably the best way to make yourself known. You get some decent reviews, and then you can give the agencies something to work with. It's a good way to give your career a push." I was about to tell him of the Naumburg Competition, and my vague plans for taking another shot at it, when Carr cut through to the heart of the matter: "What would it cost?"

"Pardon me?"

"A Town Hall debut. What would it cost?"

It so happened that I had a rough idea of the minimum expenses. Renting the hall with a piano; advertising and publicizing would cost something, Larney would arrange that. My teacher, Otto Herz, could accompany me. "I don't know," I said, "about a thousand dollars. My manager, Mr. Goodkind, has the details, but it's about a thousand."

Carr took a sip of his brandy, and I found myself studying him more closely. I had seen him frequently at the club, often enough to witness the respect he commanded from the owner, the maître d', and the staff. It also occured to me that he looked tired. Carr was probably in the prime of life, but he looked a little less lively than the first times I'd seen him with Manya at Table One. Or maybe it was just that I'd never been this close to him.

Finally Carr said, "When I was a younger man, at one point in my career I was strapped. I had a world of opportunity ahead of me, but I was at a roadblock and I needed one person to do something for me. That person came through, and that's why I'm here today. I've always told myself that sometime in my life I'd do the same for someone else." He pushed his brandy away, and pulled a slim leather wallet out of his dinner jacket.

"Here's an advance," he said, as he counted out six hundred dollars in U.S. currency. "Have your manager work up some figures and let me know what else you need. Let's get you out of the clubs and onto the concert stage."

That winter Larney pulled out all the stops to make my Town Hall debut a success. Among his friends were Isadora Bennett and Richard Pleasant, two of the best-connected promoters and publicists in the business. Yul Brynner, who was just getting hot, was one of their clients, and they were in the enviable position of being able to trade tidbits on Yul for small favors from top columnists like Leonard Lyons and Walter Winchell. Larney arranged for Bennett and Pleasant to hear a private recital, and succeeded in communicating his enthusiasm to them.

They were key to our effort, because they were able to trade favors, cash in some chits, and see to it that first-string music critics would open our Town Hall invitation, keep it in their stack of "maybes," and ultimately put the Sunday afternoon performance, by a complete unknown, on their calendars: 3:00 p.m. on March 19, 1950.

When the day arrived, my teacher-turned-accompanist Otto Herz and I were occupied with the technicalities of performance. So I didn't pay much attention to Larney's business. He and Karen were clearly excited about the event, but they were always so supportive that I didn't attach any special significance to their anticipation. I was completely matter-of-fact about my preparation. It hadn't even occurred to me that I'd want my family to come down and be a part of the event; as close as we were to one another, I never urged that they attend, and they weren't there.

I knew this Town Hall debut was going to be an important rite of passage, but I didn't realize it would be the moment that would change my life. My hero, Roland Hayes, had triumphed in his debut and then remained an unknown for years. Somewhere, way in the back of my mind, was some notion that I'd have to face some reviews in tomorrow's papers. At best, I hoped, a modest success would make it easier for me to get the attention of the impresarios and agencies. If I could get one or two decent reviews, together with the *Variety* review of my club act, Larney would have something to work with.

Even when I stepped out onto the stage that afternoon, there was not a flicker of the stage fright that sometimes afflicts even the most seasoned performer. Otto Herz was playing for me, as he had so many afternoons. The preliminary chords of Heinrich Schuetz's "Eile mich Gott zu erretten" were in my ear, and in my heart — "Hurry, Lord, to save my soul." I took a deep breath, opened my mouth, and did what I came to do. All the emotion I felt was for the music, not the moment.

Nowhere in the music of that final Sunday of winter was there the vaguest notion that my life was about to change forever— that I'd be waking up the next morning with my name at the top of the column in all the major dailies; that I'd be seeing photographs of myself in all the weeklies, the monthlies; that I'd soon become practiced at plucking out the boldface type, "William Warfield," in the celebrity columns — and seeing those same two words typed neatly on so many contracts for tours and recitals.

My whole attitude that afternoon was almost blasé. If I'd had any idea of what was about to break, I might at least have urged Larney to get on the phone and try to cut some deals. But I didn't, because I didn't know. And anyway, he never had a chance, because on March 20 the phone never stopped ringing.

WILLIAM WARFIELD SCORES
IN RECITAL
(Ross Parmenter, New York Times,
March 20, 1950)

William Warfield, the baritone who was heard earlier this season in Marc Blitzstein's musical drama, "Regina," showed yesterday afternoon in his first New York recital at Town Hall that he is also a highly gifted concert singer. It was an auspicious debut.

He is endowed with a noble voice, warmth of temperament, a feeling for the stage and great sincerity. And since his discharge from the Army Mr. Warfield has worked hard to develop his gifts, first at the Eastman School of Music and then with the American Theatre Wing. In between he has sung in night clubs. Perhaps the most striking thing about him yesterday, aside from his splendid voice, was his range of style. In the three Karl Loewe songs in his lieder group, for instance, Mr. Warfield turned in quick succession from the light charm of "Kleiner Hausalt" to the lyric tenderness of "Suesses Begraebnis" to the spirited vigor of "Odins Meeres-Ritt."

It was a tour de force, for ordinarily one would think it would take a soprano to carry off the first, a tenor the second and a bass the last. Yet the singer did each practically perfectly in its own way. He had the necessary variety of approach. And the agility and range of his voice made it possible for him to summon all the necessary colors.

One of his new songs was "The Ledo Road," a narrative by John Klein about American soldiers in India. As he sang it one was apt to think Mr. Warfield's forte was for ballads. Yet one remembered that only a group before he had sung Fauré's "La lune blanche luit dan les bois" with the sweetness of tone and sensitivity of the truly lyric singer.

The baritone called his first group "Songs of the Believer" and he mingled the spirituals of his own people with the religious music of Schuetz, Perotin, Handel and Monteverdi. This revealed still another facet of his talent, for he also has the gifts of the oratorio singer.

Mr. Warfield held his listeners with everything he did, and they revelled in his voice for its pure sound, from its warm, rich depths to its particularly beautiful soft high tones. And he won them still further in his encores, when he supplanted Otto Herz at the piano and played his own accompaniments for two Jubilee Shouts.

Walter Carr wasn't in the audience that night. Larney and I called him in Toronto the next day, to share the triumphant reviews with him. And then we rang up him again, a few days later, to give him an update on the activities, including an immediate offer from the Australian Broadcasting Commission for my first international tour. I tried to describe the madness of the continuing press notices and celebrity column items that had been appearing all week.

He took a paternal pride in the proceedings, but though he was pleased, he didn't seem surprised that my career was ballooning overnight. I detected a slightly gruff impatience in his voice at the other end of the phone, that seemed to scold me. His words were brief and complimentary, but his tone suggested, "Of course you did well. All my investments do. Now stay the course."

He hadn't been able to leave his business for the March debut, but I had a performance in Rochester in May, and he drove down from Toronto to hear me, and to meet my family. It was a good day for all of us, but what I remember most vividly are his final words to me. He said, "If I ever hear of you singing in a night club again, you know I'm a very good shot. I'll give you a hundred yards and I'll catch you right in the ass."

In June, three months after the debut he made possible, Walter Carr was diagnosed with lung cancer; within days he was dead. He had never mentioned the pain he was going through. But I have no doubt that he considered his debt to life, his repayment of his own good fortune, paid in full.

By one of the strange coincidences of my life, on my first Australian tour later that year I met a young Scotch-Irish musician who came to hear me sing, and then came backstage to introduce himself. He was a fan of mine, he said. He wanted me to come hear the jazz ensemble he had put together. I don't know what gave him the confidence to insist I should give him a hearing; I'm easy to talk to, but it must have been more than that. Perhaps it was just because it was so unusual for him to have access of any sort to a musically trained American black man; perhaps he aspired to be a member of the family of music and felt that I, as an American, would understand his feeling for jazz.

In any case, though my performing schedule was hectic, I found that I couldn't refuse him the time to go to the club where he was playing, and pay him the courtesy of listening to the group. It turned out to be worth the trip — they were good, and I urged him to audition for the Australian Broadcasting Commission. I was able to impose on my tenuous ties with the commission to arrange a hearing for his ensemble.

It's one of those show-biz stories, so unlikely and yet so typical. Through my connections they gave him an audition, he did well, and the last I heard he was in England, enjoying a solid career as a jazz musician — a career that got launched at that radio audition.

I don't know what gave him the nerve to approach a black American stranger to give him a hearing. But I know what made the suggestion irresistible to me. Even at the age of thirty, I had already lived long enough to know that I had a charmed life, and I never passed up an opportunity to follow a remarkable coincidence wherever it might lead. When the enthusiastic young jazzman summoned the courage to introduce himself to me after my show, he certainly arrested my attention: "Hello, fine show, my name is Walter Carr. Do you have a minute?"

Chapter Two

MY FAMILY

My family has always been important to me. If my life has been truly charmed, the blessings began well before I came into the world. There is probably no weaker enthusiasm than the one you try to work up for someone else's family stories, but you're going to have to bear with me — or skip a few pages — because I couldn't give an account of my own life without including the people who brought me here.

Like many Southerners, I was raised in a warm extended family that went beyond blood ties. In the world of the arts you often find yourself in a different kind of extended family — no genetic relationship at all, but strong bonds nonetheless. And in the world of education it's the same: By the time I became "Uncle Bill" Warfield to an ever-growing extended family of students and proteges at the University of Illinois, I had come full circle to the nurturing environment in which I grew up.

It may sound strange to hear William Warfield described as a Southerner. I do consider myself, in some important sense, a child of Arkansas. I was lucky to be raised in Rochester, New York. But I was just as lucky to be nourished by my Southern roots. I had the best of both.

You see, I was the oldest child in my family, and all our adults were Southern born, Southern bred, spoke that Southern talk, cooked that Southern cooking. We moved from Arkansas when I was still too young to remember much. Although I have a few fleeting impressions of that early life, I suspect that most of my memories have been enhanced by stories I was told by the older folk as I was growing up in Rochester. Still, I have a rich sense of my origins.

Rochester in the Twenties and Thirties was a place where the "colored" and the Polish and the Irish and the Italian grew up in the same mixed neighborhood, where the ethnic differences that separated us were usually no more significant than the varied aromas that wafted out of our mothers' kitchens — spicy tomato flavors from the Madafferis, greens and ham hocks from the Warfields — while we played together in our adjoining back yards. I would have missed that if I'd stayed in the small Mississippi River town of West Helena, Arkansas, where I was born.

But underneath, I was an Arkansas boy from tip to toe, from my mama's milk to the stories I learned at my daddy's knee. I wouldn't have traded my Rochester childhood for any other — but I couldn't have chosen a richer heritage than the one that flowed in our Mississippi blood, even away up there on Lake Ontario.

If I hadn't been surrounded by my family — mother and father, Grandma Annie and Aunt Lillie and the rest, who knew what it was to pick cotton and truck it to market — I might have lost the roots of my culture, I might have remained forever with only half a soul. I'm lucky I was blessed with the best of both.

Roots are tricky things — the way they tangle, you can find almost anything you want to, if you look hard enough. For African-Americans who try to trace their names, the tangles can get very interesting. I can't track all the way back to the "old country," of course — but how many people of any color really can?

On my mother's side, my Grandma Annie was part Indian, she told me. Her parents, Susan and Craft Greer, were both slaves, in Clarendon, Arkansas, and weren't freed until the Civil War. Susan was half Indian, and it showed in the soft glow of Grandma Annie's smooth olive skin.

There was an Indian heritage on my father's side, too, or so the old folks used to tell us. My father's mother, Grandma Gilliam, said that our Warfield name originally came from an Englishman who married an Indian woman. The first Warfield we know of was a free black, Charles, who married a freeborn woman, Georgann, and had six children — the oldest, William, a middle son, George, and the youngest, Charles. Charles was my grandfather, Grandma Gilliam's husband.

I don't know much about Great-Grandfather Charles, but my father's father, Charles, was a very handsome man, very debonair, something of a Mississippi legend in his day. It's not clear what he did for a living — he was probably a salesman — but whatever it was, it took him up and down the Big Muddy from St. Louis to New Orleans. I never met him, but the family says that my father's brother Emmett was his spit and image. Like my father, Uncle Emmett was slender and well-built, with fair skin and greenish eyes. But like Grandfather Charley, he was taller than average, and when you see photographs of either man, you have to look twice or you'd think you were looking at a picture of a white man.

Charles Warfield was the inspiration for many a family story — and apparently he had his impact on other families as well. My cousin Idella, George Warfield's daughter, remembers her Uncle Charles well. She has told me, "Bill, if anybody comes up to you and says, 'I'm a Warfield,' they probably are. Your granddaddy left Warfields all up and down the Mississippi. No grass grew under his feet!" At some point he settled down long enough to marry my Grandma Ginny. Their union produced my Uncle Lee, Uncle Walter, Aunt Mary, and my father, Robert. They also raised another boy who was not Ginny's son, Emmett Warfield. My father, Robert, was always close to his half-brother Emmett when they were children. Later, when their fortunes took them in different directions, it would be Emmett who would play the key role in my father's career.

In his early years in Helena, Robert might have seemed destined to keep his father's randy family traditions alive. He was a completely worldly young man, famous for his skill on the guitar, the life of the party at all the local joints. He cut a fine figure with the ladies, my mother used to tell me.

My mother, Bertha McCamery, lived on a farm in nearby Ferguson, Arkansas. "Daddy" Ward — who was not her daddy — raised cotton, corn, peanuts, hogs, horses, and mules. He was also a handyman, with skills that could supplement his farming talents with a cash income.

Daddy Ward was not Grandma Annie's first husband. They had no children of their own. Bertha and her sisters, Ethel and Lillie, were all McCamerys. There were two brothers, Thaddeus McCamery — everyone called him Bud — and Murphy Greer. For reasons that were never clear to us, my Uncle Murphy was raised by Grandma Annie's parents, the Greers, and took their name. But whatever it was, apart from the different last name there was never any sense that Murphy was anything but family.

The McCamery girls were all raised in that traditional Southern style, with a certain modest reserve that is only partly successful in covering up the liveliness underneath. They were taught to behave as young ladies should. But they were also beauties, and as spirited as their mother, my Grandma Annie.

Bertha was one of those girls who is the most popular in her set, the young lady that everyone has their eye on and expects great things from. It would have caused no surprise among her friends that she was attracted to my father; he was such a "dangerous" gallant sort that all the young women fluttered around him. But it must have created something of a stir when he proposed and won her hand. Some would have considered him an unlikely catch. Others might have thought she could have done better, with someone more stable. But those would have been people who didn't see in him what she saw.

In 1918 he was twenty, a year and a half younger than she, but he carried himself with such assurance that the difference wouldn't be evident. He wooed her and won her, with his guitar picking and his footwork on the dance floor — but also with an implicit promise of great things to come.

The natural expectation would be that they would take up the life of tenant farmers, sharecroppers who would pick cotton in season and carry it to the mill where they'd be paid by weight; and then eke out their meager cash income by growing their own greens and potatoes. And so they did, at first. But anyone who knew them later could not reconcile the restless intelligence of my father, or the soft-edged resolution of my mother, with that kind of life. And I have no doubt that my father gained new purpose when he took his bride. Gallivanting with the guitar was fine for a young blade, but I'm sure he instinctively knew he was called to higher things, and my mother no doubt knew it too, very early on.

While they were still newly married, he made the decision that would change his life and his family's fortune forever. In the

Baptist tradition, you might say it was a decision that was made for him by a Higher Power — he received "the call" to the ministry.

As he later described it to me, it was not something he wanted. "It was more like Jonah and the whale," he told me. "I was having a good time. Left to my own devices, I never would have become a minister."

My mother, too, later told me it was at first an unwelcome surprise. When I was still a boy, some years later in Rochester, I remember an afternoon when she was frying some fish, and a neighbor came over to visit, bringing two bottles of beer. I had never seen her drink beer before, and I'm sure my surprise showed on my face. "Oh, honey," she explained, "I've always liked to have a beer now and then, but I gave that all up when your daddy got the calling to the ministry." She explained to me then that when she was younger she "didn't want to be a minister's wife for anything in the world." But she loved him and wanted to support him in what he did. "Whither thou goest, I will go," she quoted from the Bible. My Aunt Lillie later told me, too, "Your mother just loved to party, but she gave that all up, and never looked back."

My father had never gotten beyond what passed for the sixth grade, in the segregated school system of Helena, Arkansas. It was clear to him that he would need to complete his education if he were to follow his new calling. Immediately when he received the call, he began making plans to join the black exodus out of the South, toward the land of opportunity in the North.

I was born January 20, 1920, while the family was still in West Helena. My mother suggested I become Robert, Jr., but my father felt strongly that his firstborn should not be stuck with a "junior" label. His name was Robert Elza Warfield, but the first Warfield that we knew of in our family line had been named William. The name he chose for me was William Caesar Warfield. He must have liked the sound of that combination — maybe he had an intuitive sense for the power of a name, and wanted to give me one that would fortify my soul. I've never been completely comfortable using Caesar, or the initial C, but I like to reflect on the leonine pride and great expectations he must have felt, holding his new son, as he came up with that name that he had found in the Bible.

Considering that I was born just as my father was turning to the ministry, when I think of all the Biblical monickers he could have come up with, I suppose I should consider myself lucky I didn't become Jehosephat Warfield. Two years later my father had softened up to the idea of having a junior in the family. Or maybe he was wise enough to understand that a second son needed some distinction to set him apart from the firstborn. In any case, his next son came along in 1922 — my brother Robert Elza Warfield, Jr. Sometimes I think I might have a flicker of a memory of those early days in Arkansas, but it's more likely I've absorbed the stories my Grandma Annie used to tell me — of how they would take me out in the fields with them, grandmother, aunts, all down there picking cotton together, and I'd ride around on Grandma Annie's cotton sack, "just sittin' there gigglin' and carryin' on all day." I was a "very good baby," she testified, but she was certainly not an impartial witness. Being the first grandson, I took my Aunt Lillie's place in Grandma Annie's heart; Lilly had been her baby, the youngest among her brothers and sisters, so now I became the darling of the family.

I once described another vague recollection to my Aunt Emily. I remembered sitting on a bale of hay and looking out over a wide green expanse of tall trees, hedges, and gently rolling fields. She said, "Bill, you know what you're doing? You're describing the big door over the barn that looked out into the meadows where we lived. We used to play there, and we had to watch out that the baby — you — didn't get too close to the edge." I had to stay planted in my spot, an imperative I probably took so seriously that the moment became indelibly inscribed in memory.

About that time Lillie married a man named Dallas Lee and moved with him to Rochester, New York; Aunt Lillie became the first of our family to make that trip north. All over the South, in those years after World War I, black and white sharecroppers and Appalachian miners and back country farmers were learning of new opportunities in the industrial states up north, and a great wave of migration was beginning. From Rochester, Aunt Lillie had written of a society where blacks as well as low-income whites could get a free high school education, maybe even dream of going to college. Of course, we'd need a stake to carry us for as long as it would take to get established there.

Through the grapevine, my father learned that a strong man, willing to work hard, could make a living and save some money by working in the meat packing plants of St. Joseph, Missouri. As "immigrant labor" from the Deep South, he'd be competing with immigrants from Europe who were vying for the same jobs; and he'd be running up against much of the same racial tension that he'd be likely to experience anywhere else. In fact, he'd be leaving the relatively placid environment of a medieval economy in West Helena for the turmoil and tussle of a "big city" like St. Joe.

But at the same time my father would be breaking out of the mold, breaking away forever from a quiet but stagnant rural life that held no opportunity for him and his growing family. And he'd be paid in cash, not credit at the co-op or scrip at the company store. He'd have to do it in stages — travel alone to St. Joseph and find work, then put enough aside to be able to pay for the family's move. Once we were all in St. Joseph, he'd have to make the next step to Rochester alone again, and get himself situated securely enough to bring the family along with him. But once there, in Rochester, he would be able to go to night school, eventually get his high school diploma, and then move on toward his calling as an ordained minister.

So, still filled with the spirit of his calling, Robert Warfield made that first fateful step alone. Years later he told me of the tribulations, large and small, associated with such a daring move. Of all the difficulties of finding work and making a new life in a strange new culture, the most touching that I recall is his story of his first meal in a nonsegregated restaurant. Halfway through dinner, he dropped his fork on the floor, and sat there stricken — "I almost panicked, I was so nervous," he told me. "I was so afraid someone was going to notice me and that I would be disgraced." The Warfields had a long way to go.

That was in 1922, when I was two years old and my brother Robert, Jr., was about to be born. As soon as he could, my father sent for the family, and we spent three years in St. Joe. Grandma Annie and Daddy Ward came with us; this was not an individual escape but an uprooting of the entire family. My father's mother, Grandma Gilliam, had remarried after Charlie Warfield passed away. She wasn't part of this move, and didn't get back into the family picture for several years—but that's getting ahead of the story.

The year after we moved to St. Joe my mother was expecting again, and she was sure that this time God would give her a little girl. She even had a name picked out, one that had always been a favorite of hers: Ernestine. In April 1924 the child was born: a third son. Mother had become so resolved on that name that her little boy was named Vernestine. Needless to say, he went by the name of "Vern," and never discouraged anyone who surmised that his given name must be Vernon. We were still in St. Joe when the fourth son, Murphy Lee Warfield, was born in January 1925, two days after my fifth birthday.

That was the year Daddy was finally ready to make his next move. For over two years he had been working in that packing plant, always with his plan clearly in front of him. Now he took the next step, to Rochester, and before long he had gotten himself situated there and sent for the family to join him.

We were safely in Rochester, but in some sense we never left the South. Like American blacks everywhere, we pored over the news in the Negro press, especially the *Pittsburgh Courier* and the *Chicago Defender*. Stories that the major media rarely reported, we got to read every week: lynchings, schools and churches burned out, graphic pictures of blacks whipped and hung on trees. All the way through my teens, I carried the sense that through my parents' hardships I had been blessed with a priceless advantage.

Just as Dutch or Danish Jews must have shuddered at the stories that would filter out of Nazi Germany during those same years, we would gather for our weekly editions of information out of Mississippi, Alabama, Arkansas, and suffer to learn of things that might be afflicting people we knew, or people like them.

From our safe vantage in Rochester, I must confess, there was often the sense that all these terrible things were happening in a foreign land. By contrast, we were safe in our melting pot, surrounded by a vigorous tradition of tolerance. People went out of their way to trumpet the principles of brotherhood and mutual accommodation; they believed in those principles, and were proud of them, and proclaimed them inseparable from the idea of America itself. In the years of the reckless Roaring Twenties and then throughout the Great Depression, the same spirit prevailed.

If my first gift was the gift of life given me by my family, my second was given me by my extended family in Rochester: They gave me the chance to form my character in a climate of tolerance and remarkable good will. It's a quality of civilization that too many people today seem to have forgotten, but it used to be the norm.

Chapter Three

GROWING UP

As I've already said, my boyhood days in Rochester were about as normal as they come: lessons and sandlot games on schooldays, chores and movies on Saturdays, church on Sundays. (Except that in my household those Sundays started on Friday night and didn't end until Monday morning.) My father was fulfilling his dream of becoming a Baptist minister.

Even before the whole family had completely made the move from St. Joe and settled in Rochester, my father was in night school earning his diploma, and making his introductions in the Baptist community. He had found a new home church and had come under the wing of a mentor, the locally celebrated Dr. James Rose, pastor of the leading black congregation in Rochester, Mount Olivet Baptist Church.

Dr. Rose must have been impressed with my father's potential. From being a member of the church, my father progressed through a series of apprentice positions to his own storefront congregration across town —as assistant pastor at Aenon Missionary Baptist Church.

As a "mission," Aenon was something of a satellite to the prestigious Mount Olivet. From time to time Dr. Rose would come to our small church with the Mount Olivet choir, and my father would preach to an augmented assembly. On other Sundays, particularly when there was baptizing to be done, we would go across town to Mount Olivet and participate in their services. When I was of age — in the Baptist faith, twelve years old — I was baptized in Mount Olivet's large heated pool, completely immersed as is our tradition.

Those early years of my father's ministry must have been hard on the family, but you'd never know it from the mood around our house. A fourth son, Murphy, named for Uncle Murphy Greer, had been born in St. Joseph in 1925, and a year later, when we were getting settled in Rochester, Walter was born. Five boys born in six years were a handful for the young parents, but they both enjoyed their family and we all delighted in being together.

In those first difficult years, the church was the center of our lives — not just for my father's work, but for much of our socializing as well. It was in the church, like so many young Baptists, that I had my first "theater" experience.

I can remember it vividly. Every year we had a Christmas program in the church, with all the children, from kindergarten on up, saying their piece. When I was about five years old, soon after we arrived in Rochester, I made my debut. They stood me up in the pulpit chair, and my speech was,

What ch'all looking at me for?
I didn't come here to stay.
I just come here to let ch'all know
That this is Christmas Day.

*   *   *   *

My mother was responsible for a big share of the family income. She took in laundry and did ironing for a while. And then she began to do weekend baking, starting well before the sun came up on Saturday morning, so she could deliver fresh-baked rolls and pies and cakes that folks would order. She'd bake again, early Sunday morning. By the first church service, she'd be out of her apron and in her pew, wiped clean of flour but still faintly redolent of cinnamon and allspice, the perfect pastor's wife.

This was before the era of instant powders and pre-mix, remember. In Rochester we'd buy our produce from the farmer's market whenever we could, even live chickens, and Mother would make up pig's feet, chitlins, stove-top cornbread. She'd prepare chicken stock using the feet and just about any other part but the beak. Cooking was more than a matter of cranking up the microwave; as a total process it was complex and fascinating.

She was a fabulous cook, and all the Warfield boys have turned out to be pretty good chefs as a result. That started one evening when I came home and said, on a sudden impulse, "Mom, I'll help you make dinner." I worked alongside her, fascinated with both the logic and the art — building from the raw elements into the finished product.

I was learning, and I was being entertained, but it wasn't until after dinner that I discovered I was benefiting in a way I hadn't expected. "Bill was helping in the kitchen tonight," Mother told the family as we began to clear the table. "He doesn't have to do the dishes." The result was that my brothers all figured out it was a lot more interesting to help before dinner than to be in the clean-up squad afterwards. We all learned how to cook.

My mother had a lovely, lyric, light soprano voice, and though she was too shy to use it as well as she might, it had a purity that has never faded in my memory. We had a practice, in our Sunday service, of standing up and sharing a testimonial. My mother was too shy, I suppose, too private to rattle on about what she felt. When it came her turn to testify, she sang a little song *a capella*: "This little light of mine — I'm going to make it shine." She sang the verse, and then said with a blush, "That's my testimony." And sat down. She did that, all her life; she did let it shine.

Whatever her original misgivings might have been about his calling, she was my father's perfect helpmate. A pastor, any pastor, assumes enormous responsibilities — psychological and spiritual but also sometimes physical and economic — for those he serves. No matter how young he might be, he is looked to for paternal counsel at every turn. For those who are sick or convalescing, for those who are aging, for those who are beginning to experience the confusions of youth, and for everybody in between, the pastor is expected to be all things to all people, on call twenty-four hours a day.

On top of that, the pastor has to create, every week, a message of inspiration and even scholarship, and he has to prepare himself for its delivery. Add to that the maintenance and accounting and housekeeping duties of a one-man operation like Aenon Baptist—and then keep in mind that the holidays that are for others a time of recreation are, for a pastor, the busiest times of the year — and you get some idea of the kind of burden it can be.

As he well knew, my father couldn't have done it without my mother. How they managed all that, and to raise a large family as well, still makes me shake my head in wonder. But she was devoted to my father, and supported the long hard period of his apprenticeship without seeming to give up anything of her own; and they were both devoted to their children, with a commitment that was doubtless hardened through long days of self-dedication in the Arkansas cotton fields as they were laying their plans to leave for the North.

She directed the household when he was away; and in the evening she'd become the stage manager, turning any potential family dispute into an orderly flow of activities. And whenever he was working on a sermon, she'd be after us: "Don't be making all that noise."

Though she was completely focused on raising her family, providing for her husband and her own brood, she was also full of care for anyone who needed her, family or not. She had her faith and she had her hope, but above all she had her *caritas*, her charity. It was manifested in many ways. The story of Mary is typical.

Several blocks away from our neighborhood was a thoroughfare where prostitutes would occasionally ply their trade, I suppose when police crackdowns drove them from their usual haunts. From time to time they'd stray as close as the corner near where we lived. My mother would sometimes encounter them on the sidewalk, and though there might be a distressed expression on her face, I never saw a judgmental one. And at least once, in Mary's case, my mother's care blossomed into real compassion.

One morning, when the weather was blowing cold rain and sleet, this young woman was working that corner with nothing but a light jacket, waiting for a car — any car — to pull over and offer her "a ride." My mother walked down the block and brought the woman in, warmed her up with a cup of coffee, and gave her one of her own old coats. My mother was so delicate that the contrast between the two women was striking. I held my peace, but there must have been an inquiring look on my young face, because after Mary left, my mother volunteered an explanation: "I don't know what she does and I wouldn't want to know what she does, but whatever she does she shouldn't be standing out there in the wet and cold without a coat on her back and a cup of coffee inside."

The young woman's name wasn't really Mary — I won't use her name, because she and her family became upstanding citizens of Rochester and might be hurt by a careless word here. I won't try to tell you that Mary responded to my mother's care by giving up her profession. That came later: She and her boyfriend — her procurer — finally married and raised his daughter, who later became a good friend of mine. But for the time being, Mary continued to work the streets a few blocks away. The difference was that she was no longer a stranger.

In fact, in a peripheral way Mary played an important role for me, as I was passing from blissful ignorance into inquisitive curiosity about all things sexual. I was never going to find out about the birds and the bees from my mother, and my father would sooner clear his throat and discover he had some extra work to do on next Sunday's sermon than get too technical with me on those subjects. Like many parents, they'd rather let the grapevine fill me in with the details, and if I had any *real* problems — on the subject of sex as on any other subject — they knew I'd feel free to come to them.

But I had a far better source than most youngsters who have to guess at the facts of life. I could talk to Mary, and Mary would tell me. There was never a hint of ulterior motive on her part — I was the Rev. Warfield's son, after all, and she had a devoted respect for both my father and my mother. She never initiated any of our discussions. But at the same time there was no silliness or false modesty in her answers. I could talk with her about both the mechanics and the sentiments of sex.

Even more than the broader physical questions, I was interested in her relationship with the man who eventually became her husband. How could she maintain an emotional life with someone who put her out to market? How could she keep her feelings separate from her — vocation?

She never flinched or hesitated. "Son," she told me, "when I'm with my clients I'm all business, and there's nothing there for them but a one-time service. I don't feel a thing. But when I get home, all he has to do is touch the back of my arm and all the little hairs stand straight up. You learn to keep things separate." It was an insight a teenager would never be likely to hear from his parents.

She didn't go to our church. As I learned in our conversations, she had her own religious sensibility — she could remind me who St. Mary Magdalene was, for example — but she had an equally strong social sensitivity and would never have presumed on my mother's solicitude by risking an embarrassment for her in church society.

Indirectly, my mother's tolerance and Mary's respectfully distant gratitude combined to make me a little more broadminded about social differences. That, even more than the sexual openness, was Mary's contribution to my adolescence. And of course, it was really my mother's contribution, wasn't it?

My father worshipped my mother. Once, after she handled a complex series of emotional problems among some people in our church, he spoke a sentence about her that impressed itself permanently on my memory: "If there ever was an angel that walked the earth, it is your mother."

For all her angelic qualities, Mom would let you know when she was riled. When she had to discipline one of us, it was instant, a flare-up of righteous anger and a swift spank with whatever she might have at hand. Just as quickly, she would forget the cause of her anger — so if you could avoid instant punishment, you were probably off the hook. Father was different. When you committed a spanking infraction, he would let you know, quietly, what you'd done wrong. "I'm not going to punish you now," he'd say. "I'm going to punish you later." He didn't believe that a parent should ever strike a child in anger. You'd wait until that evening, or even the next day sometimes, until the time for your spanking came. When he figured the time was right, you'd have to put your hand in his and take a smack or two of his strap in the palm of your hand, along with a verbal reminder of why you were being punished.

There were rare occasions, though, when Mother could bide her time, too — if she had trouble catching you. Little Murphy usually ran faster than she could, and I remember one evening when she tried to get her hands on him, the both of them running around our long kitchen table. "You just stand still, Murphy," she cried. "I'm going to catch you sooner or later."

Murphy knew she never sustained her anger, and figured he could outwit her by getting away; I think he ran out of the house.

But that night after we'd gone to sleep in our adjoining beds — all the boys slept in the same room in those early days — Robert and Vern and I were awakened by a bloodcurdling cry from the bed at the end. Murphy was sprawled over between two of the beds, one leg awkwardly extended back toward his bedframe, taking his spanking. My mother had come in while we were sleeping and tied his foot to the bedpost. Murphy was almost always right. Every time he ran away she would soon forget that she had promised a punishment — except this once. "I told you I was going to give you a spanking," she said. This was one time she was determined to make a punishment stick.

Both my mother and father are associated with my first memories of music. My mother would sing in her high little voice as she worked around the house, usually something from the hymn book or a spiritual. I don't think I ever heard her sing any secular music. She'd be filling the air with "Amazing Grace" or other Dr. Watts songs; there was always some kind of tune on her lips.

And my father was always singing too. He had a fine voice and he'd practice at home all week long, previewing for us whatever songs the Sunday service was going to feature. This was a time just before the more contemporary rock-em- sock-em gospel music of Thomas A. Dorsey and others was coming into vogue; my father would usually be singing spirituals.

I was sometimes there with him while he practiced playing the piano over at Aenon Baptist. His guitar-picking days were over, but not his gift for music; he became a self-taught pianist. In most of our churches, Wednesday night prayer meetings typically were not musical events, with hymns and a choir; if a hymn were to be sung it would usually be *a capella*. But my father liked to have music even for those occasions when our usual church pianist wasn't on call. He memorized entire songs by painstakingly fingering out each chord, and did a passable job of it.

That was sufficient for him, he figured, but he wanted his children to have a real musical education. And so I started early. As soon as we could afford it — I think I was about nine years old — the folks bought a second-hand upright piano for our front room, and I began to take lessons.

My brother Robert started at the same time. Two years younger than I, he would wait patiently at the dining room table while I labored through my exercises, listening as I finally managed to achieve a recognizable melody from the pieces I was learning. When I had had enough and left the piano, he would sit down and riff through the tunes I'd been playing — by ear. He could do better, faster, by listening to me, than I could by learning to sight-read and practicing for hours. Needless to say, at that age this produced more aggravation than fraternal pride!

Of course, my first "real" music boomed out from Mount Olivet's resounding pipe organ. Although I was proud of my father's Aenon Baptist, I particularly enjoyed those Sundays we spent at Dr. Rose's church because of the organ and the wonderfully spirited choir. It was at Mount Olivet, before I was old enough to know what I was hearing, that I first enjoyed some of the classics of western church music — Handel, Bach, and others — alongside the traditional Southern religious songs and Negro spirituals. It was there that classical music first became an easy and familiar part of my daily life.

In that way, at an early age I began to develop an intuition about a truth that musicologists fill volumes trying to articulate: the fact that both the "classical" and the "traditional" kinds of music are equally fundamental parts of the same great heritage — my heritage. In the spiritual environment of Mount Olivet, a concept so simple as "the family of man" came perfectly naturally. It was an article of faith. And with it, part and parcel, came an associated concept, "the music of mankind" — the continuity of all music, of harmonies for all people, everywhere.

*   *   *   *

The sacred music took on a fresh significance for me when I first experienced what Baptists refer to in different ways — as a conversion, or a new birth in Christ. But to appreciate that story, you have to know about Grandma Gilliam.

My father's mother had remarried after Grandpa Charlie died. I don't know much about the circumstances of her second marriage, or even how old my father was at the time, but by the Rochester years he had lost touch with her. It was not until some time in the early thirties, when I was in my early teens, that he found out where she was — and that she was destitute.

I don't know whether the fact of her remarriage had anything to do with his dropping contact with her; I don't know whether the estrangement from his mother, if that's what it was, had been gnawing at him; I don't know whether Uncle Emmett (who was Charlie's son by another woman though Grandma Gilliam had raised him as a brother to her own boys) had helped him find her, or perhaps simply motivated my father to reestablish contact.

I only know that at some point in those years it became important to him to knit his family back together; and that somehow he found her, and brought her home to Rochester. By this time Grandma Annie and Daddy Ward, my mother's folks, had put down strong roots in Rochester and were doing just fine. I remember them as always being the first Negroes in town to have whatever came along that was new — the first car, the first radio, the first washing machine. Grandma Annie had an eye for the modern, and an attention to detail: She knew the different models of Buicks and Oldsmobiles better than the youngsters did.

Grandma Gilliam, on the other hand, was an old-fashioned Southern woman. She was nearly blind, so she was physically dependent on the Warfields, and economically dependent too. She lived with us from the time my father found her to the day she died in her room. Throughout those early years, as the oldest child in the family, I became her companion and helper and seeing-eye dog. It was a blessing for me to have that contact with her.

She had a lively disposition, as lively in her way as Grandma Annie; but her liveliness had a fragile side, and it tended to turn inward. Maybe her problems with her eyesight made her rely more on insight. You can get a sense of her prickly humor from her comment after a prayer meeting at which one lady of the church had testified by singing a spiritual about how anxious she was to meet her Maker. As we were walking home, Grandma Gilliam was reflecting on the meeting and the still-unwashed sins of this woman, because she commented to me, "I don't know why she's so anxious — she ain't ready to leave here yet."

It says something about Grandma Gilliam's feisty nature, that she was attracted to colorful men like Grandpa Charlie, who had "left Warfields all up and down the Mississippi." She took her name from her second husband who was, she told me, "a jackleg preacher." She told me that at one point his congregation had wanted to "put him out — so he took along his big old pistol and when he got to the church meeting he put it down in front of him across the table and told them, 'The meeting is now open.'" He held onto his pulpit.

For all that, Grandma Gilliam was an old-fashioned Southern lady in every sense. She took her religion straight, with a heavy dose of prayer meetings and revivals. Her spirituality was so unvarnished and her faith so simple that I sometimes think she lived in two worlds at the same time — the one we know and the one we hope to attain. Death seemed to hold no fear for her, so completely did she believe in the continuity of those two states of being.

That sense which she communicated so naturally lent a convincing air to the ghost stories she would tell me. I would hang on every word as she told me of the "ha'nts" that were about, if I were only able to feel them as she felt them. The world of spirits that she created with her tales was wondrous but not menacing, except to those who had reason to fear retribution. She believed, like the modern physicists, that there were many invisible forces at play in our world. And *play* is the right word, because she seemed to enjoy them more than fear them.

I can think of no better tribute to her memory, and to the peaceful acceptance of the unknowable that she gave me, than to relate what happened when she died. She passed away in her sleep, without a struggle. And as soon as her body was taken to the funeral home, even before the final services, my folks told me that as the oldest son I was welcome to take Grandma Gilliam's room — my first room of my own.

It was in the back of the house, separated from my brothers and from my parents — I would be completely at the mercy of the ha'nts back there, if they wanted to get me. Yet I took the room without a moment's hesitation, without a trace of concern. Grandma Gilliam had always been comfortable with the world of spirits and ha'nts. If death was no more than a passing from this side to the other, why should it frighten me? In fact, I treasured whatever fragrance remained of my grandmother's presence there. And to this day I've never experienced any queasiness about the fact of death, or those who pass on.

That was my Grandma Gilliam. And you can see why it was only natural that we were together that night at prayer meeting when I first felt the spirit in me. Like most people who have had this experience, I can remember the precise moment of my religious awakening. It was at Aenon Baptist Church, while my father was still an assistant there. I was just about nine years old.

The pastor was a Reverend Greenleaf. He was a striking, statuesque man and a formidable preacher. We weren't what are sometimes referred to as "holy rollers," but a good Baptist preacher can always get the room rocking, even among the more staid congregations.

As Reverend Greenleaf preached, his oratory pitching and tossing toward its climax, I joined in the response, letting myself fall into the emotions and the bodily rhythms of the rest of the congregation.

And while I was saying my "Yes, Lords" and "Amens," I suddenly felt a tremor take control of my whole body. With an emotion that had nothing to do with grief I instantly burst into wholehearted tears. To my puzzlement, though I was sobbing I wanted to pray, to pour myself into prayerful emotion. It was a most fantastic physical experience. My grandmother had put her hand on mine, and when this rapture took possession of me she suddenly looked at my face. She wore a gentle smile, she showed no alarm; she seemed to recognize that something wonderful was happening that I would never forget.

Before that time I'd had a son's respect for his father's business, with a logical understanding of the importance of my religious practice. But from that moment, religion became a personal source of strength and reaffirmation for me.

It came at an important time for me, in our family life, and maybe that was no coincidence. Because just about that time my baby brother Walter died of double pneumonia. As if in some sort of cosmic compensation, my sister, Virginia, was born the same year that Walter died, in 1928. My mother finally had the little girl she had always wanted. But then, while she was still a beautiful baby, Virginia too came down with double pneumonia. Within a matter of two or three frantic days she was dead.

At that age I was old enough for the entire drama to make a strong impression. I remember my mother's openly emotional grief; she was heartbroken, and could find solace nowhere. And

I remember my father's stoic sadness; equally sick at heart, he was a pillar of strength, and his sincere faith and calm acceptance, I think, bridged the gap for us all, took us past bitterness into a sorrowful acceptance.

*   *   *   *

With the experience of religion so everpresent in my life, it's no wonder that it played such a prominent role in my early appreciation of music. But the role of public education, and the popular culture all around us, were influences that were at least as important. All my life, ever since, I've alternated between the sacred and the secular for the wellsprings of my art.

As I've said, it was in church where I grew up surrounded by beautiful music that I received my first orientation. Which means that it was in the church where I had my first experience with the ups and downs of artistic development.

After my modest debut as a five-year-old, I hardly ever missed playing in one of the church performances at Aenon and Mt. Olivet — cantatas and other presentations at Christmas and Easter, and other times of the liturgical year. One year I would be one of the little shepherds, another year a disciple, or if I was good enough (or fit the costume) one of the Magi.

It wasn't just at the holidays — in our church we were always doing recitations and other programs, nearly once a week, often using poetry that had nothing to do with religion. That was when I started to develop a repertoire of dialects, particularly for the poetry of Paul Laurence Dunbar. I especially enjoyed his "When Malindy Sings."

A generation earlier, most black protestant churches would not have tolerated so much "foolishness" — there was a time when no musical instruments of any kind were even allowed on campus at Fisk University, for example — but that had changed. In my youth, drama and music of one sort or another always played a lively part in Baptist church life.

In due time — I wasn't even in my teens — I joined with my friends in the junior choir. We were all passable boy sopranos, and for a few years we made some lively music. It's hard to imagine William Warfield hitting a high C, but I did.

Then, some time when I was still nine or so, some of our voices started to change. In the same way that a boy will look anxiously in the mirror for the first signs that he should start shaving, I heard my friends' voices going through that awkward period and listened for the tell-tale cracks in my own. They weren't there. Before long I was concerned that my voice was too much like a little boy's.

When it looked like I was going to be the last of my gang to be singing up there with the "little kids," I did the natural thing under the circumstances: I faked it. I pretended that, like the others, I could no longer hit those notes. I dropped out of the junior choir and stopped singing altogether. Between the ages of nine and sixteen I probably never sang a note, even around the house.

So that second-hand upright piano, which the folks put in the parlor just about then, arrived in the nick of time. The music inside me was going to find some way to get out, and if I wasn't going to let it come through my vocal cords, it was going to work its way down to my fingertips. There was a period of some seven years or so, until I rediscovered my voice, that my dream was of becoming a great pianist like the virtuosic and charismatic Paderewski.

First, of course, I'd need to take lessons. We had a pianist at Mt. Aenon, Mrs. Gwendolyn Edwards, who trained our little choir. She also gave piano lessons in the church. Most of her students were young adults. I told her that I'd like to learn how to play the piano, but I don't think she took me seriously at first. I never got past a pleased smile, a "Someday," and a pat on the head.

My father explained to me that she taught lessons to supplement her income — she hardly made a living wage as Mt. Aenon's choir director and accompanist. In those days I was earning my pocket change with a chamois cloth. We had a teacher whose car needed polishing several days a week, and an hour or so of effort could net me twenty-five cents each time — as much as seventy-five cents a week.

One afternoon in the late spring of 1929 I came to Mrs. Edwards's house with three quarters in my hand. She was standing at the whitewashed wooden railing, three steps up, on her front porch. "Mrs. Edwards," I called to her as she was turning to go into her house. "Look, Mrs. Edwards. I can pay for lessons." When I came up to her front step I unfolded my fingers to reveal the money I was clutching. "Could you teach me to play the piano?"

I began to explain that I could make that much or more every week, and that I would bring her every penny I earned, for however many lessons that would pay for. I remember that while I was still outlining my plan, she turned to go into the house, murmuring something indistinct, and then came back out holding a handkerchief. "Bill Warfield," she said, "come inside. We're going to start your first piano lesson right now."

That began my piano career — and Robert's infuriating self-education on our parlor upright every afternoon, when I'd finished my daily practice. For the next seven years, I dedicated a part of nearly every day to the piano. There was a particularly dramatic publicity photo of Paderewski on his recital posters, and his sharply chiseled profile was emblazoned in my imagination as I labored with my five-finger exercises. I was determined to breed for myself some of the the brooding genius of that great pianist.

Years later, after my Town Hall debut, I visited Mrs. Edwards on that same whitewashed front porch where my music career began. I never missed an opportunity to remind her how important she'd been to a young boy who was still sorting out his dreams. In one of those conversations she asked if I remembered that during my appeal she had turned abruptly and gone into the house. I did. "I was just about breaking into tears," she told me. "You just touched my heart so, you wanted to take lessons so bad you were ready to give me everything you had."

By the time I was in my mid-teens I was getting pretty good, and naturally I began to experiment with pop music — especially the lively new bebop that was just then becoming popular. I played for friends, and singalongs at parties, and that led to my first serious music job offer—playing in a small club across town. I was enthusiastic about the idea, but my father was not. "No son of mine is going to play in a night club!" He let me know, in no uncertain terms, that this new career was not going to happen. It's sometimes interesting for me to contemplate where I might have landed if I'd followed my own impulses at that point, instead of being an obedient son.

But his strictures were no hardship to me. I wasn't starved for expressive outlets, then or at any time in my youth. We lived in a flourishing cultural environment.

At Christmas we had the annual production of *Nutcracker* at the Eastman Theater. I was fascinated by Tchaikovsky's lush music, by the fantasy and inventiveness, by the ballet's combination of technical prowess and grace, and by the sheer complexity of the presentation. It was my introduction to stage production, and it showed me another dimension of music — the physical dimension, the expression of music in human form.

Not only *Nutcracker*, but also renowned concert artists like Paderewski, Rachmaninoff, Heifetz — and Marian Anderson — performed in our local auditorium. Imagine! the greatest musical talents of a generation, playing and singing for a youngster who not that long ago was sitting on a bag of raw cotton bolls in West Helena, Arkansas.

I am forever grateful for the concert series at Eastman and the continuing family-oriented and adult-oriented activities at Rochester's recreation department and institutions of higher learning. But I shouldn't give the impression that my culture was all so high-brow. We were surrounded by pop culture too, and like every youngster, after all, I had my priorities. Of all the arts available to us, nothing could top the Saturday thrillers at the movie palace.

In those days, Baptists were still ambivalent about the movies. The Bible didn't expressly condemn Hollywood, at least not by name, but going to a movie was a little too much fun to be above suspicion. So the idea of seeing a film on Sunday was out of the question — in any case, with all our church services there wouldn't have been time.

But on Saturday mornings we Warfields could troop out with the other children and stay up to date on the cliff-hangers — the adventure serials — as well as the newest cartoons, the newsreels, and of course the main features. Of all the serials, Buck Rogers was my favorite. Only later, when I was well into Washington High School in the late 1930s, would come the more provocative films like Greta Garbo in *Ninochka* or *Saunders of the River* with Paul Robeson, and then *The Emperor Jones*.

And for sheer magnitude of visual experience, nothing could compete with the radio plays and comedy series we all loved to tune in. In those years you could lose yourself completely in the imaginative world of radio. It's one of those experiences that the television generation could probably never fully understand. What we "saw" when we listened to those tales — and to the music themes that always helped to set the stage and create the mood — was not limited by a twenty-one-inch screen. The only boundaries were the infinite reaches of our young imaginations. In my house we rollicked to the adventures of *Amos and Andy*, and never had second thoughts about the possible political or social implications.

Those were all influences on our development as we youngsters learned from the culture around us. But we would never have been able to put them to use in creating new art without the arts in our public schools.

I was very fortunate that our schools, beginning at the elementary level, were so strong on arts education. Courses in music were offered during the school day, and good-quality training was available after hours, as part of a lively extracurricular program. For those who couldn't afford to buy or rent musical instruments, they could be borrowed.

The enlightened arts policies of our school district created an entire generation of music-literate youngsters, and though I'm the only one of my family to make a career in music, all my brothers and sisters studied music and nearly everyone I went to school with was able to sing and to play some kind of instrument.

As it happened, it was through those arts-in-education programs at Washington High School, where I had the opportunity to take music classes and join the chorus, that I got back on the vocal track.

My music teacher was Miss Elsa Miller, and the director of the Washington High School Chorus was Clarence P. Bilhorn. Both were dedicated teachers and sympathetic sponsors, who encouraged me to believe that the limited means of the Warfield family would be no barrier to talent, if I were willing to work hard.

Through my experience in the chorus I learned a good deal about conducting, as well as choral singing, from Mr. Bilhorn. It was an essential ingredient of the complete musical education, and had both immediate and long-range benefits for me. And through my work with Elsa Miller I got the first "break" of my musical career.

It was some time around my sixteenth birthday, and I was part of a choral exercise that Miss Miller was conducting. The Rochester school system had a superintendent of music, Dr. Alfred Spouse, who took it on himself to travel to all the music classes, trying to spot exceptional talent. One afternoon he came into Miss Miller's class.

She put us through our usual paces, and as usual I sang lightly with the rest, trying to blend in. In the years since I had quit the junior choir, my voice had changed, of course, but I hadn't gone back into vocal music and didn't know what it could do. I had kept current with my piano studies and, as I say, had enjoyed my voice only through dramatics.

But Miss Miller wasn't going to let me get away with anything today. She made me sing full out. To my amazement, and perhaps hers as well, I filled the room with music. It had been nearly seven years since I had sung with such enthusiasm. The last time I had been a pretty good boy soprano. Now I opened my mouth and discovered I was a booming baritone.

Dr. Spouse called me over after class. "Young man," he said. "You have a beautiful voice, a wonderful sound. You should develop your talent." I had become a practiced instrumentalist on the piano, but I can still remember the special pride I felt at being able to make music on the instrument that was William Warfield.

*   *   *   *

Looking back, it's easy to recognize the pattern that was developing—my increasing focus on music to the exclusion of other activities. It's a pattern that's familiar to anyone who has ever progressed from hobby to serious pursuit, whether it's sports, or ballet, or science studies. More and more I was on a trajectory toward Town Hall.

But at the time, it seemed that my life was full of all the other activities and responsibilities my friends and I shared throughout the mid-'30s. While I was still in high school I was already contributing to the household income. I had first a paper route and then a part-time job in a junkyard. One of my most successful enterprises was as a salesman for Cloverine Salve. I answered an ad in a comic book, as I remember, and when I got my stock I established a modest clientele for myself, selling pomades and salves.

The products came in handy for my hairdressing sideline, too. That was a skill I set out to master, partly because it genuinely interested me and partly because, in the mentality of that Depression era, I wanted to be sure to have a trade to fall back on. It was an easy way to make a few extra dollars too.

Being the oldest son in a family of boys, with no sister, I was fascinated by my young lady cousins and their feminine ways. I liked to get my hands into their hair, and I had a pretty good flair for it, or so they told me, and somewhere along the line someone suggested I should take a course and learn the fundamentals. I studied with Mrs. Scott's Beauty Culture School, and actually acquired a New York State License in Cosmetology and Beauty. I kept that license current for about five years, from 1937 until I went into the Army.

This was a time before afros, remember, and kinkiness was definitely not in vogue. For men or women, it was the Nat King Cole type of wave that set the style. Today, when black women have their hair straightened, it's done chemically, with safe chemicals. But in those days, a man would have his hair "conked" or "fried" with a potassium ash solution — lye! — so that it would take a wave. More than one scalp was seriously burned that way.

For women, it was done with heat. The hair would be straightened with hot combs and then curled with hot curlers; and when the hair cooled down it could be combed out into a variety of styles. Wigs were considered ridiculous — simple evidence that you had bad hair — and though hats were always in style they were disdained if used simply as a substitute for a bandana. No, if you had any style it had to show in your hair. And a woman's hair had to be done no less frequently than every two weeks, more often in the summer when sweat would undo the work, or in bad weather, or whenever moisture restored the hair to its healthy natural kink. So whether it was perspiration or precipitation, year-round I always had opportunities to make a few extra dollars.

I smile to think about it, but it was a handy trade, one that I enjoyed. Years later my training came in handy, when my wife, Leontyne, and I were on tour in Europe. Vienna is a cosmopolitan capital and you could get just about anything you wanted in the city's shops — but there were a few limits. For love nor money, you couldn't get an Austrian hairdresser who knew beans about how to treat a black woman's hair. So, with a can of Sterno, my hot irons, my steel hot comb with its thick back edge, and the right pressing oils, I did all Leontyne's daily hairstyling right in our hotel room.

*   *   *   *

Once I had rediscovered the joy of singing, basking in the approbation of Dr. Spouse and Elsa Miller, I threw myself into self-improvement. I began taking private voice lessons with Miss Miller after school, practicing at the beautiful Mason and Hamlin piano in her parlor. It wasn't long before I was ready for my first real recital, as part of a high school assembly program.

Of all the works I had rehearsed, I chose a piece that had historical significance as well as personal meaning for me. The selection, and its connections, illustrate the recursive complexity and continuity of traditions, in the world of music. If I stop to point these out along the way from time to time, it's because I have never lost my sense of awe and reverence for the universe of music we live in. It parallels religion in its scope and depth.

Harry T. Burleigh was the first great African-American composer and concert singer. He was born in 1866 and was still alive when I performed my recital in 1936 (he lived till 1949). He had studied with Antonin Dvořák, the great Czech nationalistic composer — who was, in turn, a friend and protege of the great Brahms. Brahms, of course, had written much of the literature from which I might logically have chosen. But Burleigh, who was, musically speaking, walking just a little further down the very same road, was more particularly appropriate.

Dvořák, who wove Czech folk themes into his classical compositions, encouraged Burleigh to do the same, with American Negro music. The result was a rich heritage of compositions and arrangements, including the one I performed for that high school assembly, Burleigh's "Deep River." When he published that work two decades earlier it was the first classical music to come from our tradition — that is, the first of our songs to be arranged as a solo in the classical style, carrying our musical traditions into a dimension beyond the previous choir and ensemble renditions of spirituals.

Burleigh had been born and raised in Erie, Pennsylvania, a city not unlike Rochester; and yet the traditions of the Deep South were inescapably a part of his soul. As I aspired to do someday, Burleigh bridged several worlds — North and South, European-folk and Afro-American — and brought them together in his own talent. I identified with the art and the man, and my classmates, white and black, had reason to do so as well. And that's why it was Burleigh, and not Bach or Brahms, that I wanted to show off to that high school crowd.

My first public performance was a hit, and I became identified with my talent, not only in my own mind but socially as well. From that time it became a given that I would pursue a career in music.

The fact was reinforced by the attention it earned me. I became the fair-haired boy, metaphorically speaking, that well-spoken and so-talented William Warfield, the minister's son, the one who would certainly go places. George E. Eddy, our high school principal, was also an officer of the Lion's Club. Through Mr. Eddy I was invited to perform for them, or to sing the "Star-Spangled Banner" on appropriate occasions, or to perform in solos with church choirs. Before long I was appearing with Dr. Charles Boddie, an accomplished pianist turned minister, in recitals of Bach and Handel, arias and spirituals — and, occasionally, actually getting paid!

The lessons in conducting that I had gained from working with Clarence P. Bilhorn in the Washington High School chorus now produced some of those immediate benefits I referred to.

I was rehearsing with the Inter-High Choir for one of its Saturday morning concerts, which Dr. Spouse regularly conducted. We were preparing a choral version of W.C. Handy's "St. Louis Blues" with a guest soloist, to be presented at the Eastman School of Music auditorium. It was a pretty big deal, and I felt privileged just to be involved.

In the middle of rehearsals, Dr. Spouse suddenly interrupted his own conducting with what sounded like a surprised realization: "I have an idea," he told us, out of the blue. "We have a gifted young artist among us who is showing a good deal of musical promise, and I believe he could do this work justice." To my amazement he turned to face me, and waved me to his side. "Bill Warfield," he said, "how would you like to conduct this piece for us?"

I was stunned. What could he have seen in me that made him think I was ready for this assignment? Perhaps he had been lurking at the back of the room, in his talent scout way, while I'd been learning from Mr. Bilhorn in chorus; or perhaps Mr. Bilhorn had passed the word that I was showing promise.

Whatever it was, I discovered the magic—ecstasy isn't too strong a word for it—of conducting a musical work up to the professional standards of our Eastman performances. It was an especially enjoyable experience because the smiling young voices who were responding to my direction were all my friends and musical colleagues. That Inter-High choral conducting was a real high for me.

I well remember one moment that typifies my growing confidence. I had gone to hear Dorothy Maynor performing on tour at the Eastman Theater. One of the country's top concert artists, and later the founder of the Harlem School of the Arts, she had begun her career at her father's church in North Carolina. She was only ten years older than I, so in my efforts to figure out how my career might shape up I was particularly alert to the contours of hers. Even more, I was mesmerized by her beautiful soprano voice.

When I went backstage to ask her to autograph a picture for me, she asked me how old I was. "Seventeen," I told her.

"And what are you going to do with your education?" she asked me.

"I'm going to be a singer, like you," I told her. She smiled as she completed her inscription on the photograph I had handed her. I watched her and reflected that she was as beautiful in person as she had sounded on stage. She was occupied with other guests in her dressing room, so I thanked her for the autograph and for the concert, and stumbled back out into the Rochester afternoon. When I looked down at her signature I was instantly elevated: Dorothy Maynor had written, "To a colleague."

Elsa Miller was something of an unofficial recruiter for the Eastman School of Music, in that she was a colleague of the music teachers at the University. At some point in her private lessons with me she began to talk about me with her peers, and before long the noted oratorio tenor and Eastman professor Arthur C. Kraft—all his students called him "Uncle Arthur"—began to come to our sessions. He was coaching her, improving her skills as a music teacher, as well as giving me special attention and following my progress. Before long it was a foregone conclusion that I would attend the Eastman School and develop my career. Even before that transpired, he began to take me over from Miss Miller. It was a real honor to be considered one of "Uncle Arthur's" prized students.

As early as those teenage years, I acquired the habit, if that's what it is, of shedding my anxieties and trusting that things would work out. I had reason to be anxious about finding the funds to attend Eastman. After all, I came from a large family, and the Great Depression was still afflicting us along with everyone else in the world. Although we were comfortable in the Warfield home, we didn't have a sufficient income to put one boy through college, let alone the entire household that would follow.

And yet I had a simple faith that if I had the talent they claimed I did, things would work out. There were scholarships, right? Perhaps I could earn one. In 1937, the year I was seventeen, I began to work with Elsa Miller to prepare for the annual competition sponsored by the National Music Educators League: First prize was a full music scholarship in the nationally recognized school of your choice.

That year I had to compete in the local competition in Rochester, and then on to the regionals in Buffalo, and the finals in St. Louis. The first hurdle was going to be just getting around. At that point my family couldn't afford the travel expenses. What could have been a major obstacle was overcome by my classmates at Washington High School. They presented a student production, announcing that all proceeds would go toward my competition costs.

There were several of us from Rochester who went to the regional, and several of the regional finalists went to the national in St. Louis in the spring of 1938. Rochester's strong showing was the best case that could be made for the quality of music education in our school system. One of my close friends, Anthony Giardino, made the first cut with me. We were the two top guys from Washington High, we both went to the regional, and then we both went on to the national. The only discomfort I felt, when I took first prize, was that I had beaten out Tony.

The prize gave me the option of attending a number of music schools, including Julliard. But, as I say, there never was any question that I'd continue along the track that was taking me to the Eastman School of Music.

I was the only black singer in the local or regional competitions. I don't believe there were any others in the national, either, because I was later told that I had inadvertently desegregated the Jefferson Hotel in St. Louis by becoming the first black guest ever to be registered there. My reservation was made in advance along with the other finalists. I suppose they never imagined that any of them would be African-Americans.

* * * *

Rochester was such an egalitarian environment that my youngest days were untainted by any of those psychologically damaging encounters with racism that too often blight the young lives of black children elsewhere. Hard as such confrontations can be to adults, they are unutterably destructive to a child's psyche. I was spared.

We all still believed in the idea of America as a melting pot, and my high school, like my neighborhood, was a real healthy cauldron. If some of the other ethnic groups didn't always take to Negroes all that well, it was rarely a cause of unpleasantness. If there were any problems I wasn't aware of them. I was the fair-haired boy, remember, voted vice-president of the student body, singing in recitals, "sure to go far." My father was actively involved in ecumenical exchanges with white churches, and I was a part of those events.

And you also have to remember that folks in Rochester took pride in their difference from less civilized parts of the world. The same antisegregation sentiment that characterized a woman like Eleanor Roosevelt throughout the '20s and '30s could be found in many Great Lakes and New England communities like Rochester. We all, white and black, considered ourselves integrated, and in the Warfield home we didn't feel the personal sting of racial discrimination, however appalling it might be somewhere else. If anything, for me, it was a distinction among other distinctions, to be tall and lively and talented — and black.

It wasn't until I headed into my teens that I first gave thought to racial discrimination as something close to home. Of course, I was aware of racial problems through the newspapers we read and through discussions with my father. I felt an identification with the problem, but never a sense of victimization.

I was aware, not only through the *Pittsburgh Courier* and the *Chicago Defender* as I've already mentioned, but also as a result of the annual trips my father and I made to Uncle Emmett's church in southern Virginia. We made the trip once a year — just father and eldest son — so that my father could conduct a week-long revival meeting at Uncle Emmett's church while Uncle Emmett came up to do the same for our community in Rochester. It was a sort of evangelistic cultural exchange for the churches, and a trip back in time for me as well.

In the car on the way, I noticed that he'd slow down to slightly below the speed limit as we passed out of Pennsylvania. "We're in the South, son," my father would explain. And as we went through certain small towns he knew, my father would remark, "This is one town you don't want to have your car break down in," or "You don't want to be caught out on the street after sundown in this place." We never had an incident, but these conversations with my father brought the threat to life. Of course, Virginia isn't the Deep South; I could only imagine the rest.

I associate those trips to Uncle Emmett's with several pleasant little turning points in my life. It was the first long-distance traveling I had done, a taste of what awaited. It was my first return to the South. It was an opportunity to spend long hours talking and sometimes engaging in disputations with my father, in the enforced intimacy of a car on the open road. And, most importantly, it was at Uncle Emmett's church that my father's dream was finally realized. It was Uncle Emmett who performed the ordination that made my father a fully accredited minister.

And of course — a high point for a sixteen-year-old lad — on those trips what I was racking up was valuable "flight time" behind the wheel, once I had my learner's permit and then my driver's license. That important rite of passage took place at about the same time that my father became the pastor of Friendship Baptist Church in Corning, New York, a two-hour drive from home. My father commuted there once a week, and it would have been just one more arduous chore for him if it hadn't been so much fun for me.

I looked forward to the drive. It was a heady experience, being trusted to share the driving on those journeys, sometimes in snowy weather, or on icy roads that would challenge even an experienced driver. But even more important, now that I look back, were the long hours of casual camaraderie with my father, still very much my father but in those situations a little more of a companion, a colleague, on the simpler level of sharing the driving. Of course it was still the deferential "Yes sir," and "No sir," but here at last was a meaningful adult task that I could perform co-equally. I don't remember that we had profound conversations on these trips. More typically he was mentally preparing his remarks on the way to Corning, and maybe napping on the way back. But it was a regular sharing of time together that came along at a transitional point in my young life, between my childhood and my age of real independence, a half-adult stage that was protracted enough to allow me to take things from my father he maybe didn't even know he was imparting.

*   *   *   *

I finished the twelfth grade at Washington High and started classes the next fall at the University of Rochester, of which the Eastman School of Music was a part. Actually, it was a little like entering the thirteenth grade. I continued to live at home, and I continued my music studies along with other academic courses that I might need for my degree. My life didn't change direction between my last year of high school and my first year of college.

But of course there was a difference in intensity. For one thing, I had discovered languages. I had studied French in high school, and had been active in the French drama society — I was particularly proud of the impression I had made in the role of a landlord, the *proprietaire*, in a school program. Now, at the University, my French studies went into high gear. By the time I'd finished three years of college I had qualified for a French master's course, if I'd wanted it.

French was only the beginning. In our singing studies at Eastman, as was traditional, the curriculum included basic courses in Italian, French, and German diction, to enable us to master the words we were mouthing, even with scant comprehension. But I was fortunate to have been studying for some time with Elsa Miller, who insisted that her singers acquire a real mastery of the languages. Lieder and arias were created to be recreated, not merely pronounced correctly; that would require fluency. So I studied and learned to read, to speak, and to think in those three tongues.

Now, at the college level, I threw myself into my courses. I didn't realize I was being an "overachiever" — I just wanted to do everything.

Even with my music concentration, I continued to enjoy other dramatics. I joined the local community players and then hooked up with WHAM, a local radio station that produced what they called the Texaco Theater. I used to do bit parts for them, and got frequent roles because I was especially good doing dialects.

I could do various African-American dialects whenever they were called for, but more importantly I could do a range of European accents. On radio, particularly in the days before our modern electronics and top-quality speakers, there was a real premium put on clarity of tone and enunciation. It was all done live from the studio, and you didn't have a second chance to get your point across. In the matter of dialects, the listener not only had to know instantly whether he was listening to a German character or a Brooklyn character or a black character, he also had to be able to understand every word through the static. So my vocal training paid another dividend there. My ear for accents was so good that one of my first roles in community theater was that of a very English butler.

Our dramatics classes at Eastman were not designed to train us as actors, but to bring a little theatrical technique into our performance of opera. I never formally studied the theater. I suspect I was something of a natural, though, because later, after I'd performed on stage and in films and television, from time to time I'd pick up one of the manuals on acting — Stanislavsky, Boleslavsky, something on the Actor's Studio — and I'd realize that I was instinctively doing what the masters teach. I suppose that's the whole point of the masters: They're articulating what with luck comes naturally.

It probably helped that I was living at home, because I had few of the distractions that undergraduates typically have to overcome. I may have missed some unpleasantness, too, through sheer obliviousness. I didn't know until years later that I had been recommended for the music fraternity, Phi Mu Alpha Symphonia, and turned down because I was black. "Don't you remember that time we all resigned from Phi Mu Alpha?" a former classmate later asked me. "There was a clique that didn't want to pledge a Negro, and a bunch of us resigned in protest." Now that he mentioned it, I did remember that there had been a batch of resignations; at the time I didn't focus on it. I finally heard the story long after, at a banquet on the occasion of my being named Phi Mu Alpha's "Man of the Year." It's probably just as well I didn't know it at the time.

No, I concentrated on my goals, which, as they became more concrete, became more confusing. In those college years, more and more I was determined to follow in the footsteps of Roland Hayes and Marian Anderson, but I was becoming ever more aware that their trail was sometimes hard to make out. As I was constantly reminded, there was no clear career track for me to follow. So it was a part of my long-term strategy to have a college degree to fall back on. I knew it would have to be a master's, because my fallback career plan was to teach.

In any case, I wasn't interested in simply taking the giant leap and going to New York to hustle for work. But that made the question even more urgent, especially as I headed into my senior year: What was I going to do next? As it happened, Uncle Sam made up my mind for me.

Chapter Four

ARMY LIFE

There never has been a time like December 7, 1941, in the history of our country — there certainly has never been anything like it since. In the space of an hour on that Sunday afternoon, an entire nation of millions of Americans were united in a single purpose. And it was a unity of purpose that was sustained over the next three and a half years. Families were broken up, educations were interrupted, hundreds of thousands of people left home, many of them never to return. But somehow the personal problems all merged into a larger mission, with a feeling for God, flag, and country that is probably beyond the ken of people who weren't there. If it can't be comprehended emotionally, it can't be comprehended at all.

But if it was a time for national unity, it was also a time for individual turmoil. There's no way to "keep them down on the farm after they've seen Paree." And there would be no going back to the old ways for any of those men and women who had their horizons opened out so forcefully by the hurricane of those early days of war. I had not lived a particularly sheltered life up until then, but if it hadn't been for the disruption caused by my military service, I can't imagine how I would have moved so far, so fast, from the friendly confines of the life that had been set up for me in Rochester, New York.

All of the youngsters in my area were drafted. An exemption was a rarity, and not to be coveted. We all went together to

Fort Niagara, New York, for induction. We were all slow to understand the scale of what was going on, and we thought we'd be back in a few weeks, after our "processing." Nobody in my neighborhood knew it would last so long.

While I was shuffling through the induction at Fort Niagara, I was with other kids from Rochester, even friends from my own school, from my own neighborhood. But in a matter of hours we were all on our way to basic training, and I noticed something I had never seen before. Was it coincidence, or was it my imagination? I seemed to find myself, increasingly, separated from my white friends, in gatherings of other black recruits.

By the time the bus arrived at Jefferson Barracks, Missouri, where we would receive our infantry training, it was clear. For the first time in my life, I had been forced into a totally segregated setting. I'd never been so far from family and friends, and I'd never been reduced to a serial number to be "processed." That would have been a culture shock all by itself, but beyond that was something even more shocking. At the age of twenty-two, I was for the first time placed in a realm of complete and total racial segregation, sanctioned and supported by law, by military discipline, and if necessary by military police.

I didn't dwell on the implications of this racial reality. There were certainly bigger things to worry about — and more personal considerations as well. For one thing, I quickly realized that this was no game. My brothers had been drafted at the same time I was; for the Warfield family, World War II wasn't going to be a brief interruption but a major chapter in our lives, and some of us might not come home. And on a smaller scale, like everyone else, I was so busy making my personal adjustment to military life that I didn't have much time to think about anything else. But I couldn't help registering the shock of segregation.

The military is "ordered" but not necessarily organized, especially at times of crisis like the early days of the Second World War. Our basic training put us under a strict daily regimen, but that order was sometimes against a backdrop of near-chaos. It was a world of whirling, seemingly random changes, a new sensation of receiving contradictory commands with mortal sanctions to enforce them, of hearing conflicting rumors and reports that were always buzzing around the barracks. The severest discipline I had ever experienced had been from a loving parent or a nurturing school official. Like every other young man in my company, I felt whipped around like a scrap of paper in a sudden gust, and nothing that I had ever taken for granted seemed permanent anymore.

It was hell. It was good for me.

The hardest thing to adjust to was the fact that I had to be subservient, even grovellingly subservient, during basic training, to someone for whom I had no respect. I had to invent respect where I felt it wasn't due, which is the whole principle of military hierarchy. I had to show respect for the sergeant, and he had to show respect for the lieutenant, and so on, all the way up the line.

It was never easy for me to get used to taking orders from someone "with no brains," as I felt at the time. It was a mark of my own youth. I didn't yet understand how people who seem ignorant can in fact be intelligent in ways I can't appreciate. As someone once said, "We're all ignorant. We're just ignorant about different things."

I didn't yet know there is such a thing as what the old folks call "mother wit," and that it's just as important as book-learning. And that you have to judge a man by what makes him tick, and not by what makes you tick. Eventually, over the course of four years in the Army, I met some soldiers — fellow recruits and noncommissioned officers as well — who were more clever than other folks I knew who had a slew of college degrees.

But at the beginning I was still something of a snob. Having grown up in Rochester, with all the advantages of a solid family and a good education, here I was in basic training, taking orders from someone who might not know how to read. I felt superior — in my terms, by God, I *was* superior — and it was a constant frustration to have to adjust to a system where that person had such complete control over my life.

I would like to say I got wiser and better and more philosophical, but in fact I think I only got a little bit smarter. Yes, it was a good dose of reality for me to accept all those platitudes about "mother wit." But what really changed things for me was when I caught on to how the system worked.

I was heading toward a serious confrontation with my drill sergeant, which had been building for some time. Although I tried to play down my education, and even watched my language (that is, tried not to talk like someone educated at the University of Rochester), it was clear that I wasn't having much luck. Sarge resented me and my "airs," and there was nothing I could do to prevent a showdown. I had adopted an attitude of resignation ("this too shall pass") but that wouldn't prevent the disaster, I was certain.

And then, out of nowhere, one afternoon the regimental chaplain asked my sergeant if he could requisition me for chapel duty. It wouldn't take me away from training — in fact, it would add a few activities to my schedule. He had learned from my records that Private Warfield had some musical training. He needed someone to play the small chapel organ on Sundays.

Suddenly that made a difference to the sergeant. Not that it cleared the air or brought us together or "improved our relationship" — none of that. It just got him off my back. Nobody wants to bother with you once an officer has taken some notice of you, even if it's just a passing interest, even if he wouldn't remember it the next day.

"So that's the way it works," I realized. "I can play that game." I might never get beyond private or corporal, but I recognized the flip side of subservience, and saw that sometimes it could work for me. You didn't have to wear the rank yourself to put it to use.

*   *   *   *

It was ironic that it was this call to service at the chapel that helped to ease things for me. Because, at first, there was one comfort of home that I actually enjoyed getting away from, and that was the all-consuming activity that surrounded every Sunday. For all my religious faith, how many Sunday mornings had I lain in bed a few extra minutes, thinking, "Oh Lord, there's Sunday school this morning, then church, and then church again this afternoon, there's an afternoon program and then there's BYPU (Baptist Young People's Union) tonight." There were days when I'd say, "God, I'm glad I've got a preacher for a father, but when I get away I'm going to take a rest. I think I've done all the church I need to do for a long, long time."

Now at Jefferson Barracks I came to that time. All week long, I was submerged in a new world of drill, riflery, drill, brass-polishing, drill, floor-scrubbing, and more drill, at every time of day or night. But then, on Sunday mornings, they left us alone for a few hours.

Despite its name, our camp was not literally a barracks, it was a tenting ground. During basic training that winter we lived in three-man tents, with little oil stoves which never got us very warm. It was such a rare luxury to lie under my covers and spend some quiet time by myself. I remember thinking that here, at last, was that relief I had sometimes yearned for. From being the most frantic time, Sunday had become the only quiet time. I didn't have to drill and I didn't have to get up and run around doing all those church things I did at home. I could get away from the herd for a short spell. I was still personally at peace with the Almighty, but I had no desire to march into chapel, one more cipher in olive drab, and share my worship with the same bunch of young men with whom I'd spent all week on the parade ground.

It was three or four Sundays into my Army life, once I'd begun to acclimate to the crazy routines of a military recruit, that I was able to sort myself out and create some sense of individual order. And that's when I began to feel that I was missing something important. I realized that I needed more than a generalized feeling about religion. As basic and drab as the chapel might be, I had a need for sharing my religious impulse with a congregation. I understood, in a way I had not grasped before, that religious services were more than mere rote and ritual. There was a deeper need, down there in some part of myself I had been taking for granted. Maybe I could make the chapel a little less drab.

As an aside, that was an important early experience for me to go through. Ritual may be ritual, but it's wrong to call it "empty" ritual. That was a new awareness for me, and I think about it in my art sometimes, whenever I encounter religious ritual in other forms. It doesn't have to happen in a church. There's the same profound depth of religious feeling in some of the rites of native American tribes as there is in Brahms's "Four Serious Songs." I recognize it and respond to it without expecting to understand it. Nonetheless, my religion is a constant reassurance. It gives me strength and sustenance in an unobtrusive way — it's something that I know is there, with a personal certainty that is so much more real than a theoretical proof could ever be. It's almost tangible, a "presence" to which I can relax my guard, surrender my defenses, entrust myself and all I care for, with no craven abdication — literally as a small child might completely trust in his father.

I don't make a habit of preaching to people, and God knows in my life I've worked with and befriended men and women of just about every imaginable lifestyle, with values and beliefs that are so different from those I inherited that I couldn't even place them on the map. My own religious roots have never interfered with those relationships.

My convictions have never required any kind of confirmation from others who may be taking different directions in their lives. But I would be withholding something important if I didn't make this plain: This internal conviction of mine has been the key to most of my choices in life. In matters large and small, so many times that it's hard to be specific about most of them, I've come to a point where I've felt, "Well, Lord, I've gone as far as I can go on this; it's up to You now." I've had some hard times, but I've never reached a point where I felt complete, shattering despair; I've been on the brink, but there has always been an awareness, sometimes barely conscious, that I was in a total picture much wider than my little frame could contain. Now all these feelings began to take shape in Jefferson Barracks, Missouri, in that inauspicious place and time, now that I was for the first time in my life coming to such decisions on my own.

So, on an entirely more practical level, it was ironic that the chaplain singled me out. In a very different sense of the word, I had already begun to gravitate toward chapel on my own. I was thinking of my soul, but it also probably helped save my hide as well — by getting that drill sergeant off my back.

I needed all the moral support I could get. This was a world that my upbringing hadn't prepared me for, this segregated, brutalized world of Jefferson Barracks. Weeks of struggle there had worn me down and made me wonder whether the earlier goals I thought I was working toward had been a complete sham, a romantic dream. The war could go on for years, and who knew what it would lead to? In the meantime, I was sinking into a kind of despair.

The turning point came one rainy afternoon when I had had a particularly tough day. I was feeling thoroughly browbeaten, leveled down to next to nothing, at the end of my rope. I could hardly make it back to my tent. I stumbled in and dropped myself on my cot without even bothering to light the little stove.

I had missed mail call, and anyway I had already gotten that week's round of letters from different members of the family, so I wasn't expecting anything more. But lying there I felt a crumpled envelope under me, where it had been thrown on my bunk. It had an official seal, from the trustees of the University of Rochester. I figured it was most likely more of that routine paperwork that students have to deal with, but it was comforting to see that return address and to be reminded of the world I'd left.

But when I opened it, I found it was anything but routine. It was a personal message, on the letterhead of the Trustees of the University of Rochester, and it said that my extra efforts as an undergraduate had piled up enough credits for me to graduate with my class that spring. I sank down onto my bunk with a sob. That letter was just what I needed then. Suddenly I had a complete sense of the whole thing, the entire framework and where I fitted in.

I pulled myself together. From that afternoon, throughout the rest of basic training, I had a new motivation. I knew that all I had to do was just a matter of going through the motions and taking care of business, whatever I needed to do to bring myself to the next step. It didn't have to make sense, because it wasn't going to change my ultimate direction. There was a real world out there, and I was still connected to it. Even if this war took years, it was only a temporary digression. That simple letter did it, and it gave me what I needed to piece the rest together.

That didn't mean I was going to take whatever came. On the contrary, I had to play the game and stay alert. By now it was clear that the "colored troops" were going to get different assignments from those given to white soldiers. I had qualified as a sharpshooter with my M-1 rifle, but there was little likelihood that I or any of my training regiment would be sent into combat. If I went along with the program, what I had to look forward to would be four years of manual labor in some service battalion, maybe even hauling garbage or digging latrines for the "real" soldiers.

Sure enough, toward the end of my basic training I received orders that assigned me to ordnance duties. I was big and good with my hands, so they wanted to use me as a human mule, handling carts of ammunition for artillery training. I bristled at the thought, and knew the game well enough to realize I had to take a stand. I wasn't embarrassed to cause a ruckus. If I wasn't going to get an overseas assignment, then I sure as hell wasn't going to let them wear me out in some segregated training center in the South. I protested at company headquarters that there was nothing in my records that would have recommended me for these duties. At the regimental level the colonel gave me a hearing.

I didn't kid myself that my musical background was likely to qualify me for anything significant. But wait a minute! I had taken intensive training in the languages of two of our enemies, Italian and German, as well as in French. Surely these could be put to use fighting for my country? I think I detected a skeptical smile on the colonel's part, but he could see I was serious, and that I would press my point as far up the ladder as I had to. So he sent me out for testing.

They put me through French, German, and Italian, in tests for my ability in conversation, reading, and writing. I came through with flying colors; this mule was obviously qualified for military intelligence. They tore up my ordnance papers and sent me for special duty at Camp Ritchie, Maryland.

*   *   *   *

When I got off the train at the small station — just a platform, really — I decided I had arrived in the middle of nowhere, and wondered what kind of a military intelligence camp I would find here. It turned out I was entering a whole new phase of my education, in a subject I would never have suspected.

Camp Ritchie was an extraordinary military base. Neither Army nor Navy, strictly speaking, it was an activity of "G-2." In the War Department hierarchy "G-1" referred to the top command level of the armed forces — general officers and their staffs — and "G-3" referred to the services themselves — the Army, the Navy, and so forth. "G-2," or military intelligence, was suspended between, in a kind of administrative limbo, not included in a directly subordinate role within the military.

In this little corner of the war, our mission was to prepare military intelligence teams for assignment to units throughout Europe. We were to train small all-purpose squads of seven men — three officers and four enlisted men — to cover every aspect of military intelligence wherever they should be sent. Their training would include interrogation techniques, interpretation of documents, counterespionage measures, translation, cartography and evaluation of terrain — the reading, translation, and writing of maps — every aspect of military intelligence that could be anticipated.

Quite a few of the people who came through for training were refugees, from Eastern Europe and even from Germany and Italy. Often they had applied for U.S. citizenship, and were hoping to qualify by serving in the armed forces; others just wanted to help defeat Hitler and Mussolini and return to their home country. More than once one of our European trainees would smirk when he saw our sometimes outdated maps, and correct them for us from first-hand information, showing us the back roads or pointing out where dams had been constructed, creating a lake where we showed farmland.

Our training methods were unusual. We didn't use books or give lectures. In part because so many of our trainees were unfamiliar with the English language, and in part because they tended to go to sleep during training films, the principal teaching method was the medium of live theater.

The commandos for this operation were code-named "Section 9." A group of specially trained professional actors was assembled to show, not tell, how the various intelligence techniques operated in the real world. This was a practical matter, not a theoretical one, and our subjects would be performing their duties under combat conditions soon enough. They might as well see and hear and act out what it would be like, rather than simply read about it.

We learned after the war that the intelligence teams we sent out—to operate as intensively trained special units at the division level throughout North Africa, Italy, the Normandy beachhead, across the continent, and even into Eastern Europe—were among the most effective special units in the war. Those squads could handle anything, and feedback we received while the war was in progress enabled us to refine their training to even higher levels.

The trainees themselves were an unusual lot. Because so many of them were political refugees and not the average draftee, they tended to be college-educated, sometimes professionals, sometimes technicians. Some were even musically trained. Camp Ritchie was one of those places where the guy walking around with the barbed stick picking up litter might be a Ph.D. I once watched as a general passed a private working in the yard. The private neglected to salute, and the general asked him, "Soldier, do you know who I am?" The soldier said with a polite smile, "No, sir, I don't." "I'm a general," he was told. Before the lecture got any further the private said, with an Eastern European accent, "That's a good job, general, you'd better keep it." The general shook his head in exasperation and passed on. Camp Ritchie was a little loose.

My specific function in this process was managerial: I spent most of World War II as a theater manager. During the day the Camp Ritchie theater was used for a full schedule of classes. In the evenings it became a recreation center for showing movies. I was responsible for scheduling both functions and for the up-keep of the building and the equipment. There was a WAC lieutenant in charge. She sat at a desk and was technically the one with ultimate responsibility. There was a sergeant who was supposed to be doing the work. And then there was the person who actually did it: me.

I spent my days surrounded by talented young actors, most of them New Yorkers, who knew their way around the Broadway scene. One of them was the playwright Joe Anthony, who was now developing new material for Section 9. Before long I had formed a pretty clear impression of the life they led, a life of auditions, rehearsals, close calls, lucky breaks. I became familiar with the jargon of the profession. From them I got my first taste of New York show biz from an insider's vantage point, and began to become familiar with the gossipy life of Broadway. It was in that crew that I first met Larney Goodkind, who would later play such an important role in my life.

Even my immediate supervisor was in show biz. Sgt. Forrest Daughdrill had been a New York entertainment industry press agent before the war, and had been with a firm that handled several big-name artists. We developed a rapport, and I con-sciously applied myself to learning what I could from him.

When Daughdrill was reassigned, I received my third stripe and took his place. Sgt. Warfield was now officially the theater manager — a title that sounds more impressive than it was, since the most challenging activity I faced was running the movie projector. I did get a kick out of making the preshow announcements. There was always a list of bulletins that had to be read and I was able to rattle them off in all the different languages of our trainees.

Our commanding officer was Col. Banfield, who was not concerned with the military intelligence training but with the administration of the camp itself. His concern was for running a model military base, and for making it as civilized and cultured as he could. He had a rare opportunity to excel, since so many of those who came through Camp Ritchie were a cut above the average recruit. He kept an eye out for special talent — for musicians to play in the chamber orchestra he had put together, or vocalists for the chaplain's chorales — and when he could he would divert personnel from overseas assignment to his own cadre.

Col. Banfield had a thing about making the camp beautiful, and that included seeding the lawns and planting flowers. He made it clear to me that he'd hold me responsible for the land-scaping around the theater as well as for the theater itself.

I had another encounter of the Camp Ritchie kind, with an officer who wanted to take a short cut across our yard. Col. Banfield had told me in no uncertain terms, "Don't let anybody walk on that grass, and that means a general, if it comes to that." So I literally ordered the captain (in a polite voice) to use the sidewalk.

"Who in hell are you, Sergeant, to tell a captain what to do?" he demanded. My Jefferson Barracks education came in handy: "Standing orders, Captain," I told him. "Would you rather talk to Col. Banfield about it?" The captain waved me off — orders were orders — and followed the signs around the grass, the way he was supposed to.

Of course, even colonels and generals had to adjust to the sometimes upside-down hierarchies of Camp Ritchie life. All our students, whether wearing a single stripe or a shiny star, had to follow the directions of instructors who were often corporals and sergeants. Rank didn't carry over into the classroom.

It didn't take long before I became active at the Camp Ritchie chapel. I don't remember whether the chaplain sought me out or whether I discovered him, but we became friendly and he began to depend on me to play as often as I could for services on Sundays, or to sing anthems; there was one Christmas where we put together a choral group, and I trained them to sing excerpts from the *Messiah*. Col. Banfield liked to show us off, and often invited civilians from the surrounding area to see our performances.

*   *   *   *

At the time I didn't think my situation that exceptional, but as I look back it seems ironic and faintly ridiculous. The United States was fighting for its life, all over the globe, but the nation's colored troops weren't going to be integrated into the fighting forces. There was no earthly reason for me to expect anything more than four years of menial service. And yet, here I was, part of a combat effort that was really making a difference. A combat training program, moreover, that was for all intents and purposes completely integrated.

At the same time I was also furthering my recital career and my theater education at a faster rate than I might have in peacetime. I was surrounded by Europeans who knew and appreciated classical music — the per capita proportion of music lovers was far higher at Camp Ritchie than in Rochester — and I was learning first hand from people who made their living in the show-biz world of New York. And it was all government subsidized, two decades before the existence of the National Endowment for the Arts. Some kind of charm was at work.

Of course, I can't leave the impression that life at Camp Ritchie was idyllic, in any sense. Despite the often idiosyncratic, nonmilitary nature of the place, and the chance to meet a wide range of characters that I'd never encountered before, it was still a military training camp. As often as possible I used the weekends and my leave time to get as far away from Camp Ritchie as I could afford to.

One such trip was not long after my arrival at Camp Ritchie, to attend my college graduation. Throughout my time in basic training, and now in the dusty little world of Camp Ritchie, I'd been looking forward to that homecoming. By combining leave time with a weekend, I managed to have a few days with family and friends back home.

The highlight for me was going to be the graduation ceremony itself — I was looking forward to the pageantry, the pomp, the cap and gown, the whole nine yards. And it would also be nice just to be home, in my slacks and sweater, feeling like a college-boy civilian once again.

Once I got home I found that my family preferred to show me off in my uniform on every possible occasion. So I complied and stayed starched for them. But the worst news was that the University of Rochester, out of pride for the soldiers and sailors in their student body, had requested all graduates currently serving in the armed forces to attend in uniform, not traditional cap and gown.

I was crestfallen. Of course, I went with the program, but I felt cheated of half the fun of graduating. It wasn't until some forty years later, when I accepted an honorary doctorate at the same podium, that I finally got to wear my complete academic garb; as I said in my prepared remarks that afternoon, after forty years it was a relief to finally appear dressed to suit the occasion, in full regalia.

Several times I made the trip from Maryland to New York City, my first visits there as an adult on my own. I went with New Yorkers stationed at Camp Ritchie, people who knew their way around. That was when I first discovered the pleasures of New York delicatessens. I can still taste that hot pastrami and corned beef, with the tang that I enjoyed so much after weeks of a bland Army diet.

In New York I'd stay at the Sloan YMCA, at 34th Street near Eighth Avenue, which used to be the main YMCA for service-men "on the town." It was cheap and centrally located, and I could work out in the gym. I didn't spend much time going to shows — I really wasn't oriented toward the Broadway stage — and I was never one for night clubbing. But it was an exciting taste of the Big Apple, just to be on my own in the world's greatest city. I enjoyed the architecture, the people, the street-level culture of the place; I was never a very typical tourist, but I was wide-eyed about the variety and the unpredictable novelties that were always just around the corner. When I got tired of adventuring, it was never hard to talk me into going to the movies. In those occasional aimless trips from Camp Ritchie, I developed an attraction for the excitement of New York City that would take over thirty years to wear out.

But most of my three-day passes, and even normal week-ends, found me making the trip into Washington, D.C., which was just a two-hour bus ride away. I could go in on a Saturday morning and come back Sunday night. I couldn't afford to stay in the Hotel Dunbar, over at 14th and Florida Avenue — that was the famous hotel for black entertainers and people of note, back in those days of segregation — but there was plenty to do at Lucy Diggs Slowe Hall, a dormitory-type facility at Howard University available for transient servicemen.

If you've been in the service, you don't have to ask why I'd want to get out of Camp Ritchie every chance I got. I was looking for something that every serviceman away from home is always looking for and is never going to find: some semblance of the warmth and camaraderie I'd left back home in Rochester. But if those comforts would prove elusive, there were a few consolations that would help to tide me over.

For one thing I could get a decent dinner. I always looked forward to a good homestyle meal in the cafeteria at Lucy Diggs. They had things like fried chicken, greens, cornbread — soul food — and though it was a far cry from my mother's meals, or meals I could make for myself, for that matter, if I'd had a kitchen, it was still infinitely better than the generic stuff they dished out in the Camp Ritchie mess hall.

There I could find companionship, too. There was a piano in the recreation room at Lucy Diggs, and on Saturday afternoon, as soon as I hit town, you would find me at the keyboard, practicing and playing. People would come around and it would end up as a singalong — the piano was always a great icebreaker.

The other reason for going to Washington was to go to a real church. In all my years of touring and travel, when I know I'm going to be in a new town over the weekend, I usually try to find myself a church to go to. It's almost always Baptist, but not necessarily. I ask around for "a good black church that has an organ and a wonderful choir and sings anthems," and that's usually where I end up. It was during my Camp Ritchie days that I first began this practice, and the first church I located this way was Shiloh Baptist, in Washington.

At my first visit I could see that I was going to be at home there. The pastor had a daughter, a beautiful mezzo-soprano, who sang solos with the choir. In no time at all I was taking my place in the choir stall. After my first Sunday there, the minister of music — the director of the choir — asked me to sing a solo the following Sunday. So in a matter of weeks I found myself in the bosom of an extended family. They just embraced me, as a young man from Camp Ritchie who was a talented young singer, and made me feel fussed over and cared for. I was right at home. It was a wonderful, warm, family kind of thing, and I formed friendships then that are still going strong, fifty years later.

As 1942 passed into 1943 and it became clear that the training of military intelligence teams was going to continue into the foreseeable future, I began to settle in for the long haul. That meant, among other things, that I would have to find ways of continuing my musical education.

I had already attracted attention as the "big black sergeant who sings opera," which was singular enough to get me included whenever the colonel put together a chapel presentation or recital progam. Sometimes, when Col. Banfield decided to show off the talents of his cadre, we'd have guests in from nearby towns. If they heard me sing, I'd sometimes get an invitation to perform for them off-base. I did several recitals at nearby colleges as a result. In that way I came to the attention of a New York City socialite, Mary Schlesinger, who had a summer place in the Blue Ridge Mountains not far from Camp Ritchie and who hosted soirees there from time to time. My invitations to her home there and in New York City once again opened up my horizons a few degrees wider.

In addition, I was branching out into different kinds of music. Away from the concentrated curriculum of Eastman, I was discovering the practicality of popular sounds. Bach was all very fine for the European contingent on the post, but for most GIs it couldn't compare to boogie-woogie. They wanted a lively evening of beer and piano and would ask me to play something they could sing along with. Though I had managed to improvise for these singalongs, I was developing an appreciation for more complex forms. So on one of my three-day passes to New York I bought several of Hazel Scott's books of boogie-woogie music, and applied myself to their study on a fast track. Before long I got pretty good at it. There were immediate rewards from the people I played it for. Now that I was playing music they could relate to, we soon expanded into jam sessions with other instruments, and it became a regular feature of Camp Ritchie night life.

And there were also long-term implications, though of course I couldn't know that at the time. The talent I was acquiring — a skill that my father had successfully thwarted when I was a teenager — would later come in handy to support my classical study, and even lead directly to my Town Hall debut.

There was another unlikely occurrence that gave me an early taste of the world I was moving toward. On Broadway the celebrated producer Billy Rose was preparing a production of *Carmen Jones*, due to open in December 1943. It was based on the Bizet opera but set in the southern U.S. He was looking for an actor for the role of Husky Miller. Someone associated with the production had ties to the University of Rochester and knew I'd be perfect for the part. They made inquiries and learned that I was stationed at Camp Ritchie.

John Hammond, one of Billy Rose's assistants, called me and told me to come to New York for an audition. I wangled another three-day pass, and at the audition I was offered the job. Would I be willing to take a leave of absence from Camp Ritchie and perform on Broadway? Are you kidding? It was a measure of Billy Rose's oblivious arrogance that he thought he could pull strings and have me put on "detached service" or some such arrangement to perform in his musical. It didn't happen, of course. Despite possible appearances to the contrary, after all, we were significantly involved in the war effort. So it was a near miss, but the episode would later play a significant role in the development of my career.

*   *   *   *

By far the most important outcome of my Camp Ritchie experience was wrapped up in the person of Larney Goodkind. I met Larney the way I met most people. I was playing the piano in the recreation room and he was among those who wandered by, to listen to my efforts at boogie-woogie or to the Brahms lieder that I might be practicing.

Larney was one of the actors in Section 9. He was from a musical family and was himself a very fine pianist, especially in the Brahms literature. He had also done a good deal of professional acting. When the war started he was working for Universal Pictures as a talent scout. He had an ear and an eye for talent as well as an enjoyment of good music. Through our mutual interest in the arts we became friends. Later he would become the personal manager to whom I entrusted my entire career, and he would be Leontyne Price's manager as well, among his other accomplishments. But in these early days he was just another of the remarkable people I met at Camp Ritchie.

Larney was eleven years older than I, enough older that he was something of a mentor yet close enough in age to be a friend. With his show-biz experience he was the most important aspect of my education in the years after Rochester. And with his educated and sensitive perspectives on the arts, literature, and current events, he contributed to a context that helped me sort out my career priorities.

It was becoming clearer all the time that when the war ended and my military service was through I would be stepping out into a no-man's-land. There simply was no career ladder for a black classical singer. The opera world wasn't ready for me or any other black male. Hollywood, too, offered only stereotypes for the most part, and the situation was the same for mainstream Broadway theater. The concert world was all there was, it seemed, and that was shaky at best.

I had received intimations of this situation in Rochester, of course. I always knew that the cold hard world outside would be much more difficult for me than the nurturing environment of my family and friends. Now, though the war had interposed itself, the reckoning was coming closer. It was especially important for me, at an age when young men and women are ready to launch their careers, to fall in with someone like Larney. He combined an appreciation for artistic potential with an awareness of the difficult realities of show biz, yet he was able to maintain a calm, cheerful optimism that there was no problem that couldn't be solved. That was just what I needed, and from someone savvy enough and honest enough to see the situation through untinted spectacles.

Of course, there was no idea while we were at Camp Ritchie that this artist-manager collaboration lay in our futures; but it was important that the seeds were planted.

And the future was bearing down on us. By late 1944 it was clear that the war in Europe couldn't go on forever. No one could predict how it would be wrapped up, but there was no question that it was just a matter of time.

Ironically, that fact caused some consternation among the brass at Camp Ritchie. I wondered why the commanding officers seemed unduly anxious in those early months of 1945, until I realized that the whole reason for Camp Ritchie's existence was to train military intelligence teams for service in Europe. If the war were to end there — and if we had no military intelligence function in the Pacific war (which we all figured could continue for years to come) — every one of us could expect to be shipped out to the South Pacific as part of the invasion of Japan. It would be an oriental version of the Normandy landings, and nobody had any illusions about how fierce that fighting would be.

But our commanding officers were resourceful, to say the least, and developed a refinement of their original mission. And it was to the playwright Joe Anthony that they turned to work out the details — he got the commission of his life.

They asked him to come up with an entirely new training script for the Section 9 players dealing with military intelligence operations targeted on the Japanese. He was given a new cadre of Japanese-American soldiers to work with and other experts on the Far East to consult with. The new script differed significantly from the European version, I was told. For example, the best interrogation techniques now called for extreme politeness rather than bullying threats, for maximum effectiveness.

The success of the new material meant that Larney's long-running show would not be cancelled for the coming season; they'd be going into a sequel instead, a spin-off series. Instead of the European refugees, the trainees and sometimes the actors playing the roles of the enemy would be *nisei* Americans.

Larney had left a girl behind in New York, and he didn't intend to let the war prevent him from getting on with his life. Karen was a vivacious woman of about my age, whose red hair and precise, deft gestures matched her quick wit. When appropriate she was sharp-tongued as well. She had been an actress and carried herself with that style that actresses seem to have patented. To Larney's educated taste she was straightforward and direct; but to me, at the time, she personified glamour and worldliness, crowned with a scintillating sense of humor. Like Larney, Karen was politically liberal, and continually involved in issues dealing with racial inequality, women's rights, and the like. Our discussions were mostly centered on art and theater. She had all the intelligence that Larney had, and was just as discerning. And in addition she seemed to have taken the actor's insight into character and turned it outward, so she was a very good critic and analyst of performance. She was a worldly woman, probably more so than Larney, and she knew her way around New York. She had a sister, Hennie, who was a black-haired version of the same intensity. Besides her credentials as a cosmopolitan New Yorker, Hennie knew her way around Europe as well as anyone at Mary Schlesinger's soirees. The two of them helped me set my standards high for women of intelligence and energy.

As I say, Larney had a good thing going with Karen, and when he understood that he was going to be in uniform, not for months but for years, he made sure she didn't get away. At the time our schedule — producing intelligence teams for the Italy and North Africa campaigns — was particularly busy. So he arranged for Karen to come down from New York, he found a rabbi to perform the rites, and he asked me to sing.

Karen was due to arrive on their wedding day, at the small railroad depot nearest to Camp Ritchie — just a shed, really, on the rail spur that ran out to western Maryland. When she got off the train Larney was nowhere to be seen — he was waiting on the other side of the tracks. Karen had had a long, hard journey and just wasn't comfortable to find herself south of the Mason-Dixon line, so far from the amenities of New York City. She said later she nearly got back on the train. Fortunately for Larney, for her, for everyone who ever knew them, she stood there on the roadside gravel, alone and lost, until the train pulled out revealing Larney on the opposite side.

The wedding was August 3, 1945, a Friday. It was the first Jewish wedding I'd ever seen and it was one of the most poetically beautiful I'd ever experienced. For their honeymoon Larney had rented a motel room for two weeks. He would have the weekend off; but then, beginning Monday, August 6, he would spend each night with Karen, and return to camp by early morning reveille. As it happened, the U.S. air forces dropped the atomic bomb on Hiroshima on August 6, and Col. Banfield gave everyone at Camp Ritchie the day off. Larney and Karen borrowed or rented a car and traveled to nearby Gettysburg, to contemplate the horrors of war.

Odd as it seems now, I didn't see too much of Larney and Karen on the few trips I made to New York. Larney and I were pals at work, and after the workday on the base. But, as likely as not, he'd use any free days he could arrange to get to New York

and Karen. I'd occasionally get a three-day pass and plan a trip
north, but I'd usually try to find a way to stretch the pass over a
weekend, making five days, and make it all the way to Rochester.

Most of my weekend trips were to D.C., which was far more
affordable for me. It was on one of those weekend trips to
Washington that I first experienced the overt, matter-of-fact, no-
apologies racism associated with the Old South. I should say it
was the first time I was ever aware of it, because before and since
I've blithely made my way through life, blissfully unaware of
personal slights unless they came up behind me and bit me on the
bottom.

In this case, I was on a crowded bus from Camp Ritchie into
Washington. A white woman got on the bus with a lot of
packages and sat down in the only vacant seat, next to me. I
didn't think anything of it. After a few minutes, one of the
soldiers from Camp Ritchie, a young man I knew, left his seat to
come over and ask, "Madam, would you like to change seats with
me?"

"Oh yes, thank you," she said, and he sat down beside me.
Even at that point I would have been oblivious to what was going
on. But after a minute or two, he was friendly enough to make
conversation. He said in an off-hand manner, "I didn't mean that
as an insult to you, I hope you didn't take it personally, but these
Southern white women don't like to sit next to Negroes."

At first I didn't know what he was talking about. And then
I realized what all the seat-switching had been about. For an
instant I felt an impulse to explode incoherently: "You son of a
bitch." I was arrested by a sense of wonder, not only because he
had no idea that he was offending me, but I was also amazed by
my own faulty perceptions. There it had been staring me in the
face, unvarnished, old-fashioned, dyed-in-the-wool, Jim Crow-
style bigotry — but if he hadn't opened his mouth I never would
have recognized it.

That was the gift of Rochester: that I didn't go around
picking up on all the signals that must have been out there all the
time. When I think of the enormous psychic and spiritual burden
I have been spared, which has enabled me to pursue my own
concerns and not be bothered with others' problems, I silently
thank my parents once more for their decision to lift our family
out of an environment where I would have grown up prickly-
sensitive to every slight.

Of course, the sad thing is that the lady would probably have been perfectly happy right where she was. But the same crippling code of conduct that motivated the young man to offer his seat required that she take him up on it.

That rare experience is balanced by events like the party at Mary Schlesinger's apartment in New York. She always had a very cosmopolitan group in her house, and this time was no exception. For me it was yet another case of culture shock. A few hours earlier I'd been waiting at the depot with my buddies in olive drab. Now here I was, out of my uniform and dressed casually, making conversation with her worldly friends, many of them emigres from war-torn Europe.

I think I inadvertently conveyed more of a sense of mystery than I was entitled to. Mary's friends at this soiree, and on earlier occasions at her summer home, were never quite able to completely get a handle on me. I remember talking with one of her guests, a young French-speaking woman, who interrupted our conversation to speculate that I must be from Martinique.

"No," I told her, switching to English, "I'm American."

"But born — where? — Haiti!" she guessed again, now speaking French.

"No," I said, "down South. Arkansas."

"So where did you learn your French?" she wanted to know, now getting suspicious.

"In high school in upstate New York."

She narrowed her eyes and there was a hint of irritation. "You didn't learn that French in high school," she told me. Then after a pause: "Where do you work?"

"I'm in the Army," I said. "I'm with military intelligence."

"Ahhh!" she said, waving a finger in the air, now comprehending everything. "You can't talk, I understand." And then, in English, she said in an exaggerated whisper, "Top secret," with a smile. As she walked away I heard her murmur, with amusement, "Arkansas!"

She had concluded that, since I was involved in espionage, I could have been from God knows where, Casablanca maybe. It didn't matter because she was never going to get a straight story from me. As a spy I would have told her anything — even such obvious lies as West Helena, Arkansas, and Rochester, New York — rather than reveal my true identity. Later in the evening she relaxed, we spoke of art and music and avoided compromising my military mission with discussion of classified information.

It wasn't until years later, thinking back about those good times, that I was able to see myself as they must have seen me. Especially since that whole crowd was definitely left of center in their politics, and considering the impression of strong black well-spoken males that Paul Robeson had left on their consciousness, I must have come across as a mysterious, perhaps vaguely threatening, exotic black man who spoke French and Italian and German, played Schubert and sang Verdi, and who was currently working with G-2.

That was from their vantage point. From mine, of course, I was young Bill Warfield, this wide-eyed kid who's living in the barracks, first time away from his home in Rochester, New York. In ways I couldn't completely appreciate at the time, I was gaining valuable social experience. And if I simultaneously enriched their fantasy life, well, it's wonderful how this world works sometimes.

I stayed at Camp Ritchie until I was mustered out in March, 1946, when I headed back to Rochester. I still wasn't sure exactly what I should be doing next, but figured that I should have that master's degree for security. The music department was welcoming me with open arms, and I couldn't imagine a better way to restore the priorities that had been interrupted by Pearl Harbor.

At home I found a new set of relationships. My mother recognized that the boy she had sent off to war had come home a grown man. For one thing, I had lost weight; I had trimmed down from the sometimes pampered fair-haired boy to a lean, athletic ex-G.I.

My father's change was even more significant. He had always been the man of the house and, though he was never a tyrant, while we boys were growing up there was never any question about who was in charge. Daddy never had to give orders — it was usually sufficient that he "believed this would be best," and whatever "this" was, that was what transpired.

Now, however, he had three grown sons who had gone off into the service. Vern had been in the European theater, Robert in the Far East, I had been in G-2. Now that we were all together again, we all evidenced the same undiminished respect for our parents, the same tendency to deference. But on my father's part there was now a new respect towards us — and the relationship just naturally turned from paternal and filial to something more like friendship. I have to admit it was a little awkward at times; in some part of every man, father is ever Father.

Chapter Five

ON THE ROAD

The new year 1946 was a happy time for the Reverend and Mrs. Warfield. All their sons had returned from the war healthy, trim, without a scratch. That was the year my father stepped up to his new pulpit, as the pastor of Mount Vernon Baptist Church, which is still the home church for the Warfield family; to this day my brother Thaddeus is minister of music there.

I got back to Rochester in time for the spring semester. My intention was to take classes that spring, then through the summer, and on for another full year. Then I'd have my master's degree, which would qualify me to teach music. In the meantime I would be laying my plans for whatever career opportunities might present themselves.

From what I'd picked up through Larney and his friends, there were two facts of show-biz life I knew for certain. First, breaking into the business was going to take time, persistence, and a lot of making the rounds; I would need to build up a stake to carry me through. And second, I would need a master's degree to fall back on. Too many performers learn too late that they can't make a living from what they earn on stage. Todd Duncan, among others, had already shown that a university base can support a flourishing concert career.

But teaching was more to me than a crutch. I was looking forward to teaching just as much as I was looking forward to a performing career. Throughout my life my better teachers had all been important to me. I enjoyed the school environment, the spirit of educational excellence, the enthusiasm of the young men and women inspired by a desire to study and to learn.

But I hadn't been back in the music department for more than a few weeks when Dr. Howard Hanson, the director of the Eastman School of Music called me into his office.

"You had a call, Bill," he told me. "Do you know Herman Levin?"

"The New York producer?"

"He's trying to reach you."

"Reach me?"

"They want you to audition for the singing lead in the national touring company of the musical *Call Me Mister*."

I was stunned. *Call Me Mister* was a Broadway hit. I had read that it was due to go on the road, crossing the country, playing in all the major theaters. It would mean breaking into the business at the top level, in a steady job, rather than walking the boards trying to scare up work.

It would also mean a chance to gain experience in a featured role and to put some money aside. The tour could last a full year, maybe more. I had been prepared to do walk-ons and take pot luck with casting, and here was an opportunity to start out in style.

I didn't hesitate — at least, not at first. There was no way I was going to pass up the opportunity to audition. I called Herman Levin's office and made an appointment for the very next day.

I was on the train to New York City the following morning and in front of the producer and the director that afternoon. I sang one song for them — I can't remember what I did, but it wasn't Brahms — and read a passage of the script. They didn't keep me in suspense. After about two minutes of private discussion, Herman Levin offered me the contract: "Have your agent look it over and get back to us as soon as possible." My head was spinning as I left them and caught the afternoon train back to Rochester. I didn't have an agent, of course, but I did want to talk to Dr. Hanson. On the train I reflected on the odd workings of fate: It seems I had been recommended to Levin by John Hammond, who had met me briefly back when Billy Rose had tried to get me released from active duty for his production of *Carmen Jones*. That fleeting encounter, it turns out, was the first break of my performing career.

Back in Rochester with Dr. Hanson I was having second thoughts. All my instincts said to go with the show, but some part of my more logical brain was urging prudence. Dr. Hanson resolved it for me — he was all for my seizing the opportunity. "Take it," he said. "See how you like it. You're welcome to come back, whatever happens. You won't lose any academic credits. Give it a try."

So I turned around and headed back to New York, with just one suitcase. We were in rehearsal for only a week or two, since most of the cast had already performed with the show during its New York run. I can hardly remember anything of that brief period in New York, except that they put me up in a hotel. It was my first taste of hotel life, and I found that I liked the concept of someone else worrying about the linens and the basic house-keeping — George Bernard Shaw had it right when he called hotels a "refuge from home life" — and so I looked forward to a year of it.

The musical revue *Call Me Mister* had opened in April 1946 as one of the biggest hits of the Broadway season. It was a mild social satire with music and lyrics by Harold Rome. Rome had made his name a few years earlier with a socially conscious amateur theatrical prepared for the International Ladies' Garment Workers' Union, which caught fire and became Broadway's biggest musical up to that time: *Pins and Needles*. His new hit *Call Me Mister* was less politically pungent. It hung loosely on the theme of citizen-soldiers returning to civilian life. Though it was mostly all in good fun, it did take some not-so-affectionate backward glances at the military and a forward look at the social scene that the vets returned to deal with. There was an authenticity about the humor, because everyone in the cast, men and women alike, had served in uniform.

The show featured a melange of material, from tap dancing to a serious ballet sequence (a soldier's dream of the corner drugstore) to all-out Copacabana-style chorus numbers. Just to give some feel for the work, there were tony moments of arch comedy (a Noel Coward version of Air Force life as imagined by a G.I.) and torchy spells, like the blues ballad sung by a no-longer-needed WAC who finds herself treated like army surplus. Some of the best material was written for the role they were offering me, including a poignant reverential homage to FDR, "Face On A Dime," a rollicking number, "The Red Ball Express," and the show's most moving number, "Goin' Home Train."

So you can imagine the variety of the company of performers I found myself in, and the peppery spirit I was surrounded by, in my first professional show-biz experience.

One of the first friends I made in that company was a singer and dancer my age, Lou Ampolo. Shortly after rehearsals began the company manager paired us up as roommates for the tour. That would be another first for me — the adjustments involved in getting along with a roommate. As things turned out, the choice that had been made for me by the company manager was the selection of a life-long friend.

Rehearsals went by in a flash, and then, for the first time in my life, I was on the professional stage and on the road.

Our tour took us to New Haven, Boston, Philadelphia, Cleveland, Detroit, Chicago, and then across the continent to Los Angeles and San Francisco. Except for my summer trip to Virginia, and the commuting to Corning, I'd done very little travel as a child. Even during my Army days my traveling had been more like shuttling from Point A to Point B rather than touring. Now I was off to see the country. It was heady stuff for a young performer in his first show.

Once again I had landed myself in an extended family. A theater company that works well together can be like a clan of relatives. In my first and only such experience we all got along like close kin. Wherever we went, we'd check into hotels with cooking facilities and pool our resources. We'd hang out together after the show and we looked out for each other. In those days, with blacks and whites traveling together, sometimes that mutual support became a necessity.

One of my new friends from that production was William Marshall, an actor whose career like mine was just getting started. Before long he'd be lighting up the marquees in New York and Hollywood in roles as varied as Frederick Douglas and Blacula. At the time he was, like me, just getting his footing. For all the qualities we had in common, he and I were of two completely different mentalities.

He was a tall, well-built man with a powerful voice and a physical presence that was arresting. He was also deeply involved in the social movements of the day. When we remember the civil rights revolution of the 1950s, we forget that it got its momentum in the 1940s. It was in 1947 that Bayard Rustin organized the first Freedom Ride, sponsored by CORE, the

Congress of Racial Equality. It was in 1947 that Jackie Robinson became the first African-American to play on a major league baseball team, the Brooklyn Dodgers. And it was in 1947 that A. Philip Randolph began his organizing efforts to create the League for Nonviolent Civil Disobedience Against Military Segregation. As the cold war was heating up, and the U.S. was fighting a propaganda war that pitted Democracy against Repression all around the world, the kind of segregation that I had encountered in the Army was untenable. The following year Truman would show how easily — at a single stroke of the pen — integration could be effected, when he signed the famous ban on segregation in the armed forces.

And though the world would have to wait nine more years for Rosa Parks to challenge state law with her famous refusal to move to the rear of a city bus in Montgomery, Alabama, it was in 1946 that Irene Morgan won the same fight regarding federal law, in the U.S. Supreme Court, after she refused to move to the rear of an interstate Greyhound bus in Richmond, Virginia.

William Marshall was up to date on all these movements, and his involvement was an important part of my education. In particular, he was following the ups and downs of Paul Robeson's career, and I was particuarly interested to know more about that. Where Marshall and I were of different mentalities was in our perceptions of personal slights due to racism. I was generally oblivious; he was easily insulted. In Boston, in Cleveland, in Chicago, it could be as simple as buying a newspaper from the corner stand. He would look at me with a kind of wonder. "You're very naive," he'd say. "Look around you! Did you see the way that person looked at you?" and he would laugh a bitter laugh.

We'd go out for a sandwich, and I'd be figuring out what I was going to order while he would be casing the joint. Then he'd deliver his verdict: "We're not wanted here." He was right: The waitress was taking her time getting around to us, while other customers who came in after us were waited on promptly. He was right: The manager was sullen, and there were unfriendly comments coming from that corner of the room that were audible if we cared to listen. He was right: I had simply not noticed before he mentioned it, and would probably never have paid any attention. I didn't know fast service from slow service, or concern myself with motivation. I would wait; he would fume.

Of course, there were occasional incidents when even I could catch on. I remember once while we were in Chicago, Lou Ampolo and I had gone into a diner in the Loop for a cup of coffee. I asked for sugar, which was then served in a bowl and not the paper packets we have today. I stirred in a spoonful, took a deep swallow, then had to spit it back out over the cup and saucer. The waiter had given me a sugar bowl filled with salt.

I bristled, but Lou Ampolo probably did the right thing when he said, "Come on, let's get out of here, it's not worth it." All the big race riots, lasting for days and resulting in scores of injured and dead, including the ones just the year before in Tennessee and Philadelphia, had blown up out of just such minor incidents as this.

That was the climate that was always around us then. Neither William Marshall nor I were on the barricades of the movement — each of us, in our own way, worked out our commitment on a different kind of stage — but temperamentally you could say that Bill Marshall and Bill Warfield represented opposite extremes within our own band of the spectrum. He didn't miss a single nuance of even unconscious racism. I shrugged it off; racism was going to be the racist's handicap, not mine.

Like my charmed environment at Camp Ritchie, the family of the *Call Me Mister* company provided the perfect alternative to those concerns. We were all so close that I made some lifelong friends on that 1947 tour.

There was a young dancer who was already showing he had the stuff to excel, Bob Fosse. Even then, as a hoofer in a minor role, Fosse was full of pizzazz — a real standout. There were two comedians that kept us in stitches on and off stage, Carl Reiner and Buddy Hackett. Whenever we were in a town longer than two weeks, Carl would bring his family to travel with the tour; he'd usually get a short-term lease on an apartment rather than a hotel room. The Reiner apartment would become the gathering place for the rest of the cast. I ate many a meal at the Reiners', dangling his little boy Rob on my knee.

I learned a good deal from Lou Ampolo. He had a solid foundation in classical ballet, as most show dancers do, and when we found time on the road I got him to give me some of the fundamentals, to the point where I could actually rip off a pretty passable triple tour. I was fascinated by the lore and language of ballet, and impressed by the daily discipline. I was intrigued that an art form so physical and athletic could simultaneously be so ethereal. I'm still drawn to ballet and occasionally I surprise dancers by speaking their jargon.

That first tour proved to be an invaluable year-long education in show business. I was surrounded by people at various stages of their careers who could tell me how things really worked, and I could test what they told me through direct observation. My first impression was that I had found myself thrown into a cultural explosion as dynamic as any the world has ever seen. The '40s going into the '50s were exciting years for show business. It was a great time to be in New York, a great time to be making the rounds and looking for your big break.

What was going on in New York was in part the result of all the talent that came flooding into New York City after the war. It was given special vitality by the G.I. Bill, which could be used for acting, music, and dance lessons just as well as for study in other fields. There was an enormous number of talented people pounding the pavement and making the rounds knocking on doors. There was a great spirit of optimism in the air, a sense that opportunity was all around you, that anything could happen. All that dynamism resulted in a burst of cultural energy that amounted almost to a renaissance.

Wherever you were, you felt a part of an extended life in art. In Boston with *Call Me Mister*, some of the younger members of our acting company went out for spaghetti after the show with some of the kids in another touring production, *Private Lives*. The star of that show liked to go out with the "kids," so Tallulah Bankhead became a chum. One of the young actors who tagged along, trying like the rest of us to keep up with all the adventures, was Marlon Brando.

Another time, again in Boston, someone in our company had a pair of friends who performed in a comedy team. We just had to see their crazy act, he said. These wacky youngsters looking for their lucky break were Dean Martin and Jerry Lewis.

And of course there were many more, people that nobody's ever heard of, bright faces who had a good time and then settled down to other creative careers as agents or business people or teachers. But they were all a part of that same great swirl of creativity, all of us cheerful, confident, mutually encouraging. We were all just getting started, the world was as young as we were, the sky was the limit — and in the meantime, we were having fun. I suppose we should have had some sense of trepidation about our careers, but we were too busy trying to take the next step. We were infused with an unshakable sense of hopeful anticipation. We were the people they wrote the song about: "There's no business like show business." Life was all expectancy.

The critics and journalists were part of that creative ferment. The younger critics sometimes joined the ratpacks that mixed together artists, actors, writers, and miscellaneous nightowls. Even the more established critics were considered a part of the world they covered, not aloof and unapproachable. It was during *Call Me Mister* that I first met Claudia Cassidy, the respected critic and chronicler of the arts in Chicago. I was at the Blackstone Theater in that city in the summer of 1947, and I did what I always tried to do when I came close enough to someone I respected: I decided to ask for her advice. It never occurred to me that it might be presumptuous for a performer to impose on one of the country's leading critics. I just called her up and asked if I could come over and talk to her, knowing that she knew the scene. When I arrived at her office at the *Chicago Tribune*, filled with books and newspapers and magazines falling off the shelves, I found her a little nonplussed by this road show performer talking about the classical concert career he was planning. But she was completely gracious. I remember her suggestion, which I wasn't ready to take: She said that maybe I could rent one of the smaller theaters in Chicago and do some concerts.

In 1951, the year after my Town Hall debut, the impresario Harry Zelzer and his partner and wife, Sarah, brought me back to Chicago for a concert. Of course I paid my respects to Claudia Cassidy. I discovered, even before my performance there, that I had an immediate, intense rapport with her—her glowing reviews subsequently made my Chicago debut a triumph.

I didn't have any ulterior motives, back in 1947 when I asked if I could pick her brains, but it turns out I was planting seeds of what has since become a lifelong relationship. She felt, correctly, that she had played a part in the launching of yet another career. No one minds being asked for advice; it's surprising how rarely young people overcome their reticence to ask for help.

It was during that time in Chicago that I made the first preliminary arrangements for my career move to New York.

Call Me Mister was booked at the Blackstone Theatre, on the edge of the Loop, for three months. Lou and I decided we could follow Reiner's example and rent a West Side apartment, available on a short-term lease, rather than a hotel room. We were relatively settled there and we had time to do some planning for what was going to happen after the tour. It was none too soon, we knew, because after Chicago we had just the stint on the West Coast and then the tour would end. I had already pretty much decided I was going to try my luck in New York. The clincher was when Lou and I agreed in Chicago that, since we were compatible roommates, we would continue to room together in a New York apartment after the tour. Lou had a good sense of where to locate, so all those logistics were going to be handled for me.

I was very receptive to advice from all quarters. From talking with Lou and other actors I was getting a good idea of how it would work. Even before I was settled in a place to live I'd get myself over to the offices of Actor's Equity Association. I had been required to join Equity, the actor's union, when I was cast in *Call Me Mister*. The Equity offices were a hangout for everyone looking for work, and served as the unofficial hub of the great central nervous system of show biz. I needed to plug into that grapevine, to let them know that I was in town and available for work.

Then I'd begin to scan the newspapers for work. Of course there were the trade papers — *Variety* and other show-biz weeklies. But even the major dailies would list casting calls for shows. Whenever there was a role for a black actor who could sing a lot and dance a little, I'd want to go over there and get an audition.

At the same time I'd want to do as so many other veterans were doing, fill out the forms and begin taking classes on the G.I. Bill. They'd cost me nothing, they'd give me training, and they'd keep me in daily touch with working professionals in the business — what is called networking today. My first choice would be to enroll in the American Theater Wing — both for the acting classes and for the professional contacts.

But even in this preliminary stage I kept my true goal in sight. I would want to use some of my G.I. Bill scholarship subsidy for voice lessons too, and for lessons to continue to enrich my repertoire. The Broadway stage wasn't going to be my life, it was going to be an accessory. So I'd have to make the classical musical connections as well. That might mean classes at Julliard.

Or it might be just as useful to find good teachers and study with them privately. I'd figure all that out when I got there.

But the still unanswered question was, how would I be able to support myself while I was getting started? I was frugal and had managed to save a little, but only a little. I would need an income. That was the missing link in my plan. One option that was certainly not open was to call my folks for money. They had their own financial concerns, and while I knew I was welcome to move back in with them and continue on scholarship at Eastman, I could never bring myself to ask them to support me in New York City.

In retrospect, the answer to my question was the most likely answer, from a most unlikely source.

Some nights, after the show, we'd all go out to a local club to unwind. One night during our Chicago stay, when we'd had a few drinks in a local piano bar and the piano player had called it a night, I got up to fool around on the keyboard for a while. It became a singalong. I played whatever the others wanted to hear, in whatever key they liked — show tunes, pop tunes, boogie-woogie, the kind of mix that I'd play in the rec room at Camp Ritchie.

We took a break and I remember that one of the girls told me, "Wow, Bill, you've got it made." I wasn't sure what she meant.

"Your piano, your singing," she said. "You're one guy who'll never have to worry about paying the rent. Between jobs you can always go play the clubs and cocktail lounges." I still didn't have a complete sense of what she was talking about, but I got her main point. I had been pushing around the various parts of the puzzle, ideas of what I'd do when the tour ended. And now the pieces all fell into place. I could finally lay down all the basic elements of a career plan. I would make the rounds, take the classes, and chase my muse in New York, as planned. And I would pay the bills by working in night clubs as a pianist and singer. It was far less secure than the notion of getting a degree and teaching but it gave me enough to go on. In that casual conversation in an after-hours club, it became clear to me that I was headed for the insecurities and anxieties of a new life in New York, rather than the certainties of my old life in Rochester.

Chapter Six

THE BIG APPLE

When I hit New York, as planned, I went directly to General Artists Corporation, to make an appointment for an audition, and to the Equity offices, to let the theater world know I was available. While I was doing that — literally on the same afternoon, as I recall — Lou Ampolo was making our living arrangements for us.

For the first few months we shared quarters at the Americana Hotel on West 47th Street, between Sixth and Seventh Avenues, waiting for rooms to open up for us at the Woodrow Wilson Hotel Apartments across the street. The Wilson was well known as an artists' residence, and it would be perfect for our needs, but in the tight housing market of postwar New York City there was a lengthy waiting list.

The Americana was an actors' and dancers' hangout, too, for performers even more transient than those at the Wilson. The rooms there were smaller, and had no cooking facilities — electric burners and hot plates were not allowed, and of course there were no refrigerators in the rooms. As I recall, the bathroom and showers were down the hall. It left a lot to be desired. But it was my first New York address, and I was excited to be in the center of the action. I was young and flexible, and made the adjustments easily. No kitchen? — That didn't stop us from cooking up a storm. We had to do it all on the sly, of course, and after dinner we had to tuck the hot plate way in the back of the closet where it wouldn't be noticed by the maids — not that the maids were all that thorough! We bought our perishables in small quantities, and in those winter weeks we were able to use the fire escape outside the window as our refrigerator. I'd pick up ham hocks and greens and whip up a pretty good main course with one skillet on one burner. That was where I perfected my stove-top cornbread.

That brief time in the Americana was my most authentic taste of the life of a show-biz "gypsy," and while I wouldn't have missed it for the world — you haven't been baptized in the business if you haven't paid those dues — I was very happy when the Woodrow Wilson let us know an apartment was available.

Of course, the Wilson was no Waldorf-Astoria, either. But there we had two separate rooms and enough sunlight to make the place cheery. The rooms were clean and the price was right. And now that we had a kitchenette we could do some real cooking. We could make our trips to the grocery without having to sneak in the milk and eggs. Lou taught me a thing or two about Italian cooking, but I surprised him by showing off a few Italian dishes of my own repertoire— thanks to the ethnic diversity of our neighborhood in Rochester. In two months at the Americana I'd gotten so used to the improvised arrangements that, for the first week in the new place, every time I needed something from the refrigerator I instinctively turned toward the window with the fire escape.

The Wilson could be a pretty wild place, which worked to our advantage. Since the standards were lax, there were no objections to my bringing in a small spinet piano, so I could practice in the room. There were studio spaces in New York that you could rent by the hour. At Nola's on Broadway at 53rd it was seventy-five cents an hour for a small room and piano, if I remember correctly. But when every nickel counted, being able to bring in my own piano made it possible for me to study many more hours than I could have otherwise.

One reason why Lou and I turned out to be such compatible roommates might be the fact that there were many times when I was out of town, and later, out of the country; and then Lou was often out of town when I was there. Still, off and on, we shared that hotel apartment for nearly three years, until I got married.

One of the priceless characters at the Wilson was Lulu Shoemaker. She was the major domo — I suppose her title was head housekeeper, but everyone knew she was the generalissimo. She ran that place like it was her own little duchy, and she kept everyone in line — the other employees, and the guests as well. Early on she became my champion and my friend. She'd take it on herself to warn me of guests that she thought I should avoid — "So and so, down the hall, don't you be messing with them: They're trash." Or, "Don't you go up to the fourth floor tonight, there's going to be a lot of trouble up there" — referring to a party being planned that she considered too wild for me.

Lulu kept me entertained with wild stories of guests who managed to exceed even her world-weary tolerance of New York extravagances. She was sharply discriminatory between "real people" and "fakes," between "classy" and "no-class." Fortunately for me, she categorized me as someone who needed looking out for. What might have been no more than a mutually condescending give-and-take between a resident and the lady who supplies your linen, over time became a real friendship.

The Wilson was at its liveliest whenever the fleet came in; any fleet would do. Our hotel ended up being the scene of many a nautical celebration, no doubt because there were so many single ladies living there. The Wilson made room for just about every lifestyle that New York had to offer, black and white, young and old, foreign and domestic, party girls, dancers looking for work and writers casting about for material (which was right there under their noses). In all that creative ferment, one more black baritone, pounding out piano exercises on the spinet in his room, was hardly going to cause a stir. In 1954, as I was preparing to move out of the Wilson, I went to see Alfred Hitchcock's new film, *Rear Window*. Its pageant of urban vignettes, set around a courtyard in an unconventional block of apartments, reminded me of life at the Wilson.

Almost immediately after I arrived in New York I was on the fast track with my studies and my job search. Keeping my appointment with General Artists Corporation, I played and sang in a small GAC studio, concentrating on popular music, of course. They were optimistic that they would be able to find me work.

My luck held, too, when I went to the American Theatre Wing to see about finding a good voice coach. I was sent to talk to a professor in their Veterans Training Program — Otto Herz. When I rang his doorbell, I was greeted by a tall, slender, almost gangly gentleman who looked to be in his mid-fifties but showed not a trace of gray. He had an ebullient energy that was more evident in his eyes than in his somewhat restrained manner. Despite the casual lifestyle of the American Theatre Wing, he was nattily dressed. I had spent enough time with refugees at Camp Ritchie to know by his accent that, despite his German name, he was from Hungary.

Otto certainly looked the part of the intense, dedicated music professor. Some of his intensity was doubtless due to his Eastern European origins and his intellectual appetites. He had indeed been born in Hungary and had received the best European education; as I later learned his doctorate, from the University of Bratislava, Slovakia, was in political science. While still a young man, engaged in the world of politics but lured by the world of the arts, Otto had studied piano with the respected Karel Hoffmeister at Prague, and in 1933 became a professor at the Fodor Music Conservatory in Budapest. He came to the United States as part of a tour, as accompanist to the violinist Zino Francescatti, in 1939 — just as war was breaking out across Europe.

If Otto had not already made a final choice between politics and arts, he probably did so then. He decided to leave his European life behind, and stayed to become a naturalized American citizen. In 1940, at the age of forty-six, he began a new life as assistant conductor of the New York Opera Company and as a member of the faculty of the New York College of Music. I sang for him that afternoon and watched his eyes light up. He could see that here was something to work with. For my part, I was pleased to have such a well-schooled musician as a private coach, to continue to develop my voice.

I would also need to enlarge my repertoire, to expand the range of classical literature beyond the basics that I had studied at Eastman. Once again, I was fortunate to be matched with a recognized master in the field, Yves Tinayre. A little older than Otto — he was approaching sixty when I met him — Yves had a voice that was still strong and mellow, and slightly flavored by the crisp French of his native Paris. As a younger man he had started on the path that I hoped to follow myself: He had been a celebrated lyric tenor in Paris, London, and Vienna. But he had been pulled away by a greater love for musicology, and had devoted himself to the transcription of hundreds of original manuscripts from all over Europe — music for solo voice dating back to the 1500s. Yves was versed in even earlier music. In his recitals for the BBC in London, for example, he specialized in very rarely heard ancient songs, French, German, and Italian, going back as far as the twelfth century. He himself had studied with the masters of his day, Leopoldo Gennai in Milan and Victor Beigel in London.

I mention those names, though today they're little more than entries in a music encyclopedia, to make a point. This is as good a place as any to try to share some sense of the hallowed traditions of classical music. "In my father's house are many mansions," we're told by St. John. He could have said the same thing about the inspired realm of music. Follow the heritage with me: Yves's teacher Victor Beigel (1870-1930) had been a child prodigy and later a pianist who then became an internationally famous teacher. Beigel in his earlier days had studied with Woldemar Bargiel among others. Bargiel (1828-97), a composer and disciple (and relative) of Schumann, had studied under Mendelssohn's supervision at the Leipzig Conservatory. Thus, through only two or three generations, I was in a direct, face-to-face and soul-to-soul line of descent with the immortals of the art.

One of the joys of this life of music is the tradition of personal transmission, from one master to the next, down through the ages. It's a form of apostolic succession, and the chain is unbroken. It is true that music has sometimes made quantum leaps; new influences, some of them very raw indeed, have jazzed things up along the way. But always behind those novelties there is a long, continuous series of links that stretches back through the Romantic and the Classical masters, through the monasteries, literally to the ancients themselves. And that's not a paper chain or a merely theoretical tracing of influences, but a human chain, a "laying on of hands" from one generation to the next.

Thomas Jefferson is said to have wished for his new republic an "aristocracy of talent" to replace the Old World aristocracy of blind inheritance. Whether we have been or ever will be able to achieve such a thing in our society, in the art world we're halfway there. We have a "pedigree of talent," a flowering family tree of art that can be traced in reverse from some of today's most promising students back through teachers who have themselves learned from the masters, who learned from masters in their turn. The great artist becomes a teacher, and the art is enriched, not only by his performance but also by his willingness to help shape the next generation. I was very fortunate to be able to study with both Otto Herz and Yves Tinayre, and doubly fortunate that I had the G.I. Bill to subsidize what would otherwise have been unaffordable to me.

The Naumburg Competition was an important incentive in those work sessions. It gave us a concrete goal. As it turned out, I didn't win the prize, but the competition became the organizing principle for all my study and practice. It was through that preparation that I developed such an extensive repertoire. It was through the successive stages of the competition that I was able to measure myself against the best that the field had to offer. It was through the finals that I became convinced of my own relative merit among my peers.

It helped that I received unsolicited feedback from people who should know — like Elsa Fiedler, sister of the Boston Pops' Arthur Fiedler, who was the regular accompanist for Naumburg competitors. She was enormously helpful. She became my biggest fan, and cheered me after I had lost a second time: "I don't understand why you didn't win it. You were far and away the best." I may not have gotten a Town Hall debut out of it, but I got plenty of fringe benefits from my involvement with the Naumburg. I never discourage a music student from competing in prestigious competitions like the Naumburg and the National Music Scholarship Awards.

I worked with Otto in his studio up on 79th Street off Riverside Drive. In good weather it was a pleasant walk up Broadway from the Woodrow Wilson. Yves worked out of his apartment, about twenty blocks north. The added attraction of Yves's place was that the building was owned by Duke Ellington. Ellington's sister lived there, and from time to time you could catch a glimpse of him on his way to or from a family occasion.

Those were wonderful days, at midcentury, to be young and energetic and charged with an almost mindless optimism. I filled every hour with some variety of purposeful activity — even when I was larking, I was consciously soaking up experiences that I knew would be useful. When I wasn't studying with Herz or Tinayre I was making the rounds, going on audition calls. When I wasn't doing that I was rehearsing. Friends called me a practice-holic, because I couldn't get enough.

Soon the breaks started coming. The first offers I received were for out-of-town clubs and cocktail lounges. In the cocktail lounges I'd generally be twenty minutes on, twenty minutes off, all evening. As I progressed to night clubs, the performances became more formal. Instead of background music, I'd present an entire show twice, occasionally three times, a night.

The agents at General Artists Corporation thought I was tremendously talented, and that was encouraging. Every time they sent me out on a contract, the reports came back enthusiastic. GAC's game plan was to keep me in development, with steadily growing audiences and good reviews; then, when the time was right, to bring me into a cafe in Greenwich Village and "develop" me into the cafe society that had already welcomed Harry Belafonte and Lena Horne.

It sounded like a reasonable plan, for their purposes. Of course my primary interests were in another direction, but I could hardly expect GAC to care about my classical bent. I was just grateful to have the gigs they booked, because money was always tight and Lou and I were always living hand to mouth. Pooling resources, we usually managed to make ends meet. At one point I was so low I had to go to Grandma Annie for a fifty-dollar loan. At another low moment I had no idea how I'd be able to pay my share of the rent — which came due the very day that my tax refund check arrived. As I say, it was a time for paying my dues as a performer, and though there were some tense moments I always had some deeper conviction that things would work out.

And in the meantime I was having a good time adjusting my middle-class, middle-America perceptions to the adventures of life in the big city — the whole range from the sacred to the very secular.

One of the first things I did when I got to New York in 1947 was to establish church membership. This time I didn't have to do a lot of asking around — the church I was naturally drawn toward was the celebrated Abyssinian Baptist Church in Harlem, pastored by the flamboyant Adam Clayton Powell and his assistant, Pastor Licorice. I knew they had a great choir headed by

Howard Dodson. In those early years I was up there every Sunday that I was in town.

I never connected with the music intelligentsia in Harlem — the heyday of the Harlem Renaissance was before my time — but if I missed the action on Saturday nights I was nonetheless a Harlemite on Sunday morning.

Saturday nights you were more likely to find me with the theater crowd in the Broadway district. There was a bar called the Rustic Cafe on 45th Street between Sixth and Seventh, frequented by actors and writers, artists and dancers, and every kind of character you'd expect to find in the bistro nightlife of midcentury midtown New York. Eartha Kitt was then a hoofer on Broadway and she and her friends would float into the Rustic after a show. And on a good night Lady Day herself would be by around closing time. Billie Holliday had a seat at the bar that everyone understood was hers, and often she'd be there with her friend, Lenny. She'd drink her gin and talk and talk, and I listened to her stories for hours, long after the bar was supposed to be closed.

Though I don't remember the Broadway bars being segregated, the Rustic was a white-owned establishment where blacks just happened to feel particularly comfortable. Whenever a show happened to have blacks in the cast they'd usually head on over afterwards, often bringing their white friends with them. The owner, Bernie, was our bartender and father confessor. He kept a neighborhood feeling about the place. Of course, it was literally in my neighborhood, or close enough. Whenever I came back into town from one of my gigs I tended to head straight for the gang at the Rustic.

It wasn't until I rediscovered Larney Goodkind that I began to find some shape in my career. Actually, Larney rediscovered me. I hadn't seen him since Camp Ritchie. When I had first come to New York from Rochester, in those few hectic days of rehearsal for *Call Me Mister,* I never took time to give him a call. An entire year of touring had passed in the meantime, followed by several months of activity as I got myself situated with GAC and the American Theatre Wing. Whenever I gave a thought for Larney, I assumed he'd gone back to Universal Pictures, and made another mental note to look him up one of these days.

In that season of ups and downs, he came back into my life at a low point. I had come down with the flu and had been bedridden for a week. Larney had run into Joe Anthony, the playwright we both knew from Camp Ritchie days, who told him I was in town and where I was staying. He and Karen decided to come around and say hello. What they found was a sniffling, bedraggled convalescent — a lousy way to renew an old acquaintance.

But Larney was a real tonic for me. For one thing, he and Karen made it their business to doctor me with hot tea and chicken soup. For another, he made me give him a full accounting of my progress with classes and club bookings.

He was now an independent literary agent, Larney told me. He had been eased out of Universal Pictures by the new regime that had taken over there during the war years. As a returning vet he was entitled to his old job for a period of at least one year, but on the 365th day, he told me, they let him go. Karen was also working on her own, also a literary agent, so they both operated out of their apartment in midtown.

It was clear that Larney's work, though lucrative, was not completely satisfying to him. For all his expertise, he was too much in love with music to be satisfied with what he was doing. Through his friends and contacts in the music business he had plenty of outlets, but his talents seemed to yearn for a more direct involvement.

We talked generally, without a specific commitment on either side — but in that short period of reacquaintance, we agreed that Larney would keep his eyes open and let me know if anything interesting turned up. He'd take a 10 percent commission of anything he found as my personal manager. We didn't sign a contract. I don't know if we ever had a contract until much later, when some accountant said it was formally required.

Larney managed to help me line up a few things, nothing worth mentioning but enough at the time to reassure me that he was looking out for me. And I was a frequent guest at the musical evenings that he and Karen would host. He would have friends over, and sometimes friends would bring friends — and sometimes those friends were people like the producer David Merrick, who happened in one night — or publicists and agents and others to whom I was being subtly introduced.

Larney knew I was oriented toward a concert career, and that in the meantime I didn't need his sponsorship of my club career, which GAC was managing. But he did keep a sharp lookout for theater work, because he knew that a theater connection could later enhance a recital career and catapult it into another dimension. He started small: The first theater job he wangled for me was in an off-Broadway production, *Set My People Free*.

Marty Ritt was the director. Larney knew him, and had read that he was directing this Dorothy Heyward play for the Theatre Guild at the Hudson Theatre. He got on the phone and told him, "Marty, I'm going to send a kid down, see if you can find something for him to do with the production. Trust me," he told Ritt, "you'll be able to put him to work."

Ritt gave me a bit part, at the Equity minimum of $90 a week. The total of twelve weeks would mean another thousand dollars of income, but more importantly it would get me in circulation on the theater scene.

The play told the true story of Denmark Vesey, a South Carolina slave who planned an insurrection in 1821; the revolt was aborted when a "faithful servant" told his master what was going on. One critic wrote that if the insurrection had worked the play might have too — as it was, neither went anywhere. As Brooks Atkinson pointed out in the *New York Times*, the staging depended on what amounted to a formula for black plays in the post-*Porgy and Bess* era, including "spirituals, superstitions, incantations and lithographic crowd scenes."

But, Atkinson also noted, the effect was "always interesting and occasionally engrossing — due no doubt to the force and magnetism of the acting." Another critic wrote that "the entire cast is admirable," which seemed to be the consensus, however shaky the play's story might have been. So we completed a respectable if modest run of thirty-six performances.

The company for *Set My People Free* was like a small family. My role was a small one, but the mood was so informal that Marty Ritt thought nothing of asking me to pitch in and help with other aspects of the production. He saw that I knew music, so he'd ask me to work out a harmony for a piece in the show. The next day he'd ask me to take a few singers and put together some background spiritual music. It never occured to me that these chores weren't in my job description. It was a tremendous learning experience for me, and I pitched in with all the enthusiasm I had felt when I was taking extra classes at Eastman or at Washington High School.

Larney also found me work in the musical *Regina*. Again, the money wasn't going to make me rich — $40 a week for four weeks of rehearsals, and then an out-of-town tour to New Haven and Boston before the New York opening. It would all come to something over $1,500. But I was working.

Like *Porgy and Bess*, this was a show the newspapers had to send both their music and their drama critics to cover. That ambiguity might have presented problems for audiences, too, because— like *Porgy* — *Regina* suffered from an identity crisis. Was it serious music, or was it a musical melodrama? In fact, it was both. As music it merited the attention of the New York City Opera, which later added *Regina* to the repertoire. As melodrama it never took.

Marc Blitzstein had written both the score and the libretto, based on Lillian Hellman's highly successful play *The Little Foxes*. Jane Pickens performed the title role of a woman who out-schemes her scheming male relatives to take charge of the family fortune. The story was told in an artfully erratic mix of song, recitative, and straight dialogue — including a touch of the song-speech, the *Sprechstimme*, of Alban Berg. The effect was some-times to create a superficial appearance of arbitrariness in the arrangement. It must have suffered from word-of-mouth, not because audiences didn't enjoy it or couldn't understand it but because both the details and the overall effect were so hard to describe.

My role of Cal was not a major role. It figured in *Regina* (and in *The Little Foxes*) to underscore one of the drama's themes, of racial exploitation. But it was memorable in its small way, and there was a charming little aria that Cal sang to Regina's brow-beaten sister-in-law, Miss Birdie. Looked at from that perspec-tive, it would be my professional classical music debut.

It was also an opportunity to watch a work in development and pick up a few pointers. I was fascinated by the way the show came together, and by the collaborative role a performer can play. It was an important lesson in the creation of serious music, not previously available to a young man who had concentrated on the classics — the product of collaborations of yesteryear.

Right up to the opening in New York, Marc was still rewriting. At one point Jane Pickens complained, "There's no aria for Regina." He went home and penned a strongly defiant aria for Regina to sing before going to confront her brothers. That was virtually written overnight.

My aria disappeared just as suddenly. The song "didn't work," I was told, and while we were in the New Haven tryouts it was taken out. I couldn't see the point of that. The song was there to solace the weepy Miss Birdie; it was a lovely song and had a meaningful function. It seemed to me that without that moment there was an emotional gap. Then, in Boston I think it was, they restored the song. But now it was the maid who sang to Miss Birdie, not Cal. I later heard that there was discussion about how unnatural it would be for a black man to be singing a song of comfort to a white lady. As long as I was going along grinning, "Yes sir, no ma'am," it was fine. But let it seem that a black man might actually have the power of consolation over a white woman, and that was too much. In those days, those kinds of changes were often made after the New York opening, to soften the work for the Southern cities of the touring circuit. But this change was made for New York sensibilities. There's no rancor in my recollection of this incident. But it serves me as a reminder of how racial mindsets creep into our lives without being explicitly racist.

Regina opened at the 46th Street Theater on October 31, 1949 — the night after Todd Duncan and William Marshall opened in another serious musical, Maxwell Anderson and Kurt Weill's *Lost in the Stars*, down the street at the Music Box. They did a little better with their South African racial tragedy than we did with our scorching opera-melodrama. We limped along into December, they ran into July. It's hard to imagine such serious works opening in the holiday season these days.

Regina had a personal importance to me that I didn't know until later. It was my introduction to the respected producer Cheryl Crawford. I knew her as the person who had revived *Porgy and Bess* during the war. I didn't know that she would eventually play an important part in my own career. But I was pleased to come to the attention of any producer, and particularly one whose career might hold any sort of affinity for mine.

At that point, I was completely uncertain that I even had a career. I was full of self-confidence, but not sure where to apply it. I was like clay, willing to be molded. That was a point in my life when it might easily have gone either way. You can see the same development, perhaps, in the extremely talented Robert Guillaume. He's an intensely trained classical performer. He was clearly destined for the concert stage, in the tradition of Roland Hayes, when Fame tapped him on the shoulder and made him the multitalented star he has become — in the movies, on television, in music — everywhere but on the concert stage. Ask him if he's happy with his success? Why wouldn't he be? Why shouldn't he be? I'd be too.

The drive was there, all right. I knew I had to be performing, I had to be singing, I had to be playing, and if it turned out I was going to be on an opera stage, that's great, and if it turned out I was going to be another Nat King Cole, that probably would be great too. At that point in my life I would have been happy doing anything that stretched my talents to their limits.

There were certainly allurements in the nightclub career I was building. Like the night in Johnstown, Ohio, when Victor Borge was in town performing somewhere else, and someone had told him, "Hey, you have to go over and catch this kid's nightclub act." So he was in the house. I had just finished the Toreador song from *Carmen*, winding up my set, and I looked up and there he was. He came over with real interest, and shook my hand. "I'm impressed," he said, and he took a few minutes to satisfy his curiosity about who I was and where I'd come from. It was a short chat, and I was enormously flattered, of course, but what was even more impressive to me was that later in my career, when I had progressed from night clubs to my concerts, whenever we met he would recall the time he "discovered" me in Johnstown. To this day, now that we're friends, even at our ages, to him I'm still the "young man" in that nightclub who surprised him by going from boogie-woogie to the serious music that no one expected from me.

What would life have been like? It was through this night club preparation that I met Walter Carr, and that led to my Town Hall debut. I've often wondered what my life would have been like if the timing had been out of sync, if GAC had had time to develop their night club career track for me before my concert career track caught up with them — that is, before my Town Hall debut settled the question. I would have happily followed the Muse in that direction, I have no doubt. After all, they were the experts, and it's hard to argue with success, no matter how it comes your way. I'd like to think I would have fallen into a category comparable with Nat King Cole. I don't know how it would have played out. I'd like to think that a part of me would

always be regretful that I hadn't put my classical training to more
direct use, but I can't truthfully say that. I'd probably be happy
wherever I landed.

There were even moments of deep satisfaction, in that life
of nightclubs and pop music. They might have been enough to
fill my need for great music. I was able to mix just enough of the
classics into my act to sustain some sense of continuity with my
long-range goal. Not just the occasional *Messiahs* with the
Rochester Oratorio Society, even moments in the clubs.

One night I'll never forget. It was at the Club Norman,
during the Christmas season, and one patron of the club wanted
me to sing "Ave Maria." I smiled, and stayed with my repertoire,
but he and his friends kept asking for the song, every time the
applause died down from my last number. I smiled and shook
my head, and goodnaturedly told them, "No, no, no," and went
on with my program.

I suppose in my mind's eye I could see my father's expression. As an adult I had never talked with him about it, but it was
a safe bet that he was never crazy about the idea of my doing
night clubs; I'm sure he'd have misgivings about my bringing
religious music into that scene.

But before long practically everyone in the room was
asking for the song: "Sing 'Ave Maria.'" I finally had to stop and
explain that I didn't do that song in my routine, but even that
didn't end their persistence. Finally I swung my legs around the
piano bench, facing the audience, and they could see by my
expression I was serious.

"All right," I told them. "I'll sing 'Ave Maria' —" and there
was a scattering of applause, but I held my hand up — "I'll sing
'Ave Maria' if you'll promise me you won't drink, you won't eat,
and not a waiter will move. Because this is very dear to me."

All around the room they nodded, and the waiters found a
place to stand. I played for myself, and sang "Ave Maria". They
were true to their word: There wasn't another sound or movement in the room, and I sang a second verse. My personal
feelings, the power of the music, and the magic of the Christmas
season came together in that moment. But even more, I found my
spiritual background, my classical music training and my night
club work all coming together in the same place at the same time,
for one moment of sublime personal integration. Whatever I was
feeling must have communicated, because when I had finished

there was a stunned silence over the packed room, and then a thunderous outburst of cheering and applause.

In my mind's eye, I saw my father acknowledge that moment with a tolerant grin: God doesn't have to be reserved for the church or religious music for the concert hall. I could share an experience like that, with a packed room full of revelers, at a time when no one was looking for spiritual upliftment. You don't always have to look for it — sometimes it will come find you. By the way, that performance might well have been my swan song at the Club Norman, that same December in 1949 when Walter Carr decided to stake my career.

Chapter Seven

OVERNIGHT SUCCESS

As everyone in the performing arts knows, the overnight reviews are usually available in the newspaper editions that come out in the wee hours of the morning. There's a tradition of partying after the opening performance and then going to the newsstand—or to the newspaper's printing plant—for the early editions. If the reviews are good, they're a perfect ending to a perfect day. If they're bad, they can ruin a wonderful opening night party.

I've always been one to make a brief appearance at the party, then get home for a good night's sleep. I usually don't know what the critics have to say until someone calls me the next morning and reads the reviews to me. That habit started on the road with *Call Me Mister*, when we'd be reviewed by the local press every time we opened in a new city. It carried me through the openings of *Set My People Free* and the out-of-town and New York openings of *Regina*. And so, on the night of March 19, 1950, I wasn't going to wait up. Even though it was Town Hall, even though this opening was far more important to me personally than any other I had experienced.

I didn't expect, as I've already said, the reviews to be either unqualifiedly good or embarrassingly bad. I thought with a little luck we'd get some quotes that Larney Goodkind could put on a sales brochure. If the critics were generally favorable, Columbia Artists would have something to work with in their attempts to book me in recital.

In fact, the last thing in the world that I expected, from what are traditionally restrained music critics, was to read headlines like these: "Baritone Warfield Superb in Concert Debut," in the *Telegraph-Sun*; a rave review headed "Unusual Baritone" from Irv Kolodin in the *Saturday Review*; "Great New Voice" headlined in *Newsweek*, or the *New York Times's* cheery "William Warfield Scores in Recital."

My phone never stopped ringing that morning of March 20, 1950, as Larney called to read me the reviews and friends called to wish me well. But the real action had started the afternoon before, even before the house had cleared following the last wave of applause.

One of the people in the audience was Nell Fleming. An American by birth, she had been a musical star for years in Australia. Now, in her second career, she was a talent scout, working as a producer for the Australian Broadcasting Commission booking performers for tours. She and Larney had known each other for years.

Nell was among those who rushed up to Larney immediately after the performance, flushed with excitement. But she had more to offer than her enthusiasm. She wanted to know if I might be available for a tour of the Australian continent. As their fall season had already begun Down Under, I'd have to leave almost immediately. If Larney thought there might be a possibility, she would wire her head office in Sydney, insisting that I should be booked without delay.

The Australian Broadcasting Commission's arrangements would be hasty. But since ABC was a government commission, and since they put a premium on being out in front with the latest new talent, they had the experience and the connections necessary for last-minute bookings. They were able to make arrangements that a commercial producer wouldn't have been able to do. For them, I was a "coup." As they phrased it in their promotional literature, "The ABC was indeed fortunate to be early in the field, as Warfield — the surprise success of the recent New York concert season — is unlikely to be available again for many years to come."

Larney put it all together almost overnight. Within two weeks of my debut I had a contract for my first international tour. My head was still spinning — it had all happened in what seemed like a virtually instantaneous chain reaction, from the Walter

Carr conversation to the Town Hall debut to the concert halls of
Sydney and Melbourne. In early March I had been counting my
pennies; by April I was a celebrity. By May I was sorting through
offers for fall concert dates, from among the flurry that Columbia
Artists had been lining up. By June I was off, winging my way
over the Pacific on my first international tour.

Larney made the trip with me. We traveled by British
Airways, on one of the propeller planes that made these long
hauls in the days before the airlines switched to jets. In those
days the planes had sleepers. The first leg of our trip was from
San Francisco to Hawaii, the second to the Fiji Islands. By the
time we arrived in Australia, I was adjusted to the time zone and
well rested in my airborne pullman.

The ABC paired me with an excellent pianist, John Douglas
Todd. His repertoire was as wide-ranging as mine, so it was a
good match. That was essential, because our rehearsal schedule
would be as demanding as our performance schedule. We were
booked so tightly that I had to perform four different programs.
We rehearsed morning and afternoon, beginning almost immediately after my arrival. He was an excellent accompanist.

It's worth recounting those programs here, to recall how
demanding such a tour can be.

One program opened with a Handel suite: "Invocation"
from *Radamisto*, "Honour and Arms" from *Samson*, "Oh, Sleep,
Why Dost Thou Leave Me?" from *Semele*, "Thy Glorious Deeds
Inspired My Tongue" from *Samson*, and "Dank Sei Dir Herr."
That was followed by Schubert lieder, "Der Wanderers Nachlied"
and "Am Feierabend." And then, before the intermission, Hugo
Wolf's "Fussreise," "Nun Wandre, Maria," and "Trunken Müssen
Wir Alle Sein." Following the intermission, I sang Quilter's "Go,
Lovely Rose" and "It Was a Lover and His Lass," Bury's "There
Is a Ladye," and Lane Wilson's "The Pretty Creature"; then M.
Lund Tyson's "Sea Moods," Malotte's "Sing a Song of Sixpence,"
Jacques Wolfe's "Sailormen," and John Klein's "The Ledo Road."
And I closed with spirituals arranged by Burleigh: "Wade in de
Water," "Joshua Fit de Battle of Jericho," "My Lord, What a
Morning," "Scandalize My Name," "Go Down, Moses," and
"Oh, Didn't It Rain."

Another program began with Bach's "Komm Süsser Tod,"
and two Handel pieces, "Where'er You Walk" from *Semele* and
"Hear Me, Ye Winds and Waves." Then Brahms's "Die Mainacht,"

"O Wüsst Ich Doch den Weg Zurück," "Vergabliches Ständchen," and "In Waldeseinsamkeit." And then a suite of chansons: "Beau Soir," Paul Bourget's song to music by Debussy, Delibes's "Bonjour, Suzon," Fauré's "Après un Rêve," and Victor Hugo's "La Cloche," to Saint-Saëns's music. After the intermission I performed Fritz Kreisler's arrangement of "The Bonney Earl O'Moray," Frederick Keel's "Mother Carey," Ernest Charles's "The Sussex Sailor," and two Herbert Hughes pieces, "The Men from the Fields" and "The Fiddler of Dooney." Then Grant Schaeffer's "The Sea," Stanford's "The Bold Unbiddable Child," Paul Bowles's "Cabin," Marion Bauer's "Minstrel of Romance," Dunhill's "Clothes of Heaven," and Ernst Bacon's "Brady." My closing songs for that program were self-arranged and self-accompanied spirituals, "Sometimes I Feel Like a Motherless Child," "There's a Meetin' Here To-Night," "No Hidin' Place Down There," "True Religion," "Were You There?" and "Every Time I Feel the Spirit."

Still another opened with Handel's "Te Deum," two pieces from Bach's *Christmas Oratorio*, "Mighty Lord and King All Glorious," and "Oh Lord, My Darkened Heart Enlighten," "Good Fellows, Be Merry" from Bach's *Peasant Cantata*, and Mendelssohn's "Oh God, Have Mercy" from *St. Paul*. Then Hermann von Olim's song to Richard Strauss's "Allerseelen," and Strauss's "Die Nacht." Then four Schumann songs would take us to the intermission: "Du Bist Wie Eine Blume," "Im Wunderschönen Monat Mai," "Aus Meinen Tränen Spriessen," and "Die Rose, Die Lilie, Die Taube, Die Sonne." The second half consisted of five sea ballads arranged by Celius Dougherty, "Rio Grande," "Blow Ye Wind," "Across the Western Ocean," "Shenandoah," and "Mobile Bay"; then Howard Swanson's "The Negro Speaks of Rivers," Sam Raphling's "Homesick Blues," the traditional "Water Boy" arranged by Avery Robinson, and Gershwin's "It Ain't Necessarily So" and "I Got Plenty o' Nuttin'" from *Porgy and Bess*. I closed that program, again at the piano, with spirituals I had arranged myself: "I Steal Away," "I Know the Lord Laid His Hands on Me," "Swing Low, Sweet Chariot," and "Heav'n, Heav'n."

My fourth program for this tour began with "Eile Mich Gott zu Erretten" by Heinrich Schütz, Pérotin Le Grand's "Homo Vide" (which I sang unaccompanied), and Monteverdi's "Psalm CL," and then Schubert's "Wohin" and "Totengräbers

Heimwehe," followed by Loewe's "Kleiner Haushalt," "Süsses Begräbnis," and "Odins Meeres-Ritt," to carry us to the intermission. Then the nine songs of Fauré's "La Bonne Chanson." And spirituals to close: "I'm Going to Thank God" in Dett's arrangement, Burleigh's arrangements of "Deep River" and "Lil' David, Play on Your Harp," and Hall Johnson's arrangements of "City Called Heaven" and "Honour, Honour."

Altogether I performed a total of thirty-five concerts between June 11 and September 22 of that year. We did four recitals in Sydney, four in Melbourne, three or four in every city where we performed; guest appearances with the symphony orchestras in some of these same cities; and other special engagements — and they all required a fresh repertoire. I never repeated myself, never did the same piece twice in the same city.

That tour-de-force is a tribute to the comprehensive approach of my two principal coaches, Otto Herz and Yves Tinayre. In our time together, Otto and I had covered almost the entirety of the Schumann "Dichterliebe" and "Liederkreis," Brahms's "Four Serious Songs," a good deal of Schubert, including more than half of the "Schöne Müllerin" cycle of Schubert, and much more. The many ancient and contemporary works I studied with Yves spanned a range from Monteverdi works that he himself had discovered and transcribed, to the entirety of "La Bonne Chanson" of Fauré, and a good deal of Debussy. All those extra credits of "overachieving" at Eastman, and then the many hours of work with Otto Herz and Yves Tinayre, developing new repertoire, now made it barely possible to pull off this tour-de-force — but barely! With encores, I think I used every scrap of music that I knew to stretch across that performance schedule.

This was the first time I had ever endured a schedule as demanding as this. After this first international tour, Larney tried to make sure that I was never asked to maintain such a breakneck pace. But, as it turned out, it was a good baptism by fire, and I taught myself a few survival tricks for such tours.

One of my biggest concerns, after caring for my voice and my physical stamina, was that I might appear an ungracious guest. My hosts were doing so much for me — receptions, soirees, high teas, special audiences with VIPs — and I wanted to somehow do it all without risking exhaustion.

Fortunately, I figured out how to make most of their social patterns suit my needs. I would sleep late, have breakfast at their morning tea time at about ten, then excuse myself for practice. I would use their high tea in the afternoon as my lunch break, and then excuse myself for a brief rest before the performance. Afterwards I'd take my dinner late, usually at one of the banquets or parties they had planned. Whenever I was expected to join in a toast, or just drink socially at a reception, I made sure my glass was filled with ginger ale. In this way I was maintaining the discipline I needed to keep myself together—I sang, I rested, I ate — and still I was managing to keep up with all the social obligations. With a little creative time management, their customs fitted my regimen "to a tea."

On the tour there was not much time to be a tourist. I was not only meeting a tight schedule, but also covering an entire continent in the travel between appearances. I do remember a few of the places where I managed to relax a little, notably King's Cross in Sydney; and I did get a strong sense of the wonderful wilds in Australia's outback. But most of my time was spent between the big hotels and the concert halls.

A few highlights do stand out:

I sought out an opportunity to see how the native Australians lived. I had a good time with them at a boomerang meet, and was fascinated by their expertise.

In Sydney I visited the zoo, where I was posed with the animals for publicity photos. I'm one of those people who have an inherent, irrational fear of snakes; I even avert my gaze when a snake comes up on the movie screen. It's one of those mild phobias that many people share. It was at the Sydney zoo, posing for publicity shots, that one of the keepers came up from behind me and said, "Here, Mr. Warfield," and put a thirty-pound boa constrictor in my arms.

The cameras clicked, and I forced an automatic smile, holding this scaly, slithering mass in my arms like a new father holding a squirming baby — so shocked I was numb, I suppose, because while they got the shots they wanted I was standing there playing the role of someone who didn't mind handling a great wriggling, writhing snake, instead of being young Bill Warfield who couldn't think the word "snake" without discomfort. I was much more comfortable with the wallaby they perched on me.

There's one aspect of the world of performance that doesn't change, no matter where you go, and that's the appetite for publicity. It was in Sydney, on my final night before heading off to Brisbane, that someone took us out to a nightclub where they had a lively dance band. I was ready for a good time, and threw caution to the winds while I danced up a storm, my own improvement of the twist by way of boogie-woogie.

I guess I was getting a little acrobatic, because I came down hard on my toe at one point, and had to limp off the dance floor, grinning and still having a good time. Before the evening was over, though, my injury became painful enough to convince me I should have a doctor look at it. At a nearby emergency room they did x-rays and discovered I had indeed broken my toe. A cast was required.

The next morning, limping toward the Brisbane plane, I was escorted by a solicitous publicity woman who was pleased that I was on the mend but rather wished, if I were to break my toe and wear a cast, I had done it at the beginning of my Melbourne tour, not at the end: "Now Brisbane will get all the publicity," she fretted. I had to wear that cast for the rest of the tour.

My strongest impression on the entire tour, however, was the quality of my audiences. I was amazed at the cultural level throughout Australia. In part because of the Australian Broadcasting Commission's music programming, and in part because the educational system there puts such a high premium on culture, I found that there was an enormous appetite for classical music in even some of the roughest rural districts. You could take a string quartet into the outback and have a packed house — with program selections considered too esoteric for mainstream concert audiences in middle America.

Larney was with me on this first tour, partly because I was completely new to all this, and partly because we had scheduled the tour so quickly that there were a host of minor details — as well as extra recitals or guest appearances still to be added — that required a manager's attention.

Even half the globe away, some part of Larney was back in New York laying plans for the next move. We were still in Sydney, the first stop on the Australian tour, having breakfast together when Larney opened a local newspaper to peruse Hedda Hopper's column, which was syndicated all over the world. He rattled the pages and said, "Listen to this: 'Arthur Freed has still not found an actor for the character Joe in his film version of *Show Boat*.'"

I could hear the wheels starting to whirl in his head. "I'm going to get the ABC here to lend us a sound engineer," he said, "and we're going to cut an audition record."

Larney saw the magnitude of the opportunity and knew he'd have to act quickly. As much as he had looked forward to the jaunt across Australia, he had to head back. After setting up the recording studio arrangements for me in Sydney, he didn't wait for me to record the disk. He hurried to wrap up all the loose ends of the Australian tour, then caught the next plane out.

It might seem that Larney was taking a wildly improbable shot at this opportunity, but he was working an angle that gave him reason to think he could pull it off. At any rate, he had a foot in the door; he figured that if he could get me inside, my audition would do the rest. His advantage was that he had an ongoing professional connection with the head of production at MGM.

The connection demonstrates how show business works. The link was a play by Joe Anthony — the guy who had also been the link when Larney and I rediscovered one another in New York.

In the five years since Camp Ritchie, Larney had kept in close touch with Joe and continued to look for ways to promote his playwrighting talent. Shortly after the war, Joe had written a poignant family drama about Japanese-Americans, called *Some of the Sky*, and Larney had tried to interest RKO Pictures in a film deal. RKO's head of production, Dore Schary, was interested and asked for rewrites. When Schary became head of production for David O. Selznick, Larney made another pitch to have the movie produced there; Schary responded by asking for still another version. Finally Schary became head of production at MGM, and Larney tried again.

By now Schary and Larney had spent so much time in discussions that they were almost cronies. This time Schary told Larney that MGM wouldn't be interested in *Some of the Sky*, but wanted to produce another film that could benefit from some of the mother-son sequences in Joe's script. MGM would be willing to pay as much as $10,000 for the rights to just those sequences.

Larney and Joe agreed to the deal. In the process, Larney had created a valuable contact at the very studio that was now preparing to remake *Show Boat*.

Back in New York he put together a packet of pictures, clips of my Town Hall reviews, and a glowing report of my Australian tour. He contacted Dore Schary, and did a strong pitch on how perfect I'd be for the role. An audition disk would be coming, he told him, direct from Australia. While he was taking care of this business, back in Sydney I sat down at a piano in the ABC studio and cut an audition record: Bill Warfield, accompanying himself, singing "Old Man River."

But once again, some kind of charm was at work, because other events were moving on a parallel track: The producer of *Show Boat*, Arthur Freed, happened to be a good friend of Oscar Levant. Oscar Levant one evening listened to a radio interview of Peter Herman Adler, conductor for NBC Opera. Adler was talking about this "young Negro baritone" who had made an impressive debut at Town Hall: "Watch out for this William Warfield," he said to the listening audience. Oscar Levant, knowing of Freed's search, picked up the phone and called him to relate what Adler had said. That might have gone in one ear and out the other, except that the next day Freed strolled into Dore Schary's office to find the desk spread with photos of William Warfield, and an audition recording newly arrived from Sydney, Australia, accompanied by a glowing letter from the Australian Broadcasting Commission praising my tour.

Freed and Schary listened to the record, looked at the pictures, and made their decision on the spot. Larney let me know by cable that when the Australian tour was over I was to report to MGM in Hollywood.

Chapter Eight

HOLLYWOOD

I don't know what I was expecting when I hit Hollywood. But as everyone says who's gone through the experience, whatever I thought I was getting into — it was something else again.

I got there in the fall of 1950, still only a few months after my Town Hall debut. As the object of MGM's long and difficult casting search, I was welcomed with the enthusiasm that usually greets the Prodigal Son. Except that the welcoming committee wasn't large: I seemed to be just about the only performer on the lot. The part of Joe — the same role that Paul Robeson had played in the 1936 version — was not a large one. But it was critical to the atmosphere of the movie. And of course, it required a soulful rendition of "Old Man River."

As everyone knows, a film is not shot in the same sequence that it is finally shown on the screen. I think even I knew that, at the time. But I was a little taken aback at the notion that my very first chore — before I'd seen the set or met a single actor — would be to sing the final on-screen version of "Old Man River." Later it would be dubbed into the action of the movie. This was the reverse of the usual process of dubbing, as I'll explain later.

Not counting the audition record I'd made in the ABC studio in Sydney, this would be the first professional recording I'd ever done. I was impressed by the elaborate setup of the large sound studio. This was in a time before the sound engineers could lay down the separate tracks electronically. The recording

was done with a full, live orchestra, together with the singers —
in this case, just a soloist — and any other sound effects that
would be a part of the sound track during the takes.

An orchestra, fully deployed, is complicated enough. Add
to that the many microphones and mike cables, the amplifiers
and preamps that were used in recording, and all the technicians
that were darting about directing this operation, and you can
imagine the busy complexity in which I would have to do my
work. They expected the recording to go on all day, and had a
contingency plan to continue on the following day if necessary.

Larney had managed to get me a copy of the score they'd be
using. I had been able to go to work with it immediately on my
return from Australia. Now the moment had come, and as I
listened to the orchestra tune up and waited for my cue, I felt the
same tingle of anticipation that I would feel for any stage performance — no more, no less. As I recall, I was mostly fascinated by
the entire process, and entertained myself by guessing why
certain mikes were placed where they were, or what the acoustic
reasons would be for the orchestra seating arrangement, which
differed from what it would be in a symphony hall.

When the orchestra was ready, I was asked if I were set. I
smiled and nodded. The conductor's baton fell, the music
swelled, and when my cue arrived I opened my mouth and sang
the song.

It sounded pretty good to me, but of course, I was in the
middle of it. As my vocal part ended, before the orchestra was
finished, I stood silently and avoided rustling my sheet music, as
I had been instructed. Finally, the last strains ended and the
room was dominated by a stunning silence.

Then someone shouted "Clear!" and a bell rang, and
suddenly there was a rustle of instruments and sheet music, a
murmur of conversation from the musicians, and over where the
director and his musical director and their assistants were sitting
there was a restrained conversation going on. I waited for their
next instructions. I knew I had done just the first of what would
be a long day of efforts. One of the technical workers, wearing a
set of headphones, gave me a cheery thumbs up. So at least I
hadn't disgraced myself.

Before our second take, the directors had to hear a playback
of the first take. The conductor joined them in a huddle as the
music we had made once again filled the room. I noticed that they

exchanged glances during the playback, and then one of them called for silence.

They listened to the music a second time. A certain suspense seemed to be building in the studio, though I couldn't be certain of the cause. It all made me a little nervous, especially the incredulous expressions that were beginning to appear.

Then one of them said, in a disbelieving voice, "I think we have a take!" That caused a stir that I still didn't understand. "Get Mr. Mayer!" he said, louder this time. "Get Mr. Mayer down here!"

Five minutes later, Louis B. Mayer was on the set of his latest musical. Looking preoccupied, he glanced around the room, nodded in my direction and toward the conductor, and then took the director's chair facing the speakers.

I watched as he sat nodding gently with the music. Someone close to him said that by the end of the song there were tears in his eyes. As the music ended, he stood, nodded his head, and all around the room, smiles lit up, lighting other smiles, like an outbreak of little brushfires. "It's a take," he said, and the studio erupted in a shout.

Like everyone else, I was prepared to be working all day, going through the music over and over again, through many attempts to make it perfect. I imagined I'd have to do it perfectly, each time. What I didn't know was that I wasn't expected to do it perfectly on the very first take.

Of course, it wasn't just that my singing was on the mark. What was equally remarkable, in a room full of things that could go wrong, was that everything — the conductor and his orchestra, the technicians' balance of the microphones on the strings and the percussion and the horns, the condition of the equipment itself, the absence of any stray noises — everything came together so perfectly on the very first take. They talked about that on the set for weeks, and I understand it's still a bit of Hollywood lore — the one-take "Old Man River."

So that day's recording was a lot shorter (and a lot less expensive — was that what brought those tears to Mayer's eyes?) than we had expected. In fact, everything about that film went pretty smoothly, as I recall, a good experience all around. For me, it was like being in another kind of college arts curriculum. Throughout the filming, whether I was in the shot or not, I studied the process. My learning curve was still heading almost straight up. I was unabashedly curious about everything that was going on, and everybody, from gaffers up to the producers, indulged my wide-eyed interest in their profession.

During those first few days in Hollywood I encountered an equally strong curiosity on the part of many of the stagehands I met about my travels. They had obviously heard that there had been problems and delays in casting my role, and that I had finally been hired while on tour in Australia.

They were understandably inquisitive about things Australian, and I was happy to tell them what I could — thanks to those PR trips to the zoo, the excursions to the boomerang demonstrations, and the like. I told them about the unique features of the platypus, and the kangaroo's pouch, how koalas munch eucalyptus, how boomerangs come back around, and how the year's seasons were inverted, with Christmas in the middle of the summer.

One morning, a particularly intense gaffer screwed up his courage to probe a little more personally. "What about race relations?" he wanted to know. While I was ready to relate what I could, I wasn't sure exactly what aspect he was asking about.

"Well," he hesitated, "I mean, how do they — how are you — aborigines treated?" And at once I understood that the stagehands (and who knows how many others?) had skimmed the newspaper stories and drawn the conclusion that MGM had gone down under in its search and found a native Australian to play Joe. Australia is a long way away, and as I think back about it, I suppose I had been creating the temporary impression among those stagehands that European culture had made serious inroads in the culture of the Australian bush country. I wonder if he thought me a typical aborigine, or one of the better educated?

He watched quizzically as I cracked up. He thought I'd picked up my vocal training while I was out running around the fields with kangaroos! When I stopped laughing, I let him down as gently as I could. "I was born in Arkansas," I told him, and watched as his face fell. I kept learning from them, about lighting, sound, special effects, good places to get a pastrami sandwich — but the reverse flow of information slowed to a trickle, and I think I lost a lot of whatever glamour I'd started with, in those circles.

Even the stars seemed to enjoy my curiosity and inquisi-
tiveness about the filmmaking art, and I think they got a kick out
of my innocence. I had a scene with Ava Gardner, where Joe
expresses his concern and Miss Julie condescends to reassure
him. I said my line and Ava, in character, tweaked me on the
cheek.

The director shouted "Cut! That's a take — Okay, two-
shot!" and the cameramen and lighting men started reposition-
ing their equipment.

"What's a two-shot?" I asked her, and Ava Gardner gave
me a big smile. "Baby," she said, "that means that on that gr-e-at
big screen there's going to be nobody's face but just yours and
mine." She paused for effect with that blissful smile. "And that
means they like you."

Every day was filled with so much new experience that the
time seemed to fly by. In addition to "Old Man River," there were
other tracks to be recorded, most of them with other singers.
They managed the workload in a double-pyramid form, scheduling just the few soloists first, then adding musicians who were
needed for larger numbers, ending up with the full complement
for the final recording sessions. Then they began the shooting in
reverse order, using everyone for the large, group shots, then
letting anyone go not needed for the smaller ensembles, finally
working with just those who were needed for close-up work —
two and three actors in the frame. My sound work didn't take
much time, and I had some free hours to sample the Hollywood
lifestyle.

The shooting took longer, in part because it required the
actors to match their movements with the sound track they'd
already recorded. In those days they worked with the old-style
78-rpm records, not a tape. On the platter they had also recorded
cue marks, short beeps that would occur just a few seconds before
you began a phrase, and another just a split second before you
were supposed to end a word or phrase. You had to use this
platter to practice the timing, in order to be able to synchronize
your lips with your own recorded voice.

It was important to get your own piece of it right, because
when the time came to try for a take on the set, your synchroni-
zation was one of dozens of factors that could ruin a take — like
glitches in the lighting, or the makeup, or the costumes, or the set,

or a prop, or poor positioning of actors, or a wrong gesture, or a bead of sweat or a housefly in the wrong place at the wrong time. A single actor's botched lip movement out of sync with the music or dialogue could render the entire shot unusable — an expensive mistake.

So the critical trick to be learned — in addition to everything else a young actor/singer has to worry about — was when to begin, and when to release — a phrase, a word, even in some lines a syllable. It was even more tricky because to lip-sync convincingly onscreen, you have to show the same physical strain — the same veins, the same tendons, the same air pressure in the cheeks, the same flare of the nostrils — as you'd see with a singer really singing the song. That meant that you had to create sound as you mimicked your original studio performance, and yet you couldn't make so much noise that you overrode your cues.

And then there was the reverse process, too, called "looping." For almost all the footage that was shot off the sound stage, I had to re-record my dialogue in a sound studio, looking at the film I'd made. The film was shot silent, without sound. "MOS" it's called, from the days when many of the Hollywood directors were German emigres who shot their exteriors "mitout sound."

It was a challenge to learn these new techniques. I had always been fascinated by the film medium. Now I became an avid student of the work of the cameraman, the lighting experts, the grips, all the artisans. Beyond their skills, though, I was even more amazed at how such a technical medium could result in something so artistic. I suppose it's human nature to be drawn toward the backstage view of any complicated processs — it's fun to see how things really work — and in the film world there's a backstage behind the backstage, and another one behind that, and watching how it all comes together was for me a mesmerizing pursuit.

I was in awe of the cinematic complexity involved in making something singular and whole and meaningful out of so many small bits. It has been said that the making of a great movie is today's counterpart to the medieval construction of a great cathedral, requiring the same management of complexity, the same marriage of art and craft. I don't know if I'd go that far, but I can see the comparison.

Sometimes the solutions to the technical problems could be pretty simple. For one scene they had smoke pots and all sorts of wind machines, trying to get the effect of a foggy mist at dockside. They spent an entire day on the back lot trying to get that effect right, while we did the scene over and over again. Yet when he looked at the rushes, the director, George Sidney, wasn't satisfied.

So the next morning they sent me out with the second crew and the assistant director and we used the natural fog that creeps up when the humidity and temperature are right, at that early hour. That scene in the movie, which is so perfect, is filmed in completely natural mist. The lighting is enhanced with reflectors that boost the intensity of the natural daylight, but the fog is the way God made it. That was another of those one-take shots.

Even for my brief time on screen, there were dozens of shots. A film is a spinning beadwork of thousands of images, short and long — cutaways, closeups, wide shots, momentary reactions — and far more is left on the cutting room floor than ever makes it into the movie theaters. So even for a character like Joe, with a specialized role and limited time on screen, the work takes time, and sometimes can be tedious. I was there three months, and somehow I kept too busy to have much spare time.

I did have to spend a good deal of my free time keeping my voice in shape. I had my second Town Hall recital coming up January 1951.

There was a small practice room with a piano that I was welcome to use when it was free. Nearly every afternoon I'd be there, putting my classical voice through its paces. Johnnie Mercer told me that he was walking down the alley with Ezio Pinza during one of my practice periods, when my voice came booming out of the building—I was probably singing something by Monteverdi. "Who is that?" Pinza wanted to know. "That's a new baritone we've brought in from New York, for *Show Boat*," Mercer said. Pinza was perhaps unfamiliar with the musical, or maybe he was pulling Johnnie's leg, because he asked him, "You're doing it in Latin?"

I also managed to find myself a church out there. You don't usually think of black Baptist churches in Hollywood, but I found one by asking my usual question: Which one has the best choir?

Work starts early when you're filming, so there weren't many late-night activities while I was in Hollywood. But for that brief three months, the cast became a kind of temporary family, and I remember it as a time of real camaraderie.

The center of our family life was the studio canteen, where we'd get our lunch and hang out between shots. It was a good thing we got along so well, because there really wasn't any other place for any of us to go. Even though there were sometimes long breaks, we were perpetually on call. In the canteen we spent a lot of enforced hours in each other's company, the stars along with the bit players, telling stories and picking up on the latest gossip. I was all eyes and ears, of course. For me it was a crash course on Hollywood lore, and I'd listen avidly to the tales of Tinsel Town's latest happenings, distracted only when someone like Cary Grant would wander in, munch a ham sandwich, and then wander back out.

Of those who sat around our table, Joe E. Brown was a constant cut-up. Katherine Grayson was warm, beautiful, and very serious about her music. She clearly enjoyed doing movies, but the music came first; she was something of a prima donna, in the best, original sense. She loved talking about opera, very knowledgeably, and we shared an instant rapport. Ava Gardner could be counted on for the liveliest conversation. The film was made during the time she had her big thing with Frank Sinatra, and she couldn't wait to get off the set and get back to wherever they were staying. So Ava's contribution to the conversation consisted of Frank Sinatra anecdotes — what he'd done or said or where they went the night before — and of course we were all ears.

One of the few late evenings was for the 1950 Photoplay Awards dinner. The stars of *Show Boat* had been invited to attend, probably for the publicity value.

Looking back, that period was a meaningful time for the film industry. It was midcentury; it was a time for taking stock. Like the turning of a century, there's a lot of hype associated with being at the fifty-year mark, and that awareness tends to seep into the entire culture — from advertising slogans to philosophical and religious thinkers' analyses of where we are and where we're going.

Hollywood was clearly in transition. Many of the great actors of the early twentieth century, though perhaps dimming

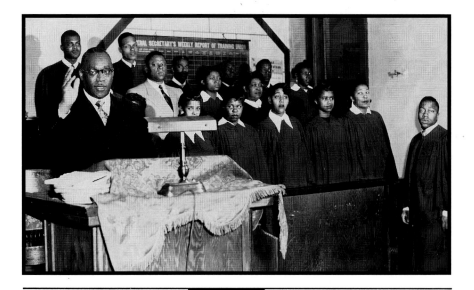

Religion and music have been important to me as far back as I can remember. This picture was taken one Sunday in 1952 at Mt. Vernon Baptist Church in Rochester where my father was pastor. That's the Rev. Robert E. Warfield, Sr., in front at the pulpit, and I'm the one in the choir in street clothes.

Elsa Miller (standing at left) was my first voice teacher. She entered me in the 1937-38 National Music Educator League's competition in which I won a scholarship to the Eastman School of Music. (Her accompanist, Dorothy Stillwell, is at the piano.)

Photo by Joe Jansen: Rochester (NY) Democrat & Chronicle

Howard Hanson, famed composer and conductor, was the director of the Eastman School of Music from 1924 to 1964. He encouraged me to leave Eastman for Broadway when in 1946 I was offered a part in *Call Me Mister*.

Otto Herz and I signing autographs after a recital. Otto, my voice coach, accompanist, and friend since 1950, was a distinguished musician in his own right. He was the assistant conductor of the New York Opera Company and associate director of the New York College of Music.

My association with Yves Tinayre also began in 1950, when I sought him out to enlarge my repertoire in preparation for my Town Hall concert. Here we are going over some pre-Bach songs in Yves's collection; he was an authority on early vocal music.

My Town Hall debut, on March 19, 1950 marked the beginning of my serious music career.

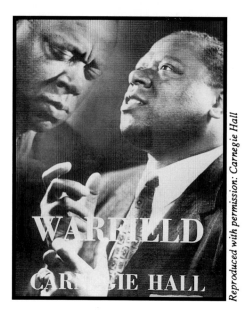

Later I had my first Carnegie Hall recital, and a stellar event it was. All my heroes attended: Roland Hayes, Marian Anderson, Hall Johnson, and of course Leontyne Price.

My most famous movie role: Joe in *Show Boat*, Jerome Kern's antebellum musical. The role had originally been played on Broadway by Paul Robeson.

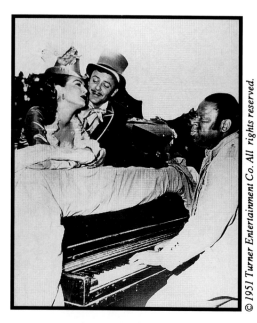

Among the stars in *Show Boat* were Ava Gardner and Robert Sterling.

Between scenes, Ava kept us enthralled with stories about her then-husband, Frank Sinatra.

After *Show Boat* was released I was a star, at least in Rochester, and in 1951 I was honored as an "outstanding representative of the youth of Rochester." Here I am presenting my parents with the silver bowl commemorating the award.

Photo by Our World

Photo by Fred Plaut

Columbia Records took this photo of great American composer Aaron Copland and me when my first recording — which included Copland's *Old American Songs*—was released. Later, in 1984, I won a Grammy Award for Copland's *Lincoln Portrait.*

Porgy and Bess: shots from the 1952 Davis and Breen production that first put me into the role of Porgy, Leontyne into the role of Bess, and us into each other's lives. That's Cab Calloway as Sportin' Life.

One of the major influences on a whole generation of black singers was Marian Anderson, the great contralto whose artistic stature was matched only by her personal integrity. She and her accompanist, Franz Rupp, came to visit Leontyne and me backstage after a *Porgy and Bess* performance in London.

In my only nonsinging dramatic role, I played De Lawd in the *Hallmark Hall of Fame* production of Marc Connelly's *Green Pastures*, first aired on October 17, 1957, and repeated March 23, 1959. Only poor kinescopes remain as records of these live television performances.

In Sydney, Australia, Larney Goodkind (far right) and I had dinner with two officials of the Australian Broadcasting Commission, Will James (left), programs director, and Charles Moses, president.

A musical ambassador has to put up with a lot of publicity shots. This wallaby was easier for me to deal with than the boa constrictor.

One of the great benefits of international touring was listening to and learning about other forms of music.

I can't read this program at all, but fortunately music is a universal language.

Leontyne's accompanist David Garvey and I are being greeted by the U.S. ambassador to Cuba and Mrs. Bonsal after our concert in Havana. The date was July 4, 1959 — only a few months before Fidel Castro came to power.

In the mid-1960s, I spent several months each year in Austria, performing *Porgy and Bess* with the Vienna Volksoper.

In 1974 I joined the faculty at the University of Illinois. There, while continuing my performing career, I finally fulfilled my lifelong plan to teach.

Over the years I've had the good fortune to meet and perform before many of our world's leaders. At President Eisenhower's request, I sang *Battle Hymn of the Republic* at a dedication for Theodore Roosevelt's home. Governor Dewey of New York is seated on the left and President Eisenhower is standing on the right.

Shaking hands with President George Bush at the Kennedy Awards, December 1990.

Photo by Ray Mickshaw, Alan Berliner Studies, Inc.

On June 19, 1991, Turner Broadcasting Company re-released the original *Show Boat* with revamped color and soundtrack. Members of our *Show Boat* company, including Kathryn Grayson and choreographer Marge Champion, gathered to celebrate the occasion.

in intensity, were still making movies; and some of the new faces were just beginning to light up.

One who made an indelible impression on us and on everyone was a young lady, flushed with excitement, who was being squired around from table to table by one of the studio PR representatives. I was sitting with members of the *Show Boat* cast, next to Ava Gardner and Frank Sinatra; Ava leaned over to Frank and stage-whispered, "Here she comes."

"Who is that?" I asked with my usual wide-eyed curiosity.

"She's one of the new gals that Fox is grooming for stardom," Ava replied, just as the new gal was led to our table and introduced around: Marilyn Monroe. The previous year she had played a small role in her first film, *Love Happy*, which also happened to be the Marx Brothers' last film. A time of transition: In *Love Happy*, Groucho was getting off his last Hollywood ogle at the very young goddess-in-progress who was just beginning to weave the spells that would help to define Hollywood for the rest of the century.

And now, at our table, she radiated that same simple, unaffected, breathy charm that soon became familiar to millions of movie audiences: "Hello, it's so nice, pleased to meet you, hello." And as they progressed to the next table, Ava leaned over to Frank again, with a knowing nod, and from the side of her mouth I heard, "She'll make it."

I had mixed feelings as I saw young Miss Monroe being led around the room. Clearly, your future in Hollywood depended on that kind of promotion. So many of the factors that made her career would be forever out of her personal control. Beyond her good looks and her talent, there would be the casting choices, the limits or largesse of publicity and promotion budgets, the fickle tastes of the film public. That night at the Photoplay Awards I remember thinking that I'd never want to become dependent on the machinery of Hollywood for my livelihood. I was fortunate that my film break came after my concert debut — when I had such a newly confident sense of who I was and what I was about — and not before.

At the time, though, I was all too willing to take whatever Hollywood had to offer. And it was clear that they liked my work, because, during the filming of *Show Boat* in the fall of 1950, I was offered the part of Jim, in a new Lerner and Lowe musical that MGM planned to make in the fall of 1951, *Huck Finn*.

This is actually getting ahead of my chronology. My second Town Hall recital and several months of touring with Columbia Artists fell between my *Show Boat* filming and my *Huck Finn* experience. But this is the best place to relate the story so that this narrative can leave Hollywood behind for good.

Huck Finn looked like a sure winner. Dean Stockwell was signed to play Huck. Even better, Gene Kelly and Danny Kaye were cast as the two riverboat rapscallions, the King and the Duke. The four of us would be costars. I'd have an elaborate song and dance number with the two biggest names in the song-and-dance business. It would be directed by Vincente Minnelli, who had just completed his wonderful *An American in Paris*.

They sent me the music early in the summer of 1951, so I could get a head start on learning my part. Of course, I wasn't known as a dancer, but those hours spent learning from Lou Ampolo hadn't been spent in vain. The script called for tap dancing? No problem, I had taken lessons in tap dancing while I was in high school, as part of an extracurricular program. That gave me the foundation, and then MGM gave me special training in tap dance routines, at the studio's dance school in Hollywood. It never occurred to me that I couldn't acquire whatever I needed in time for the beginning of filming. The fact that I wasn't a dancer just had no bearing on the assignment. I could learn.

Because of this special training, my contract called for an early start, and for several weeks I was the only actor on the set. I spent my days learning the routines and rehearsing my music. When I had had enough of Lerner and Lowe, I would go through my recital repertoire, practicing my Handel and Loewe. I waited for the studio to complete its negotiations and get started.

I had a good relationship with the director, Vincente Minnelli, who was also cooling his heels waiting for the go-ahead. In 1943, as his first feature film, he had directed *Cabin in the Sky*— one of the first general-release black films made in Hollywood, with Jack Benny's foil Eddie Anderson, Lena Horne, Ethel Waters, and Louis Armstrong. Minnelli and I had a real rapport, and he was thoughtful enough to include me in dinner parties and private gatherings at his house. I remember his little girl Liza as the kid I literally bounced on my knee.

Some weeks after I'd begun my work, Danny Kaye showed up, ready to go, and eager to get the work done because he had already committed to his next film, *Hans Christian Anderson*. But

Gene Kelly was up to his eyeballs in the cutting of the new film he'd directed and sang and danced and starred in, *Singing in the Rain*. His postproduction work was taking forever, and while the clock ran, we all knew that Danny Kaye had to be released by September. As the date approached, MGM approached David O. Selznick for an extension on Kaye's contract, but he nixed it. It was becoming clear that the project was doomed.

Danny Kaye stayed optimistic, though, and came onto the set from time to time to see how things were going. One day when he was visiting, my dance instructor asked me to do a few turns for him. With the rehearsal pianist pounding out one of Lowe's new tunes, I went through the routine for an audience of one. The closest I came to my big song-and-dance number with Danny Kaye was that private demonstration, and I treasure Danny Kaye's compliment: "Hey, that's pretty good!"

When it was finally evident that this was a film that wasn't going to happen, MGM paid off my full contract and I packed my bags for New York. Too bad for *Huck Finn*: Anyone who's seen *Singing in the Rain* and *Hans Christian Anderson* (and who hasn't?) knows that Kelly and Kaye were both at the top of their form in 1951, and I was feeling pretty good myself. It would have been a hell of a picture.

I took the money and stored away the new experiences I'd acquired. It was too bad the movie would never be made, but I'd learned by now that nothing is ever wasted, and I had no doubt I'd be able to put this experience to work somewhere else. Besides the dance practice, I'd put my other hours to work, rehearsing the music and benefitting from fresh coaching in the art of show tunes. Even when I realized that things weren't going to work out for the film, there was still plenty to see, plenty to hear, plenty to learn.

The *Huck Finn* experience didn't sour me on Hollywood, in part because I'd never gotten too sweet on the idea. Hollywood paid well and gave you a terrific audience, but the trade-off was that you lost all control. In retrospect, the cancellation of that film was probably a blessing that saved me from becoming seduced by the movies.

I could see, from my limited exposure, that the idea of building a livelihood around Hollywood projects would involve a whole series of compromises. In the long run, that would be a severe threat to the classical music career I was moving toward.

As I had already learned on Broadway, it's hard enough for a stage actor to maintain a sense of control over his own destiny. It's especially hard in Hollywood, where the superstructure of production and the delegation of creativity conspire to render the artist a part of a vast, mechanized process.

It is of course deeply satisfying to see a good performance "immortalized," to have a moment of your art frozen in time; it can also be very lucrative, compared to other artistic pursuits. From the perspective of the Hollywood producer, the money paid for talent is an always reasonable percentage of his overall financial concerns. But those seductions are outweighed by the artistic dependency that must be offered in trade. I doubt that I would have been able to resist the blandishments, if that life had been offered me. But I instinctively knew better than to pursue it, and in retrospect I'm glad I never had to make the choice.

That's in retrospect, of course. At the time I was too busy to think about such things. Between the two film experiences I headed back to the Big Apple for my second Town Hall recital, which Larney Goodkind had arranged. That meant, as well, another intensive series of sessions with Otto Herz and Yves Tinayre, adding to my repertoire. My first full season of Columbia Artists concerts began immediately after I was released from *Show Boat*. Larney had negotiated a recording contract for me as well. So throughout that whole period there was never a lull in the action.

I also made an important trip to Rochester, on personal business. At the end of that pivotal year 1950 — midway through the "American Century," the year I turned thirty, the year I started off counting my pocket change and ended up with more money than I knew what to do with — I found that I had enough in the bank to buy my parents' home for them. They would never again have to worry about how they were going to stretch my father's income to keep a roof over their heads.

It's amusing for me to review my schedule of performances (with the prices I was able to command) during that year. While GAC was making my living for me, booking me in the clubs, Larney was knocking himself out to get me some exposure as a classical artist. The year's schedule included a couple of dates later in the year that had been booked before my Town Hall debut. I honored them at the originally agreed-upon fee. (Keep in mind that the cost of living from the early fifties to the early nineties has grown by more than five times — $10,000 works out to $52,000 or so, I'm told.)

The chronological list of 1950 dates speaks for itself: Club Norman ($700), a performance of *Elijah* in Rochester ($200), a *St. Matthew's Passion* ($100), a luncheon at NYU ($60), something at Colby College ($150), and then with the Carnegie Pops ($75), and a performance at Wadleigh High School ($100). Then a performance in Washington, D.C. ($160), back to Rochester ($250), and Corning ($300), and then the Town Hall debut, for which we included a personal fee to me (I was nearly broke) of $300. At that point the list changes character: Australia (thirty-five concerts, $10,000), *Show Boat* ($15,625), San Diego, Little Orchestra ($150), and a return to Colby College ($600).

From then on, for the next twenty years, with only a few interruptions my career would be a pattern of leapfrog from one venue to another — but never another trip to Hollywood.

A final aside, and then I'll leave Hollywood alone: When the movie version of DuBose Heyward's and George Gershwin's *Porgy and Bess* was filmed in 1958-59, the studio was determined to have Sidney Poitier play the role. An all-black cast in a film with a racial theme was still considered risky in Hollywood, and producer Samuel Goldwyn insisted that only with stars like Poitier, Pearl Bailey, and Sammy Davis, Jr., would he take a chance. Neither Poitier nor his Bess, Dorothy Dandridge, could do the singing, of course, so they would have to be dubbed.

There were negotiations for Leontyne Price and me to do the sound track, but the billing would be insignificant, and the money Goldwyn was willing to pay was insultingly unacceptable. So we each refused. As it turned out, it became widely publicized that the voices were dubbed, and although Robert McFerrin and Adele Addison did a beautiful job, the overall effect was too synthetic to please either the audiences or the critics. It's not unusual for Hollywood—but amazing for anyone who loves *Porgy and Bess* to realize that McFerrin and Addison were not even in the same room when they cut those sound tracks. To produce some of America's most passionate love duets for the screen, Hollywood chose to splice them together electronically.

The film was conceived in bitterness and hostility — between the original stage producer, Robert Breen, and Samuel Goldwyn; and then between Goldwyn and his director, Otto

Preminger; and then between the tyrannical director and his browbeaten cast. Touted in preopening publicity as Goldwyn's last film and the capstone to his career, it lost a bundle. Worse, it seems to have been an embarrassment to Ira Gershwin and Dorothy Heyward, who ultimately controlled the rights — rights that Goldwyn had only leased, not purchased. The film was finally withdrawn from circulation. I'm told that the only way you can see *Porgy and Bess* today is by going to the Library of Congress and viewing the nine reels of their official copyright version in a cramped little cubicle. All the other prints have disappeared from view. It was an American art tragedy: What should have been a classic of our culture ended up in shambles.

I followed these tribulations in 1959, as the details became public. It only served to confirm my tendency to shy away from Hollywood. But by that time, I had ample first-hand experience about the ups and downs of *Porgy and Bess*, and about the antics of theater producers.

Chapter Nine

PORGY AND BESS

My personal adventure with *Porgy and Bess* began with a telephone call from Larney, while I was still in Hollywood waiting to make a movie that wasn't going to happen. Even from three thousand miles away I could hear the excitement in Larney's voice. How would I like to follow in Todd Duncan's footsteps? How did I feel about playing Porgy in an ambitious new revival of the great musical?

How can I describe what that offer represented to me? Back when I was riding on my grandmother's cotton sack, a young, white insurance salesman-turned-writer named DuBose Heyward was working on his first novel. It was set in his native Charleston, South Carolina, and it was inspired by an item in the police blotter about a local indigent who had lost the use of his legs and his problems with the woman in his life. The novel was called *Porgy*, and it became a best seller when it was published in 1925.

Dorothy Heyward, his wife, drafted a dramatization, which became the play *Porgy*. It was first presented by the Theatre Guild in New York in 1927, at the height of the Harlem Renaissance. It was a big success there and on the road.

George Gershwin's operatic treatment with DuBose Heyward's libretto had premiered in 1935, as I was going into high school. It was called a "folk opera" by the composer. The critics were mixed in their opinions — it was too "folk" for some, too "opera" for others. Though it was a personal triumph for the singers, including Todd Duncan as Porgy, that first production wasn't the success that had been hoped for.

But however challenging the libretto might be, the music was critic-proof. Throughout my musical life, beginning in the days of my high school recitals, the tunes of *Porgy and Bess* had been in the concert repertoire of every black musician, male and female, from classical to jazz to pop. "Summertime," "I Got Plenty o' Nuttin'," "It Ain't Necessarily So," "Bess, You Is My Woman Now," and "I Loves You, Porgy" were contemporary American standards for many white singers as well.

The production of *Porgy and Bess* that most people remembered was the 1942 revival by Cheryl Crawford. She was then a young producer who had started in the business as an assistant stage manager for the original production of the play *Porgy*. By stripping the opera of most of its recitatives, cutting minor supporting characters, and scaling the orchestra and chorus back to minimal size, Crawford reduced the show's operating costs and shortened it by more than a half hour. Judging from the critical reaction, she also rendered it more accessible to general musical theater audiences. Though its production costs were still too high for the show ever to be a big money-maker, *Porgy and Bess* played in New York and on the road for over two years.

Now, in 1951, *Porgy and Bess* had inspired yet another producing team to bring it back to the stage. This time it was Robert Breen, director of the American National Theatre and Academy (ANTA), and his partner, financier Blevins Davis, who had dreams of touring it, not only across the country but around the world.

The visionary Breen had big plans for *Porgy*. In those days before the National Endowment for the Arts, his enterprise, ANTA, was the closest thing we had to a federal arts institution, like the royal theater companies of Europe. Although ANTA was not really much more than a concept on paper, Breen saw it as a potential vehicle for showcasing American culture. He saw *Porgy and Bess* — for its subject matter, for its African-American musical idiom, and for the genius of the quintessentially American composer George Gershwin — as an exemplar of distinctively American art. His big plans anticipated the later state department cultural programs, and paved the way for many of them.

Breen had already produced a European tour of Ballet Theater, the first major presentation of an American dance company to the citadels of old-world ballet. His contract to make those arrangements had been signed by Blevins Davis, board president of the troupe that would later become today's American Ballet Theatre. Davis, for his part, was a moneyed and cultured businessman who had a wide-ranging interest in the performing arts. As chance would have it, he was also a lifelong friend of President Harry Truman; they had been next-door neighbors in Independence, Missouri. That connection would be useful to Breen's notion of using *Porgy and Bess* as an exercise in official cultural diplomacy.

By the end of 1951, Larney had concluded negotiations with Davis and Breen. Because the production was expensive — over seventy cast and crew members — everyone would be getting minimum pay. Larney prevailed in his insistence that I should be an exception to that policy. My film debut in *Show Boat* had established me as an up-and-coming movie star.

We did have a scheduling problem to clear up. Davis and Breen wanted me badly for the role. I later learned that Cheryl Crawford, whose advice Breen trusted, had strongly lobbied for me to do it (we had met when she produced *Regina* on Broadway). The only catch was that I had already made certain commitments to Columbia Artists, and a number of concert dates had been booked and advertised. As important as *Porgy and Bess* was to me, I had already learned something about myself while I was in Hollywood. There was nothing, *nothing*, more important to me than my concert career.

I did work with Columbia Artists to limit my concert availability to the last half of the concert season, from the 1951 Christmas season through the winter of 1952. André Mertons got on the phone with scores of presenters and worked out a complex schedule that made it possible for me to fulfill all the commitments within a three-month period. It was a difficult tour for him to schedule, and it would be physically demanding for me to perform, but it could be done.

Davis and Breen appreciated the special arrangements Larney and Columbia Artists were able to make. They agreed that there would be no problem, and my first one-year contract was signed to run through May 1953, with a three-month hole from January through March.

Their final plans were still taking shape, but they intended a tour of several U.S. cities in 1952, then a tour of European capitals into the new year. I would rejoin the company in time for the New York premiere, in the late spring or possibly as late as the beginning of the theater season in the fall of 1953. After a substantial run in New York, they would launch a second, major U.S. tour, possibly extending throughout 1954. At Davis's request, we alerted Columbia Artists that I would have limited availability for that whole year — I owed that much to the *Porgy and Bess* production.

On his tour with Ballet Theatre, Breen had experienced the terrors of a company manager dependent on the fragile health and temperaments of his star performers. One bad ankle could cause a series of programs to be reshuffled, due to the ripple effect of changing one ballet in the schedule. He also appreciated the physical demands of the lead roles in *Porgy and Bess*. Wisely, he double-cast the parts, and in fact had a continuous cycle of performers on contract or under consideration for all the major roles at all times. The fact that he would have alternates would make it even easier for us to work out any scheduling glitches. Le Vern Hutcherson, Leslie Scott, and Irving Barnes were all, at one time or another, my alternates in the role of Porgy, though it was understood that I would play the opening night performances in each new location.

Davis and Breen asked me to accompany them when they went to take a look at one of the young women they were considering for Bess. He thought I might be interested. She was performing the role of Mistress Ford in *Falstaff* in a student production at Julliard, where she was studying. She made an immediate impression on both of us as an enormously gifted singer, and when I was introduced to her in the dressing room after the performance, she struck me as a shyly self-assured woman with much more presence than a girl in her early twenties should be expected to radiate. I knew I was living a charmed life, but who could ever have predicted that by year's end I would be married to this brilliant young woman, Leontyne Price?

We started rehearsals in May. Breen didn't waste time; we were scheduled for only a month of rehearsals. With the costs he was running, he wanted us out of the rehearsal hall and in front of an audience of some kind just as fast as he could get us there.

Bobby Breen was a marvelously inventive director. Bouncy and boyish and bursting with fresh ideas, he was always looking for a new highlight to accentuate — and where the libretto lacked them, he would make them up. A quirky bit of business, a slang expression that seemed to fit, a gesture or facial expression that might underline the dialogue — he'd try anything on for size, and just as easily remove it a few days later as he tried still newer director's tricks.

He was also one of those directors who would risk throwing the performers off balance, in order to explore the emotional reaction of a new special effect. In one performance he tried the idea of a packet of stage blood — without telling the other actors it was going to happen. When the character suddenly poured forth blood from his chest, everyone else on stage gasped, and some of us nearly broke character and stopped the show to deal with the emergency, until we realized, almost as one, "It's only another Breen trick." For that performance he got the intensity of reaction he wanted from the cast, but he almost had us calling for an ambulance.

I remember him as lithe, athletic, with sharp, deft gestures as he gave us his direction. He was the kind of director that they invented sneakers for — he was always on the move as he directed, leaping from the orchestra seats in the house up to the stage to show us as well as tell us what he wanted.

One of the busiest people on the production staff, throughout rehearsals and later on the road, was Bobby Breen's assistant, Ella Gerber. She kept a thick prompt book of Breen's additions and emendations, and jotted down every improvement in the staging. As we progressed through rehearsals her book got thicker and thicker. On the road — where Breen's inventiveness continued to percolate unabated — Gerber's book probably doubled in size. Every gimmick he came up with she captured in writing. Her book became the bible of that production, and for many productions of *Porgy and Bess*, for years to come. Particularly since the alternates and new cast members would be rehearsed by Gerber rather than Breen, her influence on the staging of the show was ultimately as great as that of Breen himself.

In the long run, Ella's alacrity as the butterfly catcher of Breen's fleeting ideas probably did the show a disservice. If his trial-and-error approach had followed its natural course, new notions would have displaced previous ones. But Ella was assiduously recording every one in her notebooks. Instead of dying their natural death, they all accumulated into a cluttered collection of odds and ends, accretions on the original intentions of Heyward and Gershwin. Breen could probably have done with a bit less "help" than he got. But the effects would not begin to show for many months, and by that time *Porgy and Bess* would have become a cultural icon.

The word was that originally we were supposed to premiere at the Metropolitan Opera. There was apparently some concern on the part of Met board members that *Porgy and Bess* might be too much of a departure from their usual fare. In any case, we were off-again, on-again. Finally we were scheduled to open at the Dallas State Fair that summer, and, after a quick tour to Europe, wind up our tour at the Met. In the meantime our billing on tour would proclaim that we were a "Metropolitan Opera Production," a healthy shot of prestige for the tour.

Porgy and Bess could use all the PR trappings and prestige it could get. Despite the obvious genius of the music and the story, and the significance of those wonderful roles for the careers of so many black performers, there were always sincerely motivated activists who attacked the musical as an exploitation of stereotypes. It was produced by white producers. It was directed by a white director. Heyward was white, Gershwin was white, and it would be presented in communities like Dallas and Washington that were still legally segregated.

On that last count, the concern was misplaced. The producers were adamant that *Porgy and Bess* would not be presented to segregated audiences. Even our local stage crews had to be integrated or we didn't play.

Just as significant was the insistence of the Gershwin and Heyward estates (both originators had died tragically premature deaths by the time of our production) that *Porgy and Bess* could be presented only by all-black casts. Suggestions that white opera stars could do the roles in blackface were angrily rejected.

But most important was the strong sentiment among the cast — and among most African-American community leaders and spokesmen who made their feelings clear throughout the several productions of this work — that *Porgy and Bess* was a celebration of our culture, and not an exploitation of it. The work didn't snigger at African-Americans. It ennobled the characters it depicted, and awakened generations of music lovers and theatergoers, in America and abroad, to the universality of the "primitive" civilization of Catfish Row. Today, with the explosion of African-American culture at every level from high-brow to low-down, especially in the world of music, it seems quaint to consider that there was once a time when it was considered too exotic, or somehow needful of an apologia.

The question was reopened with the announcement of Breen and Davis's plans to tour internationally. Many who were reconciled to the performances in the U.S. felt that we were going to distort the world's perceptions of American Negroes, perhaps trivialize our social and economic problems with songs like "I Got Plenty o' Nuttin'," or provide a rationale for American racism by depicting the crapshooters, the loose women, the dopers, even murderers, on Catfish Row.

That turned out to be a completely wrong-headed anxiety. Almost without exception the reviewers in Europe recognized *Porgy and Bess* for what it was — a story of triumph, not degradation, despite our very real problems. By merging white and black perceptions, in its writing and in its performance, the folk opera transcended purely racial orientation and achieved that universality that characterizes other world masterpieces rooted in German or Italian or other ethnic themes.

One salutary effect these sensitivities did accomplish was to remove the word "nigger" from the libretto. It might be realistic, even appropriate and dramatically effective, to use that word in a "signifying" conversation between blacks. But it would be unacceptable to give the word currency — and maybe even a stamp of approval — through loose usage for mixed audiences. In particular, we wouldn't want to suggest to our European audiences that such racial slurs were considered acceptable among civilized Americans.

The international touring idea was always in Breen's game plan. As his schedule became more definite, an offer from the Berlin Festival was confirmed, even though it conflicted with the opening date at the Metropolitan Opera. Breen scrapped the Met date, and arranged with Billy Rose to play in the Ziegfield Theatre instead. He booked the show in Vienna, then Berlin, then London for a long run, and finally Paris, before returning for the Broadway premiere.

I kept an eye on the schedule changes as they were announced. I was concerned, naturally, that Breen and Davis would keep our agreement in mind — I had to keep my three months free for Columbia Artists. As things were developing, I would have to miss the Paris opening, but everything else would work out fine. While they were winding up in Europe, I'd be doing my concert dates. Then I'd rejoin the cast in plenty of time for our Broadway debut.

Rehearsals went well, and I remember those hectic days with real pleasure. Once again I was in a theater company that quickly became an extended family. The colorful Cab Calloway, who had been one of the major bandleaders and singers throughout the thirties, was playing the wicked Sportin' Life. He was a bit down on his luck since the decline of the big band era, so Calloway saw *Porgy and Bess* as a comeback for him. At the other extreme were brand-new faces like Leontyne and the striking John McCurry, an up-and-coming actor who also had an army commission and degrees in music and languages, cast as the tragic figure Crown. But throughout the company, in the many smaller roles and among the production staff, we were all like fellow travelers in a small boat, and I think we all shared the same warm feelings for one another as brothers and sisters together.

Most of all, I remember those heady days as the beginning of my long romance with Leontyne. Rehearsals can be exhausting, emotionally and physically, and theater people aren't noted for going out on dates as such. But more and more often Leontyne and I became partners when we went out with the others for dinner, and before long we were going out alone.

I was aware of the slight difference in our ages — she was twenty-four, I was thirty-two. But she was even more aware of the gap in our experience. Our backgrounds were very similar — she had grown up in a cultured and loving environment similar to my childhood home — but she was still a Julliard student, uncertain of her career. I had been on magazine covers, had toured internationally, had hobnobbed with Sinatra and Gardner and scored my success in Hollywood.

For all those achievements, I was just as uncertain of my career plans as she was of hers, but how could she know that? In age and career status we differed; but emotionally, from my standpoint at least, we were complete equals.

She later told me of the excitement in her dormitory each time she prepared for one of our dates — borrowed earrings from one friend, a borrowed stole from another, committee decisions on the type of perfume she should wear. But what I saw walking down the stairs to meet me, every time I picked her up at the International House where she was staying, was the most composed, even worldly young woman I had ever wanted to spend time with. Years later she confessed that she was the "main attraction of I-House" when she returned from our dates and told all (her account of my eating snails was a highlight), but, for all I knew from her demeanor, she had frequented that French restaurant dozens of times and knew more than I did about etiquette and comportment.

As we became closer, and I introduced her to Larney and Karen, our relationship took a professional turn as well. She signed Larney as her personal manager on the same liberal basis as his agreement with me. Without mortgaging her career, or prematurely making decisions that might later prove unwise, she now had someone actively looking out for her interests. Of course we both knew that *Porgy and Bess* was our best professional move for the next year or more. But in the uncertain careers we were each pursuing, it was not too soon to start preparing for the next move.

The time went quickly and soon we were on the road. From our first performance at the Dallas State Fair, it was clear that we had a triumph on our hands. There, and in Chicago, Pittsburgh, and Washington, D.C., we broke box office records, our ovations were endless, and even with Gerber's accumulating ledger of schtick, the production was fast becoming recognized as a definitive realization of the folk opera. At any rate, it was considered more accessible than the original, and more fully fleshed than what some called the "bargain basement," stripped-down version that Cheryl Crawford had presented.

As we progressed toward our Washington premiere and our European departure, the publicity campaign got larger and louder. We were involved in just about every kind of promotion you can imagine. The ultimate was at the Republican National Convention, held in Chicago while we were there — the one that would ultimately nominate Eisenhower for president. I was asked to open the proceedings with "The Star-Spangled Banner." Of course I was pleased to do so, even though I was a life-long registered Democrat. Nobody asked to see any party credentials. That was arranged by George Murphy, the actor politician who served as the GOP's "Hollywood connection" three decades before the Ronald Reagan era.

I had already had my share of celebrity; now Leontyne too was finding out what it was like to be in the limelight. From the very first reviews, the old show-biz cliché applied: A star was born. It might be true that Leontyne faced as uncertain a future as I did — for that matter, as uncertain as the career that Marian Anderson had once faced — but whatever the future held for her, it was sure to be stellar. That was clear from the very first performance of *Porgy and Bess*.

Dallas isn't as romantic as Paris or Vienna, but it was in Dallas, after the pressures of our first opening night, that Leontyne and I first began to realize that our feelings for one another had progressed way beyond the camaraderie of co-stars. And then it was in Chicago that those feelings took a definite form and shape.

We were performing at the Civic Opera House, the beautiful hall where the Lyric Opera performs today. Larney and Karen had made the trip from New York for our opening, and for the surprise I had in store, which I had confided to them. As I had told Larney on the telephone, I planned to propose to Leontyne in Chicago, and if she'd have me, to marry her before we left on international tour. The idea of having to go off on tour to all those romantic places, and having to spend all that time so close to her yet observing the proprieties to protect her reputation, made me want to tie the knot before we took off.

I had staged this special event with what I thought was a certain savoir-faire. The four of us were seated in a fancy restaurant in the Chicago Loop. I had ordered a bottle of champagne, and while we waited for it to arrive, I nervously fingered the engagement ring that was riding in my coat pocket. Larney and Karen had gone with me when I picked it out. They were sitting there waiting with half-smiles for my next maneuver. They knew what I had in mind.

I had seated myself next to Leontyne, on her left side, and I positioned my seat closer to her than would have seemed natural. Leontyne noticed it and I saw a quizzical smile cross her lips as we carried on our conversation. Then the wine arrived, and I became even more preoccupied with the ring in my pocket as the sommelier fussed with the bottle. While he was still doing his work, I reached under the tablecloth to take Leontyne's hand in mine. Another quizzical look as she gave me her hand, still in conversation. Under the table I fidgeted with her fingers, separating them with my own, zeroing in on her ring finger.

When our glasses were poured, we prepared to raise them for a toast. At that point, before I lifted my glass I drew the ring out of my coat pocket with my free hand, and reached under the table, toward the finger I had isolated. Now she was looking at me with slight alarm, wondering what in the world I could be up to.

If I had been as smooth as my intentions, I would have slipped the big, beautiful diamond ring on her finger in one deft move, and then, holding her hand, I would have asked her to be my wife. Instead, I fumbled the ring at the critical moment, and Larney, Karen, and I all heard it chime as it struck the lower legs of the table and began to roll.

Suddenly Leontyne was alone at the table. She and the other patrons in the restaurant were treated to the spectacle of three rear ends in the air, as we all dived under the tablecloth to find and retrieve the lost ring. Larney and Karen knew how much it had cost — several months' salary — and I was equally concerned with salvaging the special occasion I had planned.

I don't remember who found it, but after a few moments we regained our composure. This time I took her hand over the table, where I could see what I was doing, and made my humble proposal.

Did it take her by surprise? She demurely accepted, and with a blush and a smile leaned over the table to give me a kiss. In retrospect, though, it was probably more of a surprise to see her dinner companions crawling around on the restaurant carpeting. Concerning my intentions, I don't think they could have been such a great secret. I suspect she was pretty much prepared for me to make my move, and probably wondering what was taking me so long. She usually was about a half mile ahead of me in such matters.

I phoned my folks, and she phoned hers, and we began to make our wedding plans. Larney and the company's publicity people were also on the case, and before we left Chicago our engagement was announced to the world at large. We would be married at the Abyssinian Baptist Church in Harlem, by the Reverend Adam Clayton Powell. The entire *Porgy and Bess* cast would be in attendance. We would do the honors immediately after the Washington, D.C., run closed, just before we left for the European tour. Our honeymoon would therefore be a "working honeymoon," but it would be spent in some of the most romantic locations in the world.

Our schedule had us playing Washington in August. With its sultry summers, Washington is considered to be a semitropical "hardship post" for the diplomatic corps, many of whom, in those days, got extra pay as if they were posted in Rangoon. Congress is almost never in session then, and even President Truman, winding up his final year in the White House, had gone home to Independence for the summer.

But Blevins Davis had used all his White House ties to impress the administration with the significance of our production. Between his connections and Breen's ANTA credentials, the state department had agreed to substantial sponsorship of our tour. They had secured U.S. military aircraft to fly us over and back, and paid most of our other expenses (although Breen would need to make separate arrangements with commercial producers in London and Paris to finance the balance of the costs).

Davis communicated the importance of a presidential send-off, and indeed, the president and his wife, along with many members of Congress and diplomats from other countries, arranged to be in town for our opening. I remember our opening-night receiving line — the entire cast queued up to shake hands with the president when he came backstage to congratulate us.

I also fondly remember that Todd Duncan came to our opening and then came backstage to see me. He was impressed with the production and mildly envious that I had an alternate to share the performance load. But it was Breen's theatrical staging that preoccupied him. After he got past the congratulations, he shook his head irascibly. "Man, why don't you have them put some kind of spotlight on you?" he demanded. "They got you in the dark all the time." In the earlier productions, Duncan's big numbers had been staged opera-style, in a spotlight, the singer facing the audience. In ours the staging was more dramatic, and the singing was integrated into the action of the scene. I told him I would handle it all right.

The *Washington Post's* esteemed drama critic, Richard L. Coe, had been in the forefront of the movement to desegregate the National Theater only two years before. He was one of the nation's most important critics, and often set the tone for major Broadway productions that played the nation's capital before opening in New York.

Therefore we were especially gratified to accept his accolades for our production; after all the ovations, his review was the icing on the cake, and a splendid send-off for our European tour:

"President Truman last night led a cheering audience at the opening of *Porgy and Bess*," he wrote. "This is a brilliant revival. That it will be a pleasure to American audiences for years to come was clear from the opening's stunning impression on a packed house, but of equal importance is the fact that the State Department's sponsorship goes to a production of unqualified first rank."

My personal highlight of August 1952 was not that opening but our quick trip to New York for the wedding. Breen and Davis arranged a bus so that the entire cast would be able to travel together. Immediately after closing at the National, we all made the road trip to New York. If I'd been paying attention to omens, I might have detected that my carefully laid plans for *Porgy and Bess* were just beginning to show signs of unravelling at the edges.

First, Adam Clayton Powell missed the ceremony. We later heard he had car troubles; his associate pastor and right-hand man, Pastor Licorice, married us, with my father assisting. Then Leontyne and I took a commercial flight back to D.C. for our honeymoon — that is, instead of traveling with the company on the bus, we flew back and had an extra evening to ourselves. (The airline tickets were a wedding gift from our fellow cast members.) Their bus broke down on the way home, and our comrades staggered in exhausted after many extra hours on the road, just in time to get ready for the flight to Europe.

Then, as our military flight was heading out over the ocean en route to Vienna, I noticed that the sun was shining through the wrong windows on the plane. I asked a flight attendant, who held a finger to her lips. "We don't want to alarm anyone," she said, "but we've developed engine trouble and we're heading back." That began another series of maneuvers with our bags and ourselves, the other actors already exhausted from the mechanical problems on the bus; we ended up spending an extra night in the States.

However ominous those glitches might have been, they

were soon forgotten in the excitement of our European reception. It was a continuation of the accolades we had received at home, only bigger. We actually became blasé about the frequency of our half-hour ovations after every opening. *Porgy and Bess* was hailed, and we were lionized. I caused another sensation when I regaled the embassy reception with Schubert lieder. The Austrians and Germans loved the Catfish Row opera, but were scarcely prepared to have Porgy come to the reception in a tuxedo and sing their own classics in perfect *Hochdeutsch*. They were floored.

While we were in Vienna, I began to hear more rumbles of possible changes in the schedule, and I kept my antenna out. But Davis and Breen seemed assured that everything was fine, and told me not to worry. Breen was with us everywhere, continually making "improvements" in his direction, and Davis flew in for the openings.

Breen and I had a close working relationship throughout the rehearsals and the tours, but I didn't see much of Blevins Davis. His involvement in the project was primarily financial. What he didn't know about producing was compensated for by his ability to arrange financing and credit.

The only times I'd had much to say to Davis was at social functions. He was somewhat corpulent, which aged him; in his late forties, looking like late fifties, he was gregarious in a superficial way with no real warmth. He had an artificial charm that he could turn off as quickly as he could turn it on. His money had been acquired through marriage. He came across as one of those recently wealthy whose snobbery is learned rather than born; he expected servants and maître d's to bow when he made his entrance.

I got my strongest personal impression of Davis at a private lunch we shared in the hotel dining room while he was with us in Berlin. We were in the middle of a conversation when he seized a breadbasket from the table and flung it across the hotel dining room. Other patrons had to duck the shower of rolls, and waiters came running to his reproach: "When I want service, I want service!" he barked.

From Vienna we went to the Berlin Festival, to perform at the Titania-Palast. Those first two engagements were both sponsored by the state department.

The London presentation was a commercial effort by Davis

and Breen at the Stoll Theater. And here the seams started to show, the packaging started to come unwrapped. Davis and Breen, for all their visionary energy, had limitations as producers. The earlier two triumphs, funded by the U.S. government, had been short, brilliant runs. In London they were contemplating a longer commercial run. The problem with producing *Porgy and Bess* — it's still a problem today — is that, like the grand operas that always require subsidy to present, it was just too big to clear a profit, or even to pay its own way. Reviews and ovations are wonderful, but even if every ticket is sold, after all those performers and musicians and stage hands and royalties and theater management are paid off, there will still be a deficit at the end of the week. The show is just too big.

I opened in London, as planned, and then packed my bags for my concert tour back in the States. It was hard to leave my new wife, even for a few months, but we consoled each other with the awareness that this was only "chapter one" of our long involvement with *Porgy and Bess*. Our "chapter two" would open with a New York premiere that could only be brilliant, and then a long year together on the road.

The timing would be very important for our marriage. Both Leontyne and I knew the hazards of a show-biz relationship, especially when both partners have set their own individual sights so high. Children were not in the picture, certainly not anytime in the foreseeable future, so those complications wouldn't enter the equation. But even without children it would be difficult to manage a marriage and two careers, especially since neither she nor I could accurately predict our career moves in advance. With the first year together on the road, playing the romantic leads in *Porgy and Bess,* we would have time for our relationship to jell. All the little adjustments that two people need to make would come in due course. By the time we had finished the tour, we would be ready for whatever other challenges life had to offer. I was more than willing to give up a year that might otherwise be spent building up my concert career, while Leontyne's career caught up with mine. In fact, I was looking forward to it. It was in that spirit of optimism that I flew out of London for home, and began three hard months of concentrated touring for Columbia Artists.

But things were not developing as we had planned. The London ovations were as enthusiastic as all the rest, but some time after I left the crowds started to drop off, and the producers got nervous about their investment. Davis and Breen began looking for a way to break their contract with the theater management in London, so they could recoup their losses and go on to Paris ahead of schedule.

At about that same time, back in New York the producer Billy Rose was having scheduling problems with his Ziegfield Theater, which was unexpectedly dark. Billy Rose was used to getting his own way — I remembered his high-handed assurance that the U.S. Army would bend over backwards for him when he wanted me for *Carmen Jones*. Now he was telling Breen and Davis that they should bring *Porgy* in early, regardless of their other arrangements.

Breen and Davis looked at the empty seats at the Stoll and jumped at the chance. They somehow wriggled free of their commitments to the London theater management, scored a final triumphant European hit with their Paris opening and a short run in February, and headed back to New York in March. They now planned to open at the Ziegfield on March 9. I was somewhere in the middle of my Columbia Artists tour, and found out about these new arrangements in a midnight call from Larney.

It was presented to me as a moral crisis, as well as a professional dilemma. Davis was insisting to Larney that I had to do what they had done — disregard the prior contract with Columbia Artists and the commitments to the presentors in all those cities, and make a career choice based on self-interest. If I would tell Columbia Artists that regretfully I had to terminate my contract, Breen and Davis were offering me the opportunity to open in the hottest play of the season, in a role I was born to play, and then to tour nationally and internationally as long as I liked. But if I refused, although they would of course be bound to pay me through the termination of my contract in May, they would deny me a single performance at the Ziegfield in New York; I would never be seen by the New York critics opposite my wife in the title roles of this masterpiece; and I could not expect a contract for the *Porgy and Bess* tour.

Larney and I agreed, in our first phone call, that we had a moral obligation to continue as planned. There seemed to be the possibility of some compromise — we could make a few adjustments. It would be possible for me to come into New York for the opening, and then resume my Columbia Artists touring, returning from week to week to alternate a few performances with Le Vern Hutcherson. By the end of March I'd be free, as originally planned.

We both believed that we had enough bargaining leverage to achieve a compromise. Certainly Davis would want Leontyne for the tour. Like mine, her contract ran out in May. In his discussions with Davis, as her manager, Larney would politely but firmly make it clear that Leontyne would support my position in her own negotiations. The producers were taking a hard line, but we decided that was partly bluff. I was confident things would work out.

Those expectations were dashed in Larney's next phone call: He had learned from Davis that Leontyne was already signed. She later explained that she believed I too had signed with them. Without consulting Larney, she had taken them at their word, and contracted for another year. The worst news Larney saved for last: Davis was planning to go ahead without me — no compromises — if I didn't come around.

At this point the *Porgy and Bess* company had just returned from Europe and were due to open at the Ziegfield the next week. We were coming down to the wire. I suggested to Larney that I would find time in my tour schedule to come and talk to Breen myself. He thought that was a good idea. We'd always had an amicable relationship. When I called him at his office it was as if he was waiting to hear from me. "Oh, yes," he said, "I'm so glad you called. Please come in, let's talk."

He'd always been friendly, and I was sure this was something we'd be able to work out. I came to his office, and sat down opposite him at his desk. "Look, Bobby," I said. "Let's forget all the hard feelings that have been going around on this, between Larney and Blevins Davis. Let's keep our eyes on the real prize. You know Leontyne and I will be magical in the roles — we'll make Broadway history. What do we have to do to work this out?" His response was unequivocal. There was only one thing we could do: I should skip out on my contract with Columbia Artists.

"Bobby, you know I can't do that," I told him. "But I'm sure we can work out a compromise." I could see his face fall as I reiterated our alternative suggestion. He had been under the impression when I called that I was coming in to accede to his demands. It was clear to me, as Larney had already warned me, that there was going to be no give-and-take. Breen and Davis were both immovable. Despite their blandishments, they'd made up their minds irrevocably.

He also dropped another bombshell. The previous salary and billing and profit-sharing terms of our first contract would be open for renegotiation in any new contract we signed. "I'm so sorry," he said, as he fell back on the producer's ultimate recourse: "I'm sorry, but our hands are tied."

As he knew very well, it was my hands that were tied. If I was going to have the Broadway triumph I'd been working for, and if I was going to have that year on the road with Leontyne, I had no choice but to break my contract with Columbia Artists.

The next twenty-four hours were difficult for me. On one level, I was in the typical predicament of any actor dealing with any producer—for that matter, of any worker who has a problem with his boss. But on a higher, personal level I was even more hamstrung. Davis and Breen had as much power as any plantation boss ever had: They had the power to separate me from my wife for a year. And now, to rub it in, the contract they were offering represented a demotion from the contract I already had.

In their long-range plans to develop a small industry around *Porgy and Bess* so that it might finally be profitable — indefinite touring, multiple companies, film rights, and the rest — they were not only paying everyone low wages; they were also insuring that the publicity was focused on the musical itself, and not the performers. Now that the show had taken off, the advertising listed Heyward and Gershwin as creators and Davis and Breen as producers, but no other personal credits. Even the critics' quotes they ran in the ads were depersonalized. If a critic wrote that "Cab Calloway was uproarious," or "Leontyne Price was triumphant in the role," it would be "Uproarious!" and "Triumphant!" in the ad, without reference to the performer. To the extent possible, they wanted ticket sales to be independent of any individual star. The efforts were succeeding, but for me that meant that I had to get back in line with the others.

That would mean that I was expected to give up the billing and the percentage of net profit that had been originally negotiated. But Breen offered no concessions whatever in return; it was take it or leave it. He must have calculated that necessity would win out over dignity.

I talked it all over with Leontyne. She never pressured me one way or the other. She knew I had to do what I had to do. And Larney always knew that there was no real choice for me to make.

We stayed with the Columbia Artists contract. I fulfilled every one of those obligations. I kissed Leontyne for good luck on opening night, and I kissed *Porgy and Bess* goodbye.

The next few months were among the most difficult in my life. I had this notion of the manly way to behave that I'd learned from my father: stoic acceptance. I was prepared for most of the pain. I took it in stride and tried not to show how much it hurt. I had made my choice, and I was sure I was right. When you brace yourself for the worst, you can deal with almost anything.

But I wasn't ready for the loss of family. That was the clincher; that was what made it such a suffering time for me. Whenever I had to be along as Leontyne's escort, at after-show functions, it was a comfort that I had her support, and the sympathy of other members of the company. But the fact remained that I was on the outside looking in. I wasn't a part of the theater family that had been such an important part of my life. I was no longer the Prince in this little kingdom in which my young Princess Bride lived — in fact, I wasn't even a bona fide member of the family anymore, and had no rights among them. It was even within Breen and Davis's prerogatives to have me barred from backstage, if they should so desire. It was an awkward position for me professionally, an intolerable situation for me personally, and it put a heavy burden on our young marriage in its most fragile hour. It was a horrible time in my life.

My usual solution, throughout that year, was to keep myself away from most cast functions. I didn't want Leontyne to feel uncomfortable at receptions and parties, torn between being Bill Warfield's wife and Bobby Breen's star. She had hit New York like a storm, and *Porgy and Bess* paved the way for her entire career to follow. I knew that would be a complicated time for her, and I didn't want my problems to interfere with her decisions. But the consequence was that I suffered all the more because I suffered alone.

Porgy and Bess played at the Ziegfield through the summer and into the fall. Breen never stopped putting his "finishing touches" on the play, and Gerber never stopped scribbling them down. By the time the show was winding up in New York, it had so much new stage business — and so many new snippets of dialogue — that I didn't recognize it. Breen had even restructured the three-act opera into two acts.

During this New York period, Leontyne and I had been staying in my quarters at the Wilson Hotel. We were planning to make a permanent move into a new home of our own, but that would have to wait. Leontyne was about to take off for the extended U.S. tour. It was in December of 1953 when I accompanied her to the old Penn Station to see her and the cast off on the first leg of their trip. They were going back to Washington, D.C., where we had all shared such an ebullient opening before zipping off to Europe, and where Leontyne and I had spent our one-night honeymoon. Leontyne and I took some cheer from the fact that Larney had booked us together in a January performance at the Academy of Music in Philadelphia, halfway between New York and Washington (with Otto Herz at the piano). We would see each other over the holidays, and we could look forward to the rehearsal time for our recital.

But we weren't going to get the year we had planned on, being together on the road. It wasn't going to happen. What might have been the time of bonding for us was instead a time of separation, tinged with a repressed bitterness. I threw myself into my Columbia Artists touring, and concentrated on the concert career.

By now, it's probably no surprise for you to read that I discovered a silver lining in all these clouds of woe. Sometimes in show business, as in life, it is better to have lived through an experience and lost, than never to have lived through it at all.

For one thing, I made some life-long friends in that original cast. Most notably, if I had never been involved with the Davis-Breen production I might never have had the opportunity to work closely with another of the world's great artists, Eva Jessye. Since the early twenties, she had been making music with her Eva Jessye Choir, and from the earliest days of radio she had been a celebrity on such shows as the "Major Bowes Family Radio Hour" and the "General Motors Hour." I literally grew up listening to her.

Her talents stretched from spirituals to classical music — she was choral director for the first presentation of Virgil Thompson's difficult *Four Saints in Three Acts*. Then, in 1935, she was asked to be choral director for the first production of *Porgy and Bess*, a role she performed for just about every important production of *Porgy* for the rest of the century.

She was the acknowledged authority on Gershwin's original intentions, for several generations of new producers but also for me. Whenever I had a question about the music, though the composer was no longer with us there was a personal link through Eva. I especially enjoyed hearing her stories of how Gershwin derived some of his themes from street singers and hawkers — he'd go out on the streets of Charleston to listen to them, and have Eva bring them into his studio to sing out "Here comes the Honey Man!" and "Straw-ber-ries! Fresh straw-berries!" — echoes of which are in the *Porgy and Bess* score.

If I'd never worked with Eva Jessye, I'd be poorer for it.

It's also the case that sometimes you can have too much of a good thing, too early in your life. In retrospect, 1954 was a critical year for my classical music career. That year launched the most productive decade of my life, and if I'd been gallivanting across the country, buoyed by the glowing accolades in one town after another and lulled by the cozy life of a musical theater star, who knows what direction I might have taken. For Leontyne it was a once-in-a-lifetime opportunity to establish herself as a major star early enough in her life, to subsequently be able to call the shots; but for me, at the age of thirty-four, it might have been a plateau that would be too comfortable to leave behind. That wouldn't have meant an empty life, but it certainly would have meant a different one.

I told myself, "Your time will come." *Porgy and Bess* was going to be around a long, long time. I'd have another shot at it, all in good time. In the meantime I licked my wounds and got on about my business.

Chapter Ten

LEONTYNE

Leontyne and I did our first performance at Philadelphia's Academy of Music, an event that was rare enough to memorialize here; rare because we both had a strong intuition that we shouldn't let promoters package us as a husband-and-wife team.

At that recital on January 27, 1954, with Otto Herz at the piano, we opened together with Bach's "He Hath My Course Ordained," followed by Purcell's "Lost Is My Quiet" and "Sound the Trumpet."

Then I sang alone: Schubert's "Wohin" and "Totengräbers Heimweh" and Loewe's "Kleiner Haushalt," "Süsses Begräbnis" and "Odins Meeres-Ritt."

Then a short Verdi group: Leontyne solo in the aria "Pace, pace, mio Dio," from *La Forza Del Destino*; then I solo in the aria "Eri tu," from *Un Ballo In Maschera*; then the two of us performing a bit of the reunion scene and the duet from *Simon Boccanegra*.

Then a Poulenc series of Paul Eluard poems by Leontyne: "Tu vois le feu du soir," "Main dominée par le coeur," "Rien que ce doux petit visage," and "Je nommerai ton front."

We closed with duets: Roger Quilter's "It Was a Lover and His Lass," Schumann's "To the Evening Star," Sam Raphling's "Two Old Crows" and "The Potato Dance," and a spiritual, "Ride on King Jesus," in a Hall Johnson arrangement that I had revised slightly for two parts.

Leontyne and I did only about three performances together in our life. We understood from the beginning that we were going to go in our own separate artistic directions. The last thing either of us wanted was for our individual careers to be linked into what would ultimately have become a high-class novelty act.

The alternatives to individual careers were severely prescribed. Either Leontyne would have followed my route — the route taken by Marian Anderson and my other role models — which would have been a tragic loss for the world of opera. Or I would have followed hers, into the opera world — which would have been a tragic mistake for me. Because, to this very day, although the black female virtuosi have been able to reach the extreme heights of opera, black males have never received the same welcome. And in my generation, though I might have helped to make a dent in the prevailing traditions, I would have suffered a stultifying suppression of my talents.

That doesn't mean to say that an exceptional artist was prevented from making his mark, from time to time. The potential existed, of course, and any number of exceptions can be cited. Todd Duncan and Lawrence Winters at the New York City Opera, George Shirley at the Met, Simon Estes at the San Francisco Opera. Though several are more representative of a later generation, they can all be cited as exceptions to the rule.

But if there is to be a career track for the black male opera singer, there has to be ample room for the less-than-exceptional, or the striving-to-be-exceptional, as well. There are many such white performers, very few blacks. The whole idea must be to transcend the exceptional, to get beyond the exceptions, and change the rules themselves.

At the time Leontyne was making her decisions, the rules were beginning to change for women. The opera world was just beginning to open up, and Leontyne herself was one of the people who made that happen.

Her first break came in 1955, from Peter Herman Adler, the conductor of the NBC Opera Theater. Her opera debut was in his *Tosca*, on television that year. Adler became a close family friend and adviser to both Leontyne and me. It was Adler who best articulated the reasons why we should take separate career paths.

After her debut on NBC, Leontyne was offered the role of Aida at the Met. She might have joined the growing parade of black artists who were showcased from time to time by the great

U.S. opera companies, but who never really earned a permanent place in their scheme of things. Adler and Larney both advised that she should not take the role.

Adler was most adamant. "Leontyne is to be a great artist," he said, in his accented English. "She is to be one of the greats. When she makes her debut at the Met, she must do it as a *lady*, not a slave."

The way to do this, he explained, was to devote several years to building a repertoire and a reputation. She should perform with the great opera companies of Europe. She should have her debut at La Scala, in Milan. She should receive the ovations and generate the press clippings now, while she was the hottest new face to appear in the world of music, and use that momentum to come into New York as a star, not as a neophyte. Once at the mercy of the Met, always at their mercy. She should do these roles on her own timetable, not theirs. It was good advice, and Leontyne took it.

Adler gave me good advice, too — and it was the opposite advice. I had been contemplating the same investment in opera that Leontyne was preparing to make. It would have meant giving up all the concert tours and concentrating on a long period of study— re-education, really — and a long, slow progress through the stages that Leontyne would be traveling.

"In the first place," Peter Herman Adler advised me, "you're already the star. It is hard to make a beginning as a newcomer when you are already so well known. But more important is the quality of your talent. Your talent is made of many colors. Many shades, many intensities, many colors. If you make yourself an opera star, you will have to lose those many sounds and create just one sound, *their* sound. For you, now, that would be such a waste."

Larney had been giving me the same advice. And it was reinforced by Otto Herz and Yves Tinayre. I loved the literature I was singing; I loved the hours I spent in rehearsal and practice, adding to it, perfecting it. Why should I abandon everything I had been working toward, why should I relegate the love of my life to a mere avocation, while pursuing a world of opera that probably wouldn't thank me for the trouble?

Besides, Columbia Artists was clamoring for more time, and Larney was receiving requests for additional bookings. The state department, having enjoyed such success with the *Porgy and Bess* tours, saw a world of possibilities for me — solo tours in Europe, in Africa, in Asia; there was fresh interest for a return trip to Australia; and the U.S. touring was stronger than ever.

So Leontyne was headed her way, I mine. There were those few occasions when we performed together, but as a rule we made a point of keeping our work separate from our private life.

Not that our private lives were any less hectic than our professional lives. Our marriage began on the fly, and was lived in hotel rooms for the first months. And then we were on separate tours — she still with *Porgy*, I with Columbia Artists.

When we were finally together in New York City for the first time, it was a period of great stress. I was in the middle of my disputatious negotiations with Breen and Davis, and she was preparing for the most important opening night of her career. We stayed in my apartment at the Wilson Hotel (Lou Ampolo had moved out) and we postponed any decisions about finding a permanent place to live until things settled down.

While she was on tour I did some scouting around and found a house on Vandam Street, in Greenwich Village. When I showed Leontyne around, she adored it. We moved in shortly after she returned from tour in 1954. But having a house didn't make us homebodies. We were still going in our separate directions. Ironic as it seems, the most stable person in our domestic picture was Lulu Shoemaker.

When I returned from Europe, Lulu was still running things at the Wilson Hotel. She was genuinely glad to see me when I arrived home ahead of the *Porgy* company. And, if anything, she was even more delighted to greet Mrs. William Warfield when the company arrived in March.

She had met Leontyne during the early rehearsal period, when I had brought members of the cast over to the Wilson. As I expected, Lulu felt she had an obligation to look her over and let me know her opinion. What I didn't expect is that once we were married, Lulu practically adopted Leontyne as her own. Before long it was as if they were the old friends and I were the interloper. They hit it off instantly. And no wonder: Leontyne was a class act, and Lulu was a genuine original.

Originally, Lulu was from the South. She'd been born around the turn of the century, so she was already pushing fifty when I arrived at the Wilson. She had had a hard life, though I never heard a complaint — on her own at an early age, finding work doing dishes, learning to cook, helping to take care of family members who had gradually moved north, in the great black migration during World War I. Lulu liked to indulge in that age-old flirtation with the numbers game that has so often been analyzed by black sociologists, philosophers, and preachers. Even in her later life she played the numbers without apologies. "It's the law of averages," she'd explain. "Every once in a while you're going to hit." And when she did, she'd put her winnings in a savings bank account. We'd try to explain, Leontyne and I, that if she'd pass up the numbers and tuck that money directly into an interest-bearing bank account she would "hit" with more predictability. But we understood that wouldn't be half so much fun. When she died, her estate included a savings account of some $25,000, so at least she had stayed ahead of the game.

When Leontyne and I got married and bought our home on Vandam Street, it was only natural that we would ask Lulu to leave her Wilson Hotel adventures behind and come live with us as our housekeeper. Lulu didn't have to be asked twice. She had seen the house we were buying, with an entire set of rooms upstairs that would be hers. She had become weary of the life at the Wilson, taking care of transients and strawbossing the house-keeping workforce. She was ready for some equilibrium in her life, and the salary we were able to pay was probably comparable to whatever she earned at the hotel.

Lulu had family in Brooklyn that she would visit from time to time. I never met any of them, except to catch a glimpse of a nephew who might come by to pick up a loan from Lulu. She was dark, and small, and you could never be clear about her age. Like many black women, her skin never wrinkled. She was peppery and lively, and when she wore a hat it was bright — about as far as you can get from the Aunt Jemima stereotype. She was capable of drawing herself up with great dignity and turning on a glare of disapproval that might have withered a proud man.

As far as I know, Lulu had never been married and had no intention of getting married, but she did have a boyfriend from time to time. One day she let us know that there would be a new face coming around occasionally. "It's this Chinese fella," she told us, uncharacteristically a little shy. "He's from around the corner, and he's been coming around asking about me for a little while. So I thought I'd find out what that's all about. I've never had a Chinese boyfriend." They stayed friends for quite a while, and Lulu, though ever discreet, kept us up to date on the relationship. And if I ever asked, "How's the Chinese boy-friend?" Lulu would assure me, "Oh, he's fine. He's a gentleman, honey. He knows how to treat a lady."

Lulu was even closer to Leontyne, once she was in the family. Leontyne could bare her innermost secrets to Lulu, who became an adviser, a confidant, a big sister. When Leontyne and I decided we were going to separate, there really wasn't any question about what would happen to Lulu. She stayed with Leontyne and the house, and continued to take care of both of them as long as she lived.

Lulu was part of our family until she died. She kept the home fires burning when no one else would have been able to; she became the anchor our lives needed. Though Leontyne and I would often be away, in different directions and at different times, the one constant in that house on Vandam Street was little Lulu. By that time I was getting my career into high gear, and Leontyne's career was being launched, and neither of us had time to take care of the hearth and home. Lulu was indispensable.

I remember Vandam Street fondly, but the memories are spotty. There were so many nights when I was in that house alone, while Leontyne was touring. Thank God for Lulu. I never hesitated to suggest to friends that they drop by for dinner, because I knew that with just a quick call to Lulu we would have something in the oven for whomever I brought over. There were just as many nights when I was out of town on tours of my own, and Leontyne was there alone, with Lulu. And then whenever Leontyne had a major opera opening coming up, I'd volunteer to move into the guest bedroom for a few days so she could devote her every hour— waking and sleeping — to the process of preparation. That need for isolation and concentration, includ-ing a period of separate sleeping arrangements, is a common feature of life in families like ours, when one or the other is about to open at the Met.

But there were many nights full of lively memories when we entertained. The soirées at Chez Warfield/Price became major informal social events — especially at New Year's. Lulu would lay out a spread — cocktails, hors d' ouevres, lots of fairly substantial food. And there'd be dancing to the record player.

The evenings would always end up with singing. Sometimes lounge-type singalongs, and sometimes *real* singing.

A typical night might include Leontyne's principal accompanist David Garvey sitting at our piano, and Leontyne and Betty Allen doing the confrontation scene from *Aida*. Or the young composer John Carter playing a cantata based on spirituals that he had written for Leontyne to sing, or entertaining us with a Rachmaninoff movement.

It was all very stellar, and very casual. We'd put on records and people would dance — just friends and colleagues coming together for a glass of champagne.

Many of those who came and went through our lives during those years—Marge and Gower Champion, Miles Davis, Nanette Fabray, Bobby Short, Roscoe Lee Brown, Samuel Barber, Gian Carlo Menotti, and Lena Horne—in memory seem almost like characters in a colorful parade. Whenever we meet these days, they always have a tale or two to share about something that happened "that night at your place, Bill, do you remember?"

But several of the people whom I met as acquaintances of acquaintances during those lively evenings, ended up as lifetime friends. For example, one night William Marshall phoned me to ask if he might bring along a pal of his, Don Shirley. Don had been making a name for himself as a pianist—at the time, I believe, he was playing at Birdland opposite Count Basie—but it was soon evident that he was a gifted classical pianist and arranger as well. In fact, he had done superb arrangements of jazz tunes in classical style, turning Gershwin's "The Man I Love" into a fugue worthy of Bach, that sort of thing. (He still does at least one New York concert each year, and he's still bridging the worlds of classical music and jazz. These days he uses a cellist and a bass, and his trio always has at least one fresh musical surprise on the program.)

Don Shirley was well-credentialled musically, a kindred spirit. More to the point, so far as our friendship was concerned, he also had a doctorate in psychology. And he had a ruthlessly honest temperament that brooked no evasiveness whenever I came to him for sympathy or advice. He could see right through a self-serving excuse, and never let me off the hook: "Now you know, Bill, we've talked about this before—you know who was responsible for that, don't you Bill?" Whomever or whatever I had been holding responsible for the cause of my latest kvetching, Don was pretty direct in showing me that the trail usually led right back to my own doorstep.

These soirées continued, whenever Leontyne and I were in town at the same time, right up until our last New Year's Eve together.

New Year's Eve parties at our place had become the ultimate. As elaborate as our other parties were, New Year's Eve was an all-stops-out, all-night blast. We stopped trying to keep track of the invitees, because friends brought friends, and last year's invitees turned up the following year, and we knew we could count on twice as many as we ever invited.

We threw our first New Year's Eve party in 1954, and they got bigger and better in 1955 and 1956. In 1957, as we were coming to the conclusion that it didn't make sense to try to keep our marriage afloat, we decided against throwing a party that New Year's Eve. We stayed home and planned to toast the New Year in private, but all evening we kept seeing old friends — some of them from four years earlier — who showed up, stammered in embarrassment, and stayed for a quick drink. They had simply assumed that we'd be throwing our usual party.

That was the year of Leontyne's San Francisco Opera debut. She had followed Adler's advice and wowed 'em in Europe. Then she returned to her first performance on these shores (not counting the TV performance), in Poulenc's *Carmelites*.

I made the trip to San Francisco to share the premiere with her. At the opening night festivities, as is typical, no special arrangements were made for spouses and guests of the performers. We were left to mill around and fend for ourselves. There was a middle-aged man there who confided that he didn't much care for opera, and asked me, "Are you one of the husbands? Oh, great, I finally found somebody to talk to." He latched onto me, and I politely talked sports with him, or whatever it was that he was interested in. In that year my name was still more widely known than Leontyne's, but at that moment I recognized, "Tonight I'm 'Mr. Price'."

More importantly for our marriage, as I looked around myself at that 1957 debut, I realized that Leontyne really didn't need my support any longer. She was firmly established and on her way. Our marriage was a classic case of two people meeting, becoming friendly, falling in love and marrying; then going in totally separate directions, remaining friends but almost completely forgetting the original reasons they had gotten married.

When we first met Leontyne was a shy schoolgirl. I first saw her on stage at Julliard. When we started dating, by her own account she was more than a little gaga-eyed to be out on the town with William Warfield—although, as I say, she was always so cool, so regal in her bearing that I was surprised to learn, years later, that she would return to her dormitory atwitter, to regale her classmates with accounts of her date with me.

When things started happening for Leontyne it became obvious that she no longer needed a mentor, if she ever did. In 1952, when we were on the road in her first big show, our relationship offered her a lot of fringe benefits: a manager who could handle both our careers, an agent at Columbia Artists; the company of those composers and conductors and others whose careers intersected with mine; a home (complete with Lulu) and all the stability in her private life that a home represents; and of course, on my part, an educated awareness of the ups and downs of her career and the progress of her development. During that stage of any artist's career, when you have no idea how you're going to make ends meet, or even how to set yourself up in a proper apartment, there's a tremendous need for those "support services," and I was able to provide that for her.

When we married, I was for a while the pivotal point in everything that happened for her. Even her introduction to Samuel Barber and Leonard Bernstein — which, like everything else in her career, would certainly have happened sooner or later — was expedited by her association with me. That was my greatest contribution to her. Then, as her career began to take hold, there was simply much less for me to do. That initial role was now superfluous.

By the time we separated in 1958, she was an altogether different person from the woman I had married. She was still as lovely, in her soul and in her person, as the Leontyne I had first met. But professionally she had moved into a realm where the advice and the support she needed was now to be provided by an entire coterie of professionals. She was in every sense emotionally autonomous and artistically independent of anything I could give her.

And, to be honest, there were two other things that came into play.

First, Leontyne needed something I couldn't give her: dependence. Afterwards, as I've thought about our relationship, it has often occurred to me that what Leontyne required at that point in her life was a "prince consort." She was becoming, in every important sense of the word, a "queen" in the world of music, a monarch of opera. The full glory of her coronation was only a matter of time. Every princess coming into full blossom as a queen needs a foil, an appropriately accoutered gallant to accompany and attend. I was unsuited for the role since my own development had outpaced that position. I was too young to be paternal, and yet— in the prime of my career— too far along to be a prince consort. That was one role I could never play, even if I'd wanted to.

And that was the second truth: I didn't want to. I was too busy keeping up the creative pace of my own career to subordinate any part of it to anything else, even Leontyne's splendid development. Like any performer, I had too strong an instinct for survival in the treacherous terrain of show business to allow anything else to take precedence over my own career needs.

Leontyne and I understood that about one another. Many was the premiere or the major opening night when one of us triumphed and the other wasn't there — because we were busy in another city, working toward our individual career goals. I don't think it's any accident that most show-business couples have a hard time maintaining two major careers. The rule seems to be that one has to become subordinate, or the partners end up going their separate ways.

I was completely supportive of Leontyne's career. So much so that I actually felt, and very strongly, that her career was more important than our marriage. It was more than a career for her, it was a calling. And it meant a great deal beyond her own individual accomplishment: She was breaking new ground as a black woman, as well as stunning the musical world with her talent. She was changing the complexion of opera, she was single-handedly opening up a whole new world, and we all — myself, Larney, our close friends — shared a sense of mission that amplified the emotional impact of her individual achievements. The fact that I might feel somehow — for lack of a better phrase — emotionally inconvenienced, was completely overshadowed by the sense of pride I felt for her.

Still, that's no substitute for a real marriage, and ours had devolved to the point that we were using separate bedrooms. That was a gradual development. Where earlier I had occasionally — and then more frequently — moved to the guest bedroom when Leontyne was preparing her major roles (a creative process that would sometimes consume many weeks), now I was only occasionally moving from the guest bedroom back into the master bedroom. A few nights before one of Leontyne's debuts, she would move out entirely and register in a hotel near the opera, to afford herself the complete privacy from even family and close friends that she needed to keep her concentration on the role. For all intents and purposes, we were no longer living a married life.

We came to the conclusion together that our lives were on such parallel tracks it would make sense for us to live apart. The house on Vandam had become more hers than mine — she had taken care of most of the decoration, and her relationship with Lulu had become very close. It was only logical that I would be the one to move.

We were legally separated in 1958 and two years after that either one of us could have gotten a New York divorce simply on the grounds that we'd been legally separated for two years. But she didn't want to marry anyone else, I didn't want to marry anyone else, so neither of us made a move. It wasn't until 1972 — it had to do with new IRS guidelines for unmarried heads of household or something — that we got our divorce.

We were talking about it one night, and we both realized why we hadn't pushed for a divorce earlier. It had to do with our parents. Leontyne's adored me, and mine adored her. Her mother believed, "All right, one of these days when you get your career settled and he gets his career settled then you two are going to turn back to each other." And her mother just wouldn't hear otherwise. "Now did you talk to Bill?" she'd ask her, whenever any important turning point was being considered.

But my mother and father passed away in the sixties, and when her folks died, there was no longer a reason to stay legally wed. It was all very friendly, and remains so to this day.

Looking back, it would be nice to say there are no regrets, only happy memories, especially since Leontyne's friendship and loving care are still so important to me in these later years of our lives.

But there are a few regrets. I wish that I could have been by her side in some of the important things that were happening to her. There were a number of times that I considered changing around my concert dates so I could be at her next important debut. But every time the issue came up, I'd be in the middle of a tour and such an action would cause more grief than it would cure.

When Columbia Artists schedules those dates with those individual sponsors, many thousands of dollars in advertising and posters and ticket-printing and the rest is undertaken by those groups. What might seem to me like a simple matter of switching dates turns out to be a nightmare for the sponsor. Each time I'd consider it, I'd be met by the (sometimes tearful) pleas of sponsors who would be affected. I'd tell myself that surely I'd be able to catch Leontyne's next debut, and I'd let this one go, merely wiring flowers and a telegram, and then talking on the phone the next morning to see how things went.

I do have another regret — something else that I could have done nothing about. And that's the "lost *Messiah*" in Philadelphia.

We did perform the *Messiah* together, for three performances, in Philadelphia in 1956. I had performed as soloist with the Philadelphia Orchestra on their premiere European tour the year before, and had developed a solid working relationship with conductor Eugene Ormandy.

Now he wanted to record this *Messiah* with me, Leontyne, and the Mormon Tabernacle Choir. This was after Leontyne had been "discovered," but before she'd made her name.

The hottest name in opera at the time was Eileen Farrell, star of the Metropolitan. Columbia Records had her on exclusive contract, and Leontyne had signed an exclusive contract with RCA Victor.

Columbia Records also had recording rights for the Philadelphia Orchestra. They wanted to record the *Messiah* with the original voices — Warfield and Price — so Columbia called RCA to see if they would give Leontyne permission to record on the Columbia label. RCA said sure, we'll lend you Leontyne Price if you'll let Eileen Farrell do a different project with us.

As reported to me, the folks at Columbia Records were very condescending to that request. Whoever it was said, "Are you kidding, do you know who Eileen Farrell is? Not on your life."

Instead, later on, when Eileen was in Philadelphia, they recorded Eileen doing those *Messiah* arias. The recording featured Warfield and Farrell instead of Warfield and Price. But she did not do the live performance.

To this day, people in the business refer to the "lost *Messiah*" that Leontyne and I did together, but which was never recorded. What a coup that would have been, if Columbia Records had had a little more vision. That would have been the only recording that Leontyne had ever made of oratorio, and in those years she was in that light, *spinto*, flexible voice.

Leontyne and I remain close friends and confidants. Things might have been different had we spent that first year together as Porgy and Bess. Or maybe not. In any case, given a choice between a solid marriage and two full careers, I think the world is a little better off the way things worked out.

Chapter Eleven

MUSICAL AMBASSADOR

I was serving as a "musical ambassador" well before my 1956 state department tour, when that unofficial title was first used. In fact, I had been doing the job almost from the beginning of my concert career. News clips from the first Australian tour in 1951 stressed that I was not only pleasing audiences but also making new friends for the United States, and said that I was impressing every level of Australian society with the high quality of American music.

That first international tour was not an official state department trip. It was the 1952 tour of *Porgy and Bess* that marked my introduction to official channels. I flourished in that milieu, and things worked so well that Larney immediately saw the potential for building a more permanent relationship with the state department.

We started right away. There was an opportunity for a private recital during the tour, and Larney seized it. On one of our off nights in late September, during our stay in Berlin, I was scheduled for a *Liederabend*, an evening of songs, at the Esplanade-Konzertsaal. The reception echoed that at the Vienna gathering — the Berlin audience was delighted to hear their Schuetz, Schubert, Hugo Wolf, and Carl Loewe sung in flawless

German by the Porgy they had seen on Catfish Row only a few nights earlier. I gave them Fauré and a group of spirituals to close.

Back in the States, Larney was constantly reminding André Mertens of my potential in this field. My career was being loosely modeled on the precedents of Marian Anderson and Roland Hayes, but it benefitted from two enormous added advantages: the advent of international air commerce and the newly enlightened cultural policies of the U.S. Department of State.

Those two new factors combined to make the world my oyster. Where earlier concert artists had spread out their U.S. maps and planned a string of engagements linked by rail, Larney was using a globe, and Uncle Sam was more than willing to pick up the tab.

In the post-Korea days of the mid-1950s, the contest between the U.S. and the U.S.S.R. had come down to a continuous, sometimes daily, match of wits and willpower rather than military maneuvers and firepower. It sometimes seemed that the governments on both sides postured for real or imaginary audiences — the Europeans, the Latins, the Arabs, the Third World, or maybe just their own populations — using economic and social and cultural "props" rather than heavy artillery. For all its tensions and exorbitant costs, the Cold War was a vast improvement over its alternative.

It was also a pre-Vietnam era. Many younger people today can't remember the time when the U.S. was identified with Freedom with a capital F. Today's generation is more often defensive about perceptions of the U.S. as the brutal Goliath. In those days we believed we had nothing to apologize for on the international scene, beyond a certain benign complacency.

At home, the pressure was on to improve civil rights in the U.S. All people of good will accepted that black and white Americans should be guaranteed equality of economic and social opportunity. We were trying to define our way of life as superior to the Communists in every way. Racial amity became even more important.

And at a time when one of the most serious criticisms of capitalism was that it produced a soulless, materialistic society devoid of culture, a display of our artistic dynamism became politically useful.

These factors — racial and cultural — were combined in the

state department policies of the 1950s. The state-sponsored tour of *Porgy and Bess* was just the harbinger of things to come. The earlier pattern of self-exiled artists — especially artists of color — who had to be recognized in Europe before they could be recognized in their own country, was nearly over. Now the Eisenhower administration was looking for artists — especially artists of color — to advertise the dynamism and diversity of our way of life. The bureaucrats had to be convinced, by energetic promoters like Breen, that the arts would work where other methods fell flat; but once they saw the potential, administration officials responded in force.

And they discovered in William Warfield an eager, ardent musical ambassador.

The universal language of music has always been a natural bridge across cultural gaps. And within the world of music, a solo artist who can perform literally anywhere — in a concert hall or on a makeshift stage in the South American jungle — becomes one of the most efficient ways to reach across the cultural divide. Especially if that singer has a repertoire which, in itself, represents a range from Old World traditions to New World innovations. The literature of classical and modern music is inherently a living musical chronology of cultural development. And to top it all off, I was genuinely committed to the ideals I was expected to represent.

As a product of the Cotton Belt, a man whose forebearers had been sharecroppers and slaves, I had never lost the sharp awareness of my roots. And as a black American I had grown up alert to the realities of racial discrimination in my country. But, thanks to my parents and the people of Rochester, that alert awareness had never become a debilitating bitterness. I focused, instead, on the opportunities that were available in our democracy. At times when our society sometimes seems to be backsliding, it's easy to forget the spirit of hopefulness on all sides in the fifties. I truly believed that, with unrelenting effort and constant vigilance, African-Americans were succeeding in their struggle to establish their full rights alongside all the other ethnic strains in America.

I believed that I was a part of that success story — I and all other American blacks who achieved success in their fields. We now had not only the opportunity but also the responsibility to help others follow in the tracks we were laying. Just as there is a need for political leadership, there is an equal need for economic and cultural leadership. I saw my own role as a cultural leader. And I saw that entire progressive vision could unfold only in a free, equal-opportunity democracy. In a word, I believed in the American dream.

At the same time, I believed it was just that: a dream we had to work, each in our own best way, to realize. Specifically, I believed in the ultimate ideal of integration. Not in the sense that individual or cultural differences should ever be boiled away into a big amorphous melting pot. The lesson to be learned from the world of great music is the universality of the particular. Tchaikovsky and Gershwin remain Russian and American while they simultaneously represent a higher culture, a universal world of mankind, above their national distinctiveness. *Vive la différence!* with human rights for all.

All these considerations made me particularly well suited to the role of musical ambassador at large, for the U.S. Department of State.

The officials there were wise enough to know that crude propaganda doesn't work. We were clear with each other from the start: I would be free, encouraged even, to speak my mind and answer any questions honestly, however provocative, wherever in the world I might be sent. Because it was clear that I fundamentally believed in our system, they had no reservations about my speaking out on the issues. The officials calculated, I suppose, that however bad some of our problems might be, and however forthright I might be, the fact that the son of a sharecropper was standing there in a tuxedo talking candidly about those problems made a statement that boiled down to: "Only in America!"

I had already done enough foreign touring to demonstrate that I was right for the role. Besides the Australian tour and the *Porgy and Bess* run, I had performed in the Dominican Republic and Panama as part of my Columbia Artists tour in 1953. Even in those early tours, before state department involvement, whenever I performed near a U.S. embassy or consulate there would be some kind of fête. Word began to circulate that "Warfield handled himself well." That experience was reinforced during the first tour of *Porgy and Bess*.

Just as important, I had proved my drawing power — and my stamina — in the kind of concentrated schedules that the state department would want to book for international tours. Even in my domestic tours, audiences had been thrilled in such disparate locales as Nashville ("Warfield Has Few Peers As Singer," the *Banner*), and Detroit ("Warfield Brilliant in Concert," *Detroit Free Press*), in Miami ("Negro Singer Warfield Is Sensation," the *Miami Herald*) and Massachusetts ("Warfield Sings Magnificently at Mt. Holyoke," the *Springfield Union*).

In that first burst of concentrated touring in the early years of the decade, I traveled to small towns and to big cities, to college campuses and to summer festivals, to high school auditoriums and band shells and great concert halls, in just about every state in the union. While those critics were writing such nice things about me and audiences were taking my measure, I was taking their measure as well. It was a fast course in American geography and sociology for me.

I was always conscious that I was following in the footsteps of such trailblazers as Roland Hayes and Marian Anderson. Just as important, my audiences were conscious of that as well. Roland Hayes had avoided being put in situations where race would be a factor. His talent thus reached fewer people than it might have and everyone was the poorer for it.

For a slightly younger generation, Marian Anderson had suffered slights and humiliations with regal dignity and Christian charity, and had completely overwhelmed all those misbegotten objections to the color of her skin. In her 1939 triumph at the Lincoln Memorial, she had set the tone that would forever lighten the load for those, like me, who followed.

So by the time I was touring in the early 1950s, although the South was still legally segregated in most respects there was a far lesser risk that I would encounter any personal slight in hotel or restaurant accommodations.

On the trains I always traveled in my own Pullman compartment and could therefore ignore the reality of segregated coaches. When I arrived, I was met by sponsors who had been thoroughly sensitized through the experience of Marian Anderson's tours. Wherever racial discrimination was still officially tolerated, they'd be sure to pick me up at the station, whisk me past the "colored only" washrooms, and even escort me personally to my preregistered hotel room. Especially if my sponsors thought the restaurant might be problematical, they'd see to it that room service lavished attention on me. That suited me fine—like most singers on tour, I rarely had time for anything beyond preparing and resting, and I would use room service in Pittsburgh just as surely as I would in Nashville.

Of course, that didn't mean that I allowed myself to be a prisoner in my room. I remember staying in a hotel in Salt Lake City, a stop where for once I had some flexibility in my schedule and intended to spend some time on my own. It was a hotel in which Marian Anderson had stayed many times (she too preferred to use room service) and where my sponsors and I thought they'd be sufficiently experienced in the care of such exotic creatures as people of color. But after we made the reservations, the confirmation letter arrived with a proviso that I not patronize the hotel dining room. We coldly informed them that when I arrived I certainly did intend to use the dining room, and that if there were any problems with that, newspaper readers would be reading about it all over the country for weeks to come. The hotel backpedalled immediately, withdrew their request, and couldn't do enough for me.

But as a rule, the best way to avoid such encounters, for me and for most black artists in that period, was to skip touring in the South. That was a cure that was worse than the disease, because it was the South that had given us so much of our music, so much of our soul; and it was in the South that so many of our own people needed to see and hear how their culture had entwined with and enriched the greater universal culture.

In fact, I did a good deal of Southern touring, including the black colleges on the university concert series. In Atlanta I was privileged to be the house guest of the venerated Dr. Benjamin Mays at Morehouse College, but usually I was housed in college dorms or guest apartments. Even at white colleges there was hardly ever an incident.

I do remember one white college, where they'd put me up in a dormitory suite. I later learned that someone had written "nigger in the house" on one of the big white columns on the front porch. College staff were falling all over themselves trying to get it scrubbed off before I saw it, but I never noticed the fuss. I simply assumed they were trying to keep their building clean. Someone finally mentioned the incident to me. I took notice of his embarrassment — he had been trying to put forward the "New South" for me — but I shrugged it off: "Don't worry," I said, "it could have just as easily happened anywhere in the North."

The one Southern state where I never had any problem was

Texas. Texans always seemed to have a wider, more open attitude, as if it were their right to do what they damn well pleased, whether it pleased their neighbor or not. If a Texas sponsor wanted me to come sing, and if a Texas hotel wanted to put me up, no Texas redneck was going to tell a Texas sponsor or a Texas hotel manager what he could or couldn't do.

But in general we avoided the big crises by avoiding the Deep South — as did all black artists. Remember, we're talking about an era when the songs of Fats Domino had to be recorded by Pat Boone before they'd get air play — and not just in the South! But it was painful to have to avoid your home country, and it was an enormous relief when the first fruits of the civil rights movement led to the 1954 Supreme Court *Brown v. Board of Education* decision that knocked down the soft-core American apartheid principle of "separate but equal."

What was amazing to see was how quickly, after the Supreme Court decision, things began to clear up. Although there were still plenty of rough days ahead, I felt that the people of the South, white and black, had their own set of relationships. And once they were told what the limits were, they decided to just get on with it.

The attitude seemed to be, "We lost, and that's it. Times change." They held onto the status quo as long as they could, but when Samson pulled at the columns, it all came down at once. It was none of that insidious thing you get in the North. They never acknowledged they had a problem up there, so they could never deal with it so definitively.

While I was laying down a solid foundation for my concert touring career, Larney was keeping one eye on the Big Apple as well, making sure that I paid my respects to the New York critics regularly with regular Town Hall recitals and a Carnegie Hall debut. I was also booked as a soloist with all the leading orchestras, including the New York Philharmonic and the Boston Symphony.

Television was becoming an important incidental medium for classical music. Incidental, because this was well before the public broadcasting emphasis on fine music programming. But nonetheless important, once the American Federation of Musicians' ban on live music broadcasts was lifted. Beginning in the late forties, both NBC and CBS took the lead with classical music. As we've seen, it was on NBC, not in an opera house, that

Leontyne performed her opera debut.

Larney signed contracts for me to appear on Ed Sullivan's "Toast of the Town," the Milton Berle Show, the Voice of Firestone, the Bell Telephone Hour, even the Colgate Comedy Hour, to give each of these variety shows a dose of the classics.

Larney was equally busy with Leontyne's career during this period. Despite her "separate peace" with Davis and Breen, he continued as her personal manager. While she was on the extended road trip with *Porgy and Bess*, beginning in December 1953, he was making arrangements for her Town Hall debut, and judiciously booking the pair of us in the few joint appearances we made together.

As she finished out her contract — she didn't go with *Porgy and Bess* when the producers took it back to Europe in 1954 — and as I wound down my spring touring, we did manage to find some time together. In the summer of 1954 we performed at the Tanglewood Festival, the summer home of the Boston Symphony. There, in that Berkshire Mountain setting near Lenox, Massachusetts, we performed for the first time under the baton of Leonard Bernstein. That was the beginning of a long professional association and personal friendship for both Leontyne and me. We sang a group of *Porgy and Bess* songs. Bernstein asked me to record a *Messiah* with him as soon as it could be scheduled.

Later that year Leontyne and I did another of our rare joint recitals in Boston, with Otto Herz at the piano. We opened together with Purcell's "Lost Is My Quiet" and "Sound the Trumpet." She did Puccini's "Vissi d'arte" from the *Tosca* she had performed that year on NBC, and then "Summertime" and "My Man's Gone Now" from *Porgy*. I sang Bizet's "Toreador Song" from *Carmen*, Wagner's "Evening Star" from *Tannhäuser*, and Gershwin's "I Got Plenty o' Nuttin'" and "It Ain't Necessarily So." We closed together, with Mozart, "La ci darem la mano" from *Don Giovanni*, and Gershwin, "Bess, You Is My Woman Now."

Leontyne's Town Hall debut took place in November of that year. She was brilliant, and demonstrated to the critics and audiences that her unique artistry in *Porgy and Bess* was but the tip of the iceberg. It was clear to all that great things were to come.

Even before the debut Larney believed that, with care, Leontyne Price was going to be one of the immortals. When she was still a student she had caused eyebrows to raise among the cognoscenti who are always sniffing around for fresh talent. Directors and producers like Breen and artists and critics like Virgil Thompson were attracted instinctively. Peter Adler, at NBC, had made the leap past Gershwin to recognize her as a diva in the making. Discerning audiences, too, even at those student performances at Julliard, knew they were on to something special.

Now, after her triumph as Bess, Larney resisted all those who urged him to book her "while she's hot." He concentrated more on long-term career development. As Peter Adler had suggested, she would need to pull back from the concert offers and pursue a different course with the teachers and coaches, and ultimately the opera companies of Europe. Larney was concerned that if the opera world wasn't ready to open fully to a black artist, however talented, Leontyne should have a parallel set of options. He kept her on a limited schedule of performances, insuring that the public saw her often enough to be awed by her range — as an operatic talent, but also as a concert artist. The more facets that he could establish for her, the more secure she would be and the more confidently she could develop at her own pace.

The strategy worked. When things started to open up operatically — when society was as ready for her as she was for it — she was able to seize the moment. Her carefully prepared career exploded into life with her opera debut in 1957, with the San Francisco Opera as Madame Lidoine in Poulenc's *Dialogues of the Carmelites*. She went on to make musical history, as everyone knows. While the world might not have been ready for a dark-skinned diva in Marian Anderson's day, Leontyne helped to make it happen for a new generation.

But in the meantime, I wasn't on an opera track. You could say I was on a modified version of the old "exiled artists" track— modified because I wasn't an exile but an ambassador. In the spring of 1955, after two solid years of domestic touring and triumphs in New York, I was heading out once again. This time I was the lone soloist traveling with the Philadelphia Orchestra on their premiere tour of Europe. The five-week journey began in Brussels on May 17, continued to seventeen cities, and wound up in Helsinki for a final performance June 18.

It was an exhausting schedule for everyone. But it was considerably more enjoyable for me than for the musicians,

because my solos were on the program in only half the cities —
Paris and Bordeaux, Lisbon and Porto (Portugal), Barcelona,
Milan, Strassbourg, and Berlin. Of these, the most important to
me was Milan, at the venerated La Scala, where I was scheduled
to perform on Saturday, June 4.

Ormandy had his hands full. The schedule was demanding, his reputation was on the line, and the stakes were high: He
was introducing his orchestra to the most discerning music
audiences in the world. There were times when I felt that in his
busyness I was an afterthought, a colorful but perhaps nones-
sential accessory. Rehearsal time is always precious, but never
more so than when an orchestra is on the road. I sometimes felt
shortchanged, left to fend for myself as best I could during the
brief rehearsals I was given, as Ormandy had other things on his
mind.

But I noticed that Ormandy's regard for my contribution
improved enormously when the critics in these capitals focused
on my solos as a high point of the evening. Midway through the
tour, in Milan, my critical reception hit its peak. By the time the
tour was winding down, in Strassbourg and Berlin, Ormandy
and I were old friends; in fact, it was about that time he came up
with the idea of a *Messiah* for Leontyne and me, which we did the
next year.

It really was a tonic to read those Milan reviews. La Scala
is to opera what New Orleans is to jazz. Down deep in some
secret part of me, I had probably never really shaken off the allure
of the opera world. I wasn't going to devote my entire soul to
opera, but I suspect it was personally more important to me than
I cared to admit, to leave some impress on those hallowed, gilded
walls of La Scala. So I took deep satisfaction in reading, the
following day, reviews like this:

"The middle of the program began with works for singer
and orchestra. An aria from the oratorio *Samson* by Handel and
a collection of "Old American Songs" transcribed and orches-
trated by Aaron Copland, the most illustrious among contemporary American composers. Some of these songs are very beautiful, some less so. But in William Warfield all of them found a
marvelous interpreter. This gigantic Negro has a voice which is
a little difficult to define, having certain notes of the bass, all the
baritone notes, and even some of the tenor! But, in addition, this
artist has a stupendous technique with a power of expression that

is more than masterly. Although his greatest ovation followed the American songs, we appreciated him even more in the Handel which Warfield sang as a truly superlative artist."

That review in *Il Popolo* was matched by accolades from *Corriere, L'Unita,* and *La Patria.* All the exacting critics abandoned their traditional reserve (and sometimes patronizing attitude toward American artists) and gave me the kind of notices that make you wish your mother could read Italian. I appreciated kind words like those wherever I could get them, but they carried a special glow when they were talking about little Bill Warfield at great big La Scala. And don't ever tell me that good reviews have no effect on your working relationship with the maestros!

*   *   *   *

While Columbia Artists continued to book me in the U.S., Larney worked directly with the Department of State to launch me as a one-man international touring industry. His first big success was the extended tour, in 1956, and Otto Herz traveled with me as my accompanist.

As I've already said, there were no special instructions from the state department or anyone else, with one exception: For this showcasing of an American artist, they were insistent that the program include American music. They hadn't sent me this far to demonstrate that American culture was completely dependent on the European masters. That was no problem for me — Gershwin, Copland, and Virgil Thompson had always figured prominently in my repertoire. And of course the spirituals were very popular. Harry T. Burleigh, Roland Hayes, Margaret Bonds, and Hall Johnson had written the most sophisticated arrangements.

Even with this emphasis on American music, the program I took was basically the regular, typical program that I would have sung anywhere in the world. I started off with the baroque period—Handel and Bach; I usually included a group of German works—Schumann, Schubert; some French—Ravel, Fauré; sometimes an Italian aria, Verdi perhaps, as the evening's centerpiece; and of course American folk songs and spirituals. So I brought to Nigeria essentially the same material that I would bring to the concert hall in Boston.

You'll hardly ever find songs from *Show Boat* or *Porgy and Bess* on my programs. But I invariably performed them — as encores. The final encore was always "Old Man River." Throughout my career, it was a very rare occasion when I'd sing anything after that. (One of the few times was at my Twenty-Fifth Anniversary Performance at Carnegie Hall, in 1975. The audience wanted yet another encore, so I told them I would sing a hymn that had special meaning for me — on the condition that they wouldn't applaud when I'd finished. It was a song, I told them, that I was performing in memory of my parents, who by that time were both deceased. There wasn't a murmur. I sang "Must Jesus Bear the Cross Alone," and left the hall, in perfect silence.)

The African tour opened on August 18, 1956, with a performance in a school auditorium in Monrovia, Liberia. I was still adjusting to the climate, the sense of cultural disorientation that any traveler feels, and the specific routines that this tour would require — all the personal logistics that become so significant in your daily life when you're living on someone else's timetable.

The one thing that I didn't need to worry about, in those days, was jet lag. The airlines didn't use jets then. I didn't have to start adjusting to jet lag until my regular trips to Vienna began in 1965. In those earlier days, wherever we were going, it took longer to get there, and stopovers might be required, but when we got there we felt good. I sometimes wonder how much we've "progressed" since the days when I flew clipper service to Australia, in my own little sleeping compartment, with a refueling stop in Hawaii and another in Fiji, and arrived in Sydney, fit and rested and ready to work.

There were plenty of other things to adjust to. Little things, like whether you should or should not brush your teeth in the local tapwater (in some places you could), and where you're supposed to meet the local transportation (not approximately where, but exactly where), and whether the local sponsor has a piano tuner (a *real* piano tuner? or someone who tightens doorknobs, fixes plumbing, and tunes pianos). Little things like these become a jumble of priorities, all important, some critical — and getting into the rhythm of a tour takes some time.

This was a solo tour for me, but there were United States Information Service representatives who would meet me at each stop. They took care of every detail. After each engagement they would pass me on to the next USIS officer, mission accomplished. They had complete charge of my schedule, and did a good job of it. Once I realized how competent they were, how seriously they took their job, I was able to relax into the rhythm.

Like most of my tours, it was rigorous. Larney was always careful to see that my performance schedule was not too tight, so that I never had to travel and perform the same day. But when you add up all the elements — the performances; the rushed rehearsals; the coordination with theater personnel so they'll know the cues for the house lights, stage lights, curtains; the travel and hotel logistics, from check-in to repacking for the next move; the ground transportation to and from the theater; the meal arrangements; shopping, and remembering to change money, and fretting that you're getting it all mixed up and paying ten dollars for what should cost a dollar; the social obligations and other dealings with your sponsors; the press interviews, photo ops (smiling at boa constrictors), and other media obligations; trying to connect with a promised telegram of funds or personal mail at the American Express office before closing time; trying when necessary to keep track of the time changes, especially on the rare occasions when I needed to attempt a transatlantic phone call from one of those government telephone stalls; and trying to remember to send Leontyne a postcard with a big colored stamp from each African nation — add them all up, and the singing becomes the easiest part of the tour.

I'm stretching the truth with that bit about the stamps. I've always been a haphazard correspondent, at best. I never did succeed in keeping up with the time changes, and my schedule was not my own, so I didn't do a very good job of keeping in touch with Leontyne or anyone else. All those pretty stamps stayed in my suitcase. In any event, by that time Leontyne and I were pretty much going our separate ways.

So, with all that, the first stop in Monrovia went by in something of a blur. With English as Liberia's official language, it didn't feel much different from many places where I'd performed in the U.S.

I did discover, early on, that I would be making adjustments that would rarely have been required back home. The climate, for example, presented unique problems.

Almost everwhere we went, the pianos needed to be dehumidified or they wouldn't hold pitch. The most effective way to accomplish this on short notice was to use a light bulb on the end of an extension cord, and leave it burning inside the piano until performance time. That usually did the trick. But in one location the piano, and the humidity, were so bad that the piano lost its pitch during the first act. We didn't have a piano tuner, but we did find a wrench. We tuned it ourselves, during the intermission.

My first powerful impression of African culture was in Lagos, Nigeria. I remember being briefly mesmerized by the thousands of bicycles, an entire city on bicycles, and by the beautiful women balancing huge loads carried in baskets on their heads as casually and naturally as Wall Street lawyers walk with their briefcases. The armchair traveler who has seen the snapshots in *National Geographic* or watched brief clips from television documentaries can't imagine the sensation of being immersed in a culture where these ways of life are serenely, automatically incorporated into the normal activities of daily life.

Of course, with all that, I was reminded again and again that we all live in one big world. And I don't mean that in some sugary abstract sense. For instance, there was my experience in Ibadan, our second stop in Nigeria.

I performed twice in Ibadan, which meant a free day to do a little looking around. I was taken on a side trip to a small village to see some authentic traditional dances. A young man who spoke educated English had been designated as my tour guide and cultural interpreter.

All the young men were out of the village, at some males-only ritual or festival. While we were getting oriented my guide suddenly lifted his head. "The drums," he said. I strained and pretended politely to hear them; I don't think I did. My guide explained to me that the drums were "talking," saying that the chieftains were about to return. Sure enough, about fifteen minutes later the brush parted and the men of the village returned from their hunt or wherever they had been. I hadn't even heard the drums and I was impressed that this man—who, by his speech, could have been an educated black European or West Indian— knew his tribal lore.

I inquired and learned that he was indeed an African and this was his tribe. He had been born in this village. He had gone to Europe for an education but then had come back to his home to work with his own people, as a government sociologist and caseworker. He was particularly proud of the tribe's cultural traditions, and studied them not only as an anthropologist or government bureaucrat might, but as an artist who had become professionally involved.

Now he was sharing that enthusiasm with me, explaining the dance to me as I watched, pointing out the traditional symbolism of certain movements or the religious references in the rhythms. I could relate to the religious overtones, and reflected on the universality of some elements.

More and more, as I sat there soaking it all in, I was impressed with the obvious showmanship of the presentation as well. I mean, the esoteric meaning that he was telling me about was fascinating. But here there was something even more universal. This primitive ritual had all the elements that would be required to make it "commercial." The costumes had enough stuff to be accented but not so much they were cluttered. The dancers "sold" the piece to us in the audience with just enough teeth and just enough bounce. The internal repetitions established themes but never outstayed their welcome. The whole thing had enough flair to please a theater party from New Jersey. It had — choreography!

Art is truly universal, I reflected; this ancient art form was as lively as if it had been "routined" by a dance master on Broadway. I marveled on these observations and listened as he wrapped up the story of the dance — something about a village chieftain and the maiden who defended her honor.

And when he paused, obviously interested in my reaction, I couldn't wait to express the insights it had given me. "I'm impressed by the natural grace of the dancers and their reverence for tradition," I said. "But there's something even more remarkable here. In this tribal dance, I'm seeing the roots of dance as it's known in Western culture; there are even elements of what we might call vaudeville — I mean that in the best sense." I could see by his expression that he understood my enthusiasm; the whole experience had been a revelation to me and perhaps, as a sociologist, he could make it even clearer to me. I concluded, "There seems to be a tremendous amount of form in all this, a very modern sense of presentation."

I had stumbled on something particularly significant; he was obviously pleased with himself that I had recognized this quality. "Oh, ho ho," he chortled. "That's something I learned from Katherine Dunham."

I wasn't sure I'd heard it right. Surely he meant that the gifted choreographer Katherine Dunham and her African-American dance company had borrowed from these traditions in her choreography. Her striking work *Rituals*, powerfully portraying warriors celebrating the rites of passage — puberty, fertility, death, religious possession — had been seen on Broadway only a few months earlier; much of her work derived from native themes.

No, that wasn't what he meant. "While I was studying in Europe I connected with the dance troupe of Katherine Dunham, and became friendly with them," he explained. "She rather pulled me into her circle, and spent weeks asking me for authentic information about my tribe, and life in Nigeria. At the same time, I borrowed a good deal from her for my own interest in dance. When I came back to Ibadan, I worked with these women to create this dance."

I screamed with laughter and nearly fell off my log. He had "packaged" the traditional dance — I hope without losing the essentials of the authentic elements — and it was no mistake that I thought the show was ready to go on the road. The influence was working both ways: Katherine Dunham was influencing Africa.

On my way to Dar es Salaam the next day I chuckled every time I thought about it. Well, at least I wasn't far wrong when I thought it might be ready for prime time TV.

On the other hand, there were some genuine crosscultural experiences, of the sort that every artist hopes for when performing before "untutored and unlettered" audiences. I'll never forget the spontaneous enjoyment of a young audience — I think it was the trip to Ibadan — when I sang Loewe's "Hochzeitlied." When the count is awakened by the lively rustling of the celebrating elves, the Loewe libretto becomes a form of onomatopoeia, a most literate type, with the tip of the tongue tripping alliteratively to create a twittering of delightful sounds. In German, the words further the story of the scampering sprites; as pure sound, they accomplish the same effect for the ear. So when the natives heard me in that part, they broke into hilarity and applause, comprehending the pure sound effect though they could not have understood the literal meaning.

In Southern Rhodesia (now Zimbabwe) I stayed at the home of the consul-general. It was the first place I visited that had a racial policy that would present problems.

I had discussed this booking with Larney — whether or not to accept it, given the form of apartheid practiced in Southern Rhodesia. I decided to accept it in part because I thought that there might be some advantage, down the road, to my having had direct experience with the issue. My refusal to travel there would hardly have caused a ripple; this way at least I'd be better informed. It's the same dilemma that black artists and journalists and other professionals have wrestled with regarding direct experience of the Union of South Africa. There are arguments, pro and con, for both approaches.

The audience at the performance, I was assured, would be racially integrated. It would take place within the embassy, where U.S. law and not local law applied. Our ambassador made a point of mixing the audience, black and white, even to the extent of recruiting black civic leaders for the occasion.

As it happened, my Rhodesia visit was a very indirect experience. As a black man I couldn't even walk into a white post office to mail my letters. Because I would certainly have encountered problems just walking through a park and perhaps using the wrong water fountain, I was escorted by dignitaries or their deputies everywhere I went. It was all very white-gloves, but it was nonetheless clear: For all practical purposes, I was in the protective custody of the officials. It was as if I were hermetically sealed from the country and its problems. I could observe it, but I was protected from it.

I had the opposite experience in Ethiopia. The Emperor, Haile Selassie was personally interested in my visit, and obviously the word got out because I was treated like visiting royalty. An afternoon was set aside for a private tour of his palace and its elaborate, extensive grounds. I was in awe of the splendor. It was not like our grand museums, or the preserved and museumized palaces of extinct European dynasties. Here there was an echo of an earlier kind of grandeur, a living, regal magnificence, and the difference was that this palace was actually occupied, actually a home to a real, live, functioning emperor, who still did there whatever it is that emperors do.

The night of the performance the emperor was in attendance. Following the performance, I was summoned to the emperor's box and formally presented with honors. I had been primed by the protocol brigade, both U.S. and Ethiopian: If he were to speak to me in French, his language of choice, I should respond in French.

I was escorted to the imperial box and introduced to a handsome, trim, middle-aged man, very vital, with bright piercing eyes. He smiled at me for a moment, and then, in flawless English, thanked me for the performance. He presented me with a medal, in a very short ceremony. I was later told that for him to speak to me in English was intended as a personal compliment.

By the time we arrived in Cairo for a stopover, that part of the world had been through an emotional and political meatgrinder. The Suez crisis blew up in October, and though the hostilities were minimal the tension was not, and there was a ripple effect throughout the diplomatic corps, even in distant embassies.

The European dates lay ahead, and they'd be tense too: Though we weren't scheduled to perform in Hungary, we were booked for Yugoslavia. During the same weeks that Suez was boiling over, the Russians sent tanks into Budapest to suppress the 1956 Hungarian revolution, with considerable loss of life. I could hardly believe that despite those cataclysms all around us, our tour was going to continue as planned, into the Mideast and then southern Europe, right through the thick of things, before turning north.

Sitting there in Cairo, with nearly a whole day to myself, I finally had found some time to mail off a few postcards. We had arrived that day and were scheduled to stay in Cairo overnight, then fly out on a late morning plane. We had been handed off by the USIS team in Addis Ababa and were due to be picked up by the next shift in Beirut. For the better part of twenty-four hours we were on our own.

It was typical of Otto Herz to discover a way to use that time to advantage: He suggested we get up before dawn, hire a taxicab, and run out to see the great pyramids. From there, he had calculated, we could make it directly to the airport in time to catch our plane.

That was pure Otto Herz. He did the same thing wherever we happened to be, using every spare moment to experience whatever the local culture had to offer. With his training in history, our world tours were full of fresh wonder to him, wherever we went. And with his political science degree, perhaps he looked at the Suez crisis and decided that the pyramids might be permanently off limits for Westerners for years to come.

Though Otto was the older man, the greater physical demands of my performance gave him the edge in any comparison of unfettered exuberance. Which is to say, I let him take that taxi without me. After all, I was in my thirties, and I knew I'd catch the pyramids on my next trip. As it happened, I never went back to Egypt. If I found myself back in Cairo for a quick stopover next week, I'd be just like Otto, up before the sun to catch a glimpse of Giza.

Instead, I lay in my hotel room and tried to do some mental planning. I was feeling the strains of our schedule, and I knew I was about to go through another process of adjustment. With all due respect to the government planners, I couldn't help but notice that we had been performing in Africa in the summertime. Now we were headed toward Lebanon, Israel, and Turkey and then turning north. By December I'd be walking in Stockholm snowdrifts.

From New York I had shipped myself several suitcases of winter clothes to meet us en route. Now it was time to figure out what clothes I'd need for the rest of the trip. Anyone who has ever been on tour will understand how preoccupying those logistics can be.

But my thoughts kept returning to the impressions of the past few months, and how much I'd experienced. For instance, I had learned a little about how politics and cultural diplomacy really worked — what it could do, as well as where its limits lay.

I had discovered that I was good at it. Every time I got to a new location, I would hear that the word from the previous stop was all positive. In Nairobi I was met by people who'd say, "Oh they're absolutely ecstatic about the impression that you made when you were in Tanganyika." In Kampala I heard the same thing about Mombasa; and so on. So there was a feeling of personal accomplishment, a sense that I'd made a contribution, as an American, to a better perception of our country.

A typical remark, from a political attaché, went something like this: "Mr. Warfield, you have no idea. We have been trying to break through to the foreign ministry here, trying to make inroads with some of our diplomatic counterparts and we've been getting nowhere, not even an RSVP to our invitations. And now here's the minister himself, here to see your performance, and in the intermission, over cigars, we were able to casually schedule an appointment that would have been impossible to do through formal channels."

The tour also gave me some additional insights into how social systems work. In America, so much of our experience is rooted in race; even (especially?) issues of rich and poor become enmeshed in issues of race. But I discovered (of course I knew it intellectually but it's quite a different thing to be personally immersed in it) that in countries where there are no white people at all, there are still class differences between rich and poor. The whole chieftain thing, it's all about who's in charge, who's going to kowtow to whom. So, in many parts of Africa I found discrimination of the same sort I left at home, except that it was black against black, quite a remarkable thing to witness.

Another thing the African tour did for me personally was to loosen me up a little. Before, I had always been a real straight arrow, almost superstitiously avoiding any interference with my rituals for preparation. I was the typical retiring artist, more concerned with my artistic concentration than anything else on the tour. Even the systems I had contrived in Australia, to use the social schedule of a tour to replicate a studio discipline, were symptomatic of my approach. I had always felt that I couldn't allow myself too much socializing on the day I was to perform, or the night before.

Larney always made sure that all my U.S. touring contracts guaranteed there would be no obligations before a concert that might interfere with my preparation. The whole idea was, after the concert I'm all yours, for receptions or whatever, but not before.

But on the African tour, that luxury was abandoned. All at once I was thrown into a new career field that is unsparing of such amenities. I was a diplomat. I quickly realized that for each separate post of the state department, the primary point of my tour there was to further the local diplomatic mission.

From the first stop, I found myself the guest of honor at cocktail parties, going into dinner with the ambassador and his guests, and then driving with the official party to the concert hall — parting from them only as they headed for their box, and I headed for my dressing room — then back to the embassy for the postshow reception. The next morning I might meet the press, or be carted off to the game preserve, or get on a plane for my next stop — to begin another round of interviews, cocktails, dinner, and up to the stage.

I practiced a modified version of what I had already learned in Australia. Ginger ale in the champagne glass, moderate conversation before a performance to save the voice, and then a very abbreviated quiet moment in the dressing room by way of final preparation, a quick meditation to tell myself that now I'd have to get all this foolishness out of my head because I had to sing tonight.

I reminded myself that a good part of any normal preparation was mental. Anything that starts in the head, I told myself, I should be able to psych myself into. So I did what I had to, and learned that I could. Though it was nice to have all that clear time that Larney usually guaranteed, at this time in my life the preparation of my head was all the preparation that I really needed. Earlier in my life I wouldn't have been so readily able to manufacture my own environment at a moment's notice. Later in my life it would be more important to guarantee that the physical instrument got just as much attention as the spiritual part of me. But for those middle years, in my prime, I found I could loosen up.

That morning in Cairo, Otto made the plane, and we continued our tour through the Mideast, to southern Europe. For the record, that first part of our tour extended from August 18 to November 8, 1956, and included recitals in Monrovia, Accra, Lagos (two recitals), Ibadan (two), Dar es Salaam, Mombasa, Salisbury (two), Kampala, Nairobi (two), Addis Ababa (two), Beirut, Jerusalem, Tel Aviv (two), Haifa, Ankara, Istanbul, Belgrade, Zagreb, Titograd, and Athens (two).

The Mideast went by quickly. I have a strong memory of the almost mystical awe I felt when I visited the Holy Land, and realized that I was surrounded by thousands of years of history and religious lore. But my strongest impression was of the free moments I was afforded in Tel Aviv. I used that time to walk along the beach, savoring the warm Mediterranean breezes as I braced for autumn in Germany.

I also remember an adventurous night on the town in Ankara, after an afternoon reception at the embassy. The ambassador told me, "I'm going to let my chauffeur take over at this point. He's at your disposal — whatever you'd like to do, wherever you'd like to go." I had no idea what to suggest, of course, so I gave the chauffeur carte blanche — I was up for whatever he'd suggest. The next thing I knew, I was surrounded by hookahs and fatima dancing, right out of the Arabian nights. It wasn't a late night, but it was one of the most exotic I've ever experienced.

The European leg of the trip, which continued up to the week before Christmas, took us to recitals and performances with orchestras in Tübingen, Vienna, Baden-Baden, Schweinfurt, Berlin (two recitals), Hilversum, Bremen, Malmo, Stockholm, Oslo, Bergen, and London (two). We did our last performance on December 17.

When I learned that Leontyne was coming to Europe, we figured out how we could get our paths to cross in Berlin, where we could spend some time together. One night we had dinner in a restaurant that we knew would be out of the way. Nobody knew we were there, and we enjoyed a quiet, private meal. But as we were walking out of the restaurant, lightbulbs flashed and we were surrounded by reporters — it was like being back in New York. The owner couldn't resist making some calls. He didn't intrude on our meal, but when we hit the street — and were positioned in front of the restaurant entrance with the restaurant's name in the photograph frame, I suppose — we were fair game.

By the time I got to Scandinavia I was in a hurry to get home. Earlier in the year I had done the Ormandy *Messiah* with Leontyne, and now I was booked to do my second *Messiah* that year, this time in Carnegie Hall with Leonard Bernstein. Actually, it was a more complicated process than that. In addition to the Carnegie Hall presentation, he had this idea for a television version, somewhat shortened, to be performed in costume. He wanted to tape it in the CBS studio, not for a live audience. I liked the idea, and looked forward to it. But I remember that I had to summon up my last reserves of energy to make it happen.

I'll never forget sitting there at Carnegie Hall, on the edge of the stage, getting ready to do the recording, and wiping my brow and thinking, "Man, I am *tired*." It didn't show up in the recording or the performance, but I was drained. "This is really too much for me," I decided. I made a note to tell Larney that we had to spread these things around a little more. But by the New Year, after I'd recovered from the New Year's Eve party on Vandam Street, I'd forgotten all those resolutions — and got ready for another long tour.

Throughout this period I was busier than I'd ever been,

with U.S. tours as well, fulfilling the contracts that André Mertens and Larney were signing for me, traveling across the country. But Larney felt he had to keep Columbia Artists on their toes. They handled scores of artists, of course, so Larney had to make sure they realized that in this case they were dealing with not just another singer but William Warfield, and not just William Warfield but WILLIAM WARFIELD! His superlatives could be more than a little embarrassing if I happened to be in earshot when he was on the phone with André Mertens or his assistant, Nelly Walter.

Despite the fact that, with our far-flung international touring, we were continually encroaching on the weeks available for Columbia Artists to book domestic touring, Larney kept the pressure on. A letter he wrote during this period communicates some of his energy, and also illustrates, with the immediacy of Larney's current anxiety, the volume of my performances in those years.

"In advance of our luncheon this Wednesday," he wrote in November of 1956, "it may be a good idea to let you know what's been on my mind concerning Bill Warfield's bookings, which give evidence of an alarming sharp decline (for one of our greatest concert artists!)."

There followed a recitation of dates and performances, comparing Columbia Artists' bookings for the first four months of each year: forty-seven in the first four months of 1954, thirty-nine for the same period in 1955, thirty-eight for 1956, and twenty-nine for 1957. Of course, I had done scores of other performances on international tour during these years. Larney acknowledged that the state department had "stolen" some of their best dates: "I am not making a point at the moment about the fall and summer periods," he wrote, "because in 1956 we arranged for Bill's foreign tour... during which he was unavailable here. All the more reason, though, for our concern that 1957 bears so few dates (comparatively) following the very first fall season he has been unavailable in the U.S.A.

"I must point out that whenever, during the past few months, I've expressed my apprehensions, either you or Nelly have told me I had no cause to worry or that it was an obsession on my part. But, now bookings are in for the season and the Warfield engagements have fallen off to such an extent that I am really wondering about the future. . . "

Whether or not Mertens took seriously the implied threat

that Larney might seek representation for me elsewhere, I must say that his alacrity on my behalf meant that my own relationship with Columbia Artists was blissfully devoid of any pressure, in either direction. So far as the bookings themselves were concerned, as I'll soon make clear, if Columbia Artists had booked me in any more places than they did, I'd have had even more trouble than I did just keeping up with them.Those tours set the pattern for what became a lifetime of touring. To this day, there's a part of me that's more comfortable in a hotel room — more at home in a suite where someone else takes care of the linens and towels — than I am in my own place.

As an aside, I remember my mother insisting that when I performed in Rochester, I must stay with the family at home. Of course the sponsor would have provided a hotel room, but I didn't want to hurt her feelings. I had explained that a hotel room might spare her some inconvenience, but she wouldn't hear of it— until she answered the phone for the thirtieth time, opened the door to the twentieth inquiry, and had reporters and photographers traipsing through the house for the tenth time. I explained that in a hotel room you have the luxury of telling the front desk to hold calls and visitors, and she tried that until she discovered that there's no way to tell old friends and relatives that they can't have just a minute with "Uncle Bill." The next time I came to Rochester, she insisted I stay in a hotel — for my sake, not hers.

The life of touring is all about hotel rooms and tight scheduling. A performing tour is a lousy way to see the countryside, and although I am left with strong impressions of the world's cultures, I have rarely had the experience of a conventional tourist who discovers things for himself. Most of what I did was by appointment, or with the help of a loaned car and driver. Frequently my known association with the U.S. embassy made me a security concern, which meant that when I went beyond the embassy or the hotel I was expected to travel with some sort of escort to insure that I'd get back safely— another disincentive for me to go wandering the bazaars and backstreets.

Of course, I have a world's worth of impressions. Like the time I was in Benares, India, where segregation was practiced, but of a different kind: The boys were all escorted to one area of the auditorium and the girls to another, as is traditional. When a group of latecoming girls trooped in during one of my songs, a delicate Fauré piece, suddenly the hall erupted in hooting and catcalling. It got so loud I had to stop. I was concerned that something dreadful was happening, but the stage manager was surprised I'd paused. It was as if he hadn't even heard the explosion of noise, which had not yet abated. "Oh, Mr. Warfield," he said, "it's nothing." He motioned for me to go on. "Some girls have come in and the boys are naturally making the loud noise." I continued with the love song, but I doubt that it made much of an impression on children who were growing up in separate camps.

I remember an important state dinner in Hong Kong. I had not yet mastered the use of chopsticks, and no other eating utensil was provided. I had struggled with them briefly in the past, and now I simply determined that the moment had finally come for me to bear down and get it right. To make it worse, the chopsticks I was given were not the squared-off rough wooden sort with which I'd had some limited success in Chinese restaurants. This was a diplomatic function, and they were using only the best — pure ivory, smooth and round as knitting needles. It was an intense eating lesson.

In Saigon I performed in a beautiful outdoor auditorium in a park, and the crowd was standing room only. Near the end of my program I had just begun Burleigh's arrangement of "Wade in the Water" when suddenly, directly in my line of vision, I saw a young man take a step backward and disappear into the park fountain. He had to be rescued, and it caused enough of a stir that I had to stop the song. Eventually I picked up where I had left off, with "Wade in the Water," but I couldn't resist adding, "Don't take that literally, young man."

I remember the Singapore school full of little girls, seven, eight, and nine years old, impeccably dressed and speaking in their crisp British accents, where I was to teach them a spiritual. Did they want to learn it? "Oh, yes sah!" they trilled. And then as I rehearsed the words for them they repeated it for me, line by line, but giving every vowel in that American Negro song a precise Oxford line that the Queen herself would have approved. Perhaps it was the high pitch of their piping little voices that made that the most British of any accent I'd ever heard applied to Mr. Burleigh's "Steal Away."

And I'll never forget the international press conference — Lord knows which tour, or what country — for which the USIS started preparing me days in advance. They considered it an important chance to score points in the world press. Because it was an international press conference, it was important that I receive and answer the questions only in French. That was, they said, the only language in which these press conferences were ever conducted. Fortunately that was no problem for me, although the search for the *mot juste* in a language not your own is always a challenge. And when the wrong comment can cause embarrassment or even an incident, a half-hour of such give-and-take can leave you drained. So when we concluded this long session of precisely answered questions on the state of American Negroes, segregation issues, and the rest, I mopped the perspiration from my forehead one last time and gratefully accepted the invitation of our hosts to move into the reception. We all trooped into the hall adjacent to the press conference room, and everyone immediately broke into English: Every single one of those reporters spoke flawless English.

I remember looking at the beautiful black women of the Fiji Islands, and thinking — with my professional eye for the quality of their hair — how stunning they looked with their big, full afros. This was years before American blacks stopped trying to loosen their kinks, and I had a presentiment that if we ever did "go natural" we would discover a whole new kind of beauty.

That was in 1958, the year I went around the world twice, and ended up singing at the Brussels World's Fair in September.

The first trip started on January 2 — another good reason for not trying to do a New Year's party at Vandam Street that year — and extended through March 16. The program of recitals included Teheran, Isfahan, Abadan, Karachi, Lahore, Amritsar, Benares, Allahabad, Lucknow, Dacca, Rangoon (two recitals), Moulmein, Bangkok, Chiengmai, Saigon (three), Taipei (two), Ipoh, Singapore, Kuala Lumpur, Penang, Hong Kong, and Manila (two). I went around the world west to east.

Then in May I set off on my second trip for the Australian Broadcasting Commission. This time, since I was traveling with Otto Herz, I had no need of the gifted John Douglas Todd, who had accompanied me the first time and who was probably hurt that I didn't ask him again. My repertoire had changed somewhat, and in any case there was no question of replacing Otto. The tour began May 31 and included Sydney (four recitals, five performances with orchestra, one radio and one television recital), Melbourne (three recitals, four performances with orchestra), Adelaide (two and three), Brisbane (one and two), Perth (one and two), Broken Hill, Wagga, Armidale, Warwick, Toowoomba, Ballarat, Shepparton, Hobart, Launceston, Bendigo, and Wollongong. That trip I was traveling around the world east to west, heading for the Brussels World's Fair.

Since the launching of the Russian sputnik the previous fall, the U.S. seemed to be suffering a national inferiority complex. It was during this period that Nixon's "kitchen debate" with Khruschev made as its main point the statement that they might be ahead of us in space but we had more consumer goods. It's hard to remember such a time, perhaps, but in those years it was often American arts, not American technology, that reflected our national pride. *Time* magazine carried some of that tone in its review of the American arts at the World's Fair:

"Other American offerings at the Brussels World's Fair may stir assorted snorts, crank complaints, and real misgivings, but U.S. musical fare is a solid hit. Against such exotic competition as the Peking Opera, Congoese Dancers and the Bolshoi Ballet, the U.S. gets top marks for a first-rate music and dance program on a shoestring budget. 'The Americans,' wrote *De Standard*, 'are producing musical activity that can truly be called unique . . . .'

"Some of the finest solo talents in the U.S. turned up for one-night stands," the *Time* article continued, and named Leontyne and me, among a string of others who were making "a lasting impression on bedazzled Europeans."

When I think about a career as musical ambassador, I remember the small moments along with the large: celebrating the Fourth of July in Havana, Cuba, in 1959 — the last time the American holiday would be celebrated in that city for more than three decades. I toured Cuba that week, with Leontyne's accompanist, David Garvey, in recitals in Havana, Santiago, and Camaguey.

I was back in that part of the world in 1962, to perform the premiere of Pablo Casals's *El Pesebre* (The Manger), at the Pablo Casals Festival in San Juan, Puerto Rico. I repeated it there in 1963 and also presented it at Carnegie Hall. In 1966, at the Athens Festival in Greece, I presented it in the composer's native Catalan tongue.

Casals was one of those artists whose careers define an era

of music. He was an accomplished master as a cellist, a conductor, a pianist, and a composer. When he was born (in Spain) Ulysses S. Grant was president. He lived until the age of Nixon. He performed at the White House for Presidents William McKinley, Franklin D. Roosevelt, and John F. Kennedy. For everyone who worked with him, his tremendous love of music was completely contagious, and in addition there was the overwhelming awareness that you were in the presence of a living legend. I always found it curious that Casals's repertoire didn't go beyond the Romantic period, because he was thoroughly conversant with all the modern composers and knew everything there is to know about the twelve-tone scale.

Pau, as he was called in Catalan, was a political activist as well as an artist. He was an early resister to the Franco regime; in exile he worked to aid the victims of the Spanish Civil War.

I last worked with him at the *Pacem in Terris* convocation in Geneva in 1967. I once again presented the oratorio in Catalan, this time with the L'Orchestre des Concerts Lamoureux of Paris. Casals himself conducted. Martin Luther King, Jr., was in attendance for that gathering of world leaders from a hundred countries, sponsored by the Center for the Study of Democratic Institutions. I remember how I stayed close to the great man, half of me studying him as a consummate human artist who had devoted his entire instrument (including his considerable vocal skills) to his mission; the other half of me hoping to gain increased understanding from his observations on the problems of peace on earth.

My international touring extended to its sixth continent when I did my tour of Brazil in 1963, traveling to Rio de Janeiro and São Paulo to perform Bach's *St. Matthew Passion* and his two great *Solo Cantatas* for bass, as well as Brahms's *Serious Songs*.

In these ruminations on my travels, I've moved ahead of my chronology. Another era began for me in the mid-sixties with my first annual residency in Vienna, to perform *Porgy and Bess* and other works with the Vienna Volksoper. But by that time I had taken care of a little unfinished business in New York, which I should first relate.

Chapter Twelve

NEW DIRECTIONS

In 1961, ten years of travel across the country and around the world had seasoned and mellowed me. As an artist I was more mature, as a man I was more seasoned. I had been through some tough times, as I'll describe, but they had fired me up without burning me, and ultimately led to another dimension in my art.

But none of that prevented me from taking a teenager's delight in the opportunity to come back to Broadway in a new production of *Porgy and Bess*. When the offer was made by Jean Dalrymple at New York City Center, I didn't hesitate a moment.

I'm not sure how or when Jean came up with the idea for her revival. All I know is that this was one case where Larney didn't have to go out of his way — she conceived the project with me in mind.

I was all over the map those days, and I don't just mean all over the globe. Artistically I had been featured in so many different venues that people wondered what Bill Warfield would come up with next.

Only a few years before, between touring engagements I had been cast as De Lawd in the television production of Marc Connelly's comic drama *Green Pastures*. I welcomed the opportunity, even though I was under a lot of stress at the time. Leontyne and I had just about decided to pull the plug on our marriage, and I had been looking for my own place where I could start to set up housekeeping. Just as stressful was the fact that this would be the first time since my salad days that I'd be doing a role with no musical connection. It was straight drama, a new challenge for me.

But I wanted to discover whether I needed music as a veil to perform behind, or whether there was still a Bill Warfield who could project a character directly through words and emotions.

The question had an added significance. Having absorbed the full schedule of touring that they'd thrown at me, I had put my vocal instrument through some tough tests. Down deep, every young person believes he's going to live forever, and can't imagine a time when the equipment might not perform as ordered. Now, pushing forty, in excellent health but feeling the effects of my pell-mell musical adventures, I began to consider the notion that there are limits to human physical endurance.

Like every ball player who doesn't have the snap at forty that he used to, or every dancer who can't do what he once considered a simple move on stage, I occasionally had my own intimations of mortality. I had even gone through a spell of anxiety when I thought I heard serious problems in my voice — more about that later. It's hard to know one's own motivations, but I can't rule out the possibility that I wanted some insurance against the awful day when I might not be able to continue a career in music.

I remember that I had not yet moved out of Vandam Street when we went into production of *Green Pastures*, because I was laid up in bed with the flu, Lulu bringing me my chicken soup, right up till when I had to catch a cab to the studio for my first rehearsal. Those first few days were pretty rough.

But George Schaeffer, the director, was great. Under his guidance, I quickly learned the special requirements of television acting.

For film work as well as television, I had learned to tone down my actions and reactions. The sometimes exaggerated responses that work on a stage will be garish, grotesque even, on camera. In fact, the intimacy of the TV screen often calls for even less of a reaction than you'd produce in a real-life situation. An extreme close-up brings the camera right into your pores, and you deliver more "face" than anyone is ever going to get in normal day-to-day encounters. So you have to develop a new vocabulary of expressions, a new dialect of body language to fit the medium.

But that vocabulary is one thing in a domestic drama, with ordinary human emotions. It's something else in a comic or epic theater piece about confrontations between Noah and De Lawd. The challenge is to produce bombast on cue, without blowing the cameras away — and to get it just right the first time. In those days of television, of course, it was all live, with no lip-sync or second take. In that sense the *Green Pastures* experience was much closer to a stage performance than it was to the film experience I'd already had at MGM. But George Schaeffer made it work, and I was very grateful to him because it was all so new to me.

Not that I was unfamiliar with the art of acting. In fact, I was assertive in all but the fine tuning, which I happily left to George. I do remember that he was concerned about how I'd "handle" Eddie Anderson, who was cast in the confrontational role of Noah.

Eddie Anderson was one of the most recognizable characters in the world, thanks to the power of radio, the uniqueness of his voice, and the popularity of the *Jack Benny Show* on which he had first created the role of Rochester in 1937. He came into the *Green Pastures* rehearsals after we had been at it for a few days. I had been developing my character and was pretty confident with it. Now that Anderson was just getting up to speed, I was doing what performers call "marking it," holding back on the intensity levels while George Schaeffer gave him his blocking and worked with him on his delivery.

After that first day's work, George pulled me aside for some advice. "Look, Bill," he said, "this is your show. You're De Lawd. Anderson may be Rochester, but I don't want you to be intimidated by him." I managed to keep from breaking into a laugh; I toned it down to a polite smile and assured him that I'd be careful not to be intimidated. But later I cracked up at the suggestion that I was going to mute my performance in deference to Rochester. My ego is reasonably normal, but I can't imagine it would sit there and let me be upstaged once the cameras started to roll.

Thank God for the kinescopes, all we have left of television productions like *Green Pastures*. When you see recordings of old television shows, that's what you're seeing—a movie camera rigged up to film from a television screen, and a poor substitute for the real thing. I didn't get to see a kinescope of *Green Pastures* until my students gave me a videotape of it at my seventieth birthday party. For all those years in between, I knew my own performance in *Green Pastures* only through the descriptions that others had given me.

With live television in those days, throughout rehearsals you would think of your final performance as an opening night. But it would also be a closing night, the culmination of your whole artistic experience, all packaged together in one tight compartment of time. And in those days, before sophisticated recording techniques, you couldn't put the tape away and let the ratings masters figure out what month or what year it might be best to release it. It was aired as you performed it, and you crossed your fingers.

Green Pastures was aired on the *Hallmark Hall of Fame,* October 17, 1957. But that's not the one you remember. I can say that with some confidence, because if you saw it you almost certainly saw it a year and a half later when we repeated the entire process.

The problem was that, on the very night we performed what was supposed to be our once-only production, and in the identical 9:30-11:00 p.m. time slot, Mike Todd threw a party for 18,000 of his closest friends. It was aired as "Around the World in 90 Minutes" on Playhouse 90. And though it was a hopeless hodge-podge of promotional clips of his upcoming film, *Around the World in Eighty Days,* together with celebrity interviews and animals on parade (and Walter Cronkite as "anchor"; his most insightful contribution was to comment, "It's a madhouse down here"), it stole all the ratings for that evening's television audiences. One television critic summed it up as "a myriad of dancers, parading extras, bagpipers, horses, elephants, dancers, horses, dancers and horses — a resounding bust."

A few clicks down the dial, we were having better luck with the critics, and I was gratified to read the verdict on my first and only straight dramatic role: *Variety* wrote that "William Warfield was excellent as De Lawd, who, in his wrath, strikes down man, whom he has created, because mankind has become sinful. Eventually, in a highly moving scene, De Lawd learns humility from his own creatures and he becomes a God of mercy. Warfield's portrayal is authoritative and dignified, and the standout of the play."

The critics were pleased, and audiences belatedly took notice. By public demand we repeated the performance a year and a half later, on March 23, 1959.

Between those airings I managed to find myself a new place to live. I bought a house on 87th Street that I could remodel into a duplex, to use as both a home and an investment. Who knew when I might need to fall back on that rental income?

It wasn't until I moved to the 87th Street house that I began to entertain on my own. Without Lulu's professional polish, the atmosphere of my gatherings felt a lot more homey, more like what I remembered from Rochester as I was growing up. I'd do the cooking myself, for a whole different set of people from those that we had gathered together on Vandam Street. Of course, some of the same folks came around, Shirley Verette, Larney and Karen, Bill Marshall, musicians like Don Shirley and George Wilson, and their friends. But they didn't need to dress up when they dropped by on 87th Street; they came by in their sweaters and bluejeans.

At some point about this time, I decided to take seriously the problems I had been noticing with my voice. As it was soon explained to me, those problems had mostly to do with stress.

Stress—physical or emotional—is very insidious. Often it will do its worst damage without making itself evident. Only later will it surface in its full ramifications. In my case, I was told, stress damage may have begun as early as 1953, when Leontyne was opening on Broadway with *Porgy* and I was nursing my emotional wounds. Up till then I had had very few complications in my life. With only a few exceptions, I'd always been calling the shots, or letting the chips fall where they may. The 1953 events were the first that were really out of my control.

That's what trained vocal analysts told me. What I could see myself was the damage caused by my international touring, which reached a crescendo in the late fifties. And then perhaps the most emotionally stressful period would be the temporary dissolution of my home life soon after, when I made my move from Greenwich Village to 87th Street.

The voice problems only gradually became evident. Small tendencies became bad habits. I first became aware that something might be amiss on the second tour to Australia, in 1958.

When I returned to New York and my sessions with Yves Tinayre, he confirmed it — there were certain problems, notes that I wasn't hitting with perfect accuracy or that I was not holding as effortlessly as before.

Otto Herz had been with me in Australia and was able to pick up on the little indications I'd noticed myself. But because he traveled with me — and because he was, after all, concerned with his own art — he couldn't give me the accurate barometer that Tinayre's ear provided. In any case, Herz wasn't trained to to evaluate my voice the way Tinayre was. Like Larney, he could tell by listening when something was wrong, but he wouldn't know precisely where the problem lay.

The human body goes through a physical adjustment about every seven years. It's often quite imperceptible, but one way or another everything in the entire body is somehow affected, vocal cords included. In my case, the way I sounded in the late1950s, compared to my sound at my debut in 1950 at the age of thirty, showed that my voice had gone through a tremendous settling, a lowering of its range, in that period of time.

The critics had earlier mentioned that there were times when my voice would take flight and I would sound like a tenor on top — a comment that was intended as a compliment. I don't think by any stretch of the imagination that I could have sounded like a tenor at thirty-eight. In retrospect, it is clear that what I'd been doing, while my voice was settling down, was singing as before and simply ignoring the changes.

Tinayre could tell that something was wrong, but he was too closely involved in the development of my voice to be the best person to diagnose it now. I decided that I should go to see Rosa Ponselle.

Rosa Ponselle was an almost legendary prima donna. She had been a star of the Met until her retirement in 1937, still in the prime of her career. While a student, back before the Great War, she had been discovered by Caruso; shortly thereafter she was singing Verdi at the Met. For nearly twenty years she had been the opera's leading soprano.

Now, in her early sixties, recently widowed and comfortably ensconced at her Villa Pace outside Baltimore, she was a vocal coach and guru for a few selected students. It was something out of the old school: The prima donnas would abide for a month or more with the great teacher, absorbing her lessons twenty-four hours a day. At any time of the year, there might be several singers living within the compound.

I first came into contact with Rosa Ponselle when Peter Herman Adler arranged for Leontyne to sing for her. That wasn't in any sense remedial — just an opportunity for a great artist to hear and advise a woman who was also destined to become a great voice in opera. Leontyne made the trip, and I'll never forget when she returned, how she was positively luminous in the afterglow of this great woman.

"Oh, Bill," she told me, "this beautiful woman sat there and opened her mouth and just came alive with music before my eyes." Leontyne was like a woman transported. She told how Rosa would spin out her magical music, illustrating examples she was trying to explain, and, as Leontyne put it, "My stomach just about dropped out from under me, it was so incredible."

She repeated, in a kind of wonder, "I can't believe that woman can do that kind of singing. She'd be talking about something from *Aida*, and she'd say, 'My dear, maybe you should approach it with more —' and then she'd lift off into song, showing, not telling, what she was suggesting. I couldn't believe what I was hearing."

So Rosa already held a certain fascination for me. And now that I needed professional consultation, perhaps remedial work, it was time to see her for myself.

Every singer needs an outside ear to gauge what's going on. What you hear from inside is not the best measure of what's happening on the outside. Many divas have the relationship with a teacher that Leontyne has with her voice teacher, Florence Page Kimball, who never misses a performance and who continuously — on a daily basis if necessary — works to refine and correct and improve even a superbly trained voice like Leontyne's. That's one of the reasons why Leontyne has never lost any of her vocal edge.

Even the untrained outside ear can be important. Even now, if a perfect stranger starts to compliment me with a phrase like, "Your voice sounds so . . . " — whatever they say next, I'll take it very seriously. I may be able to disregard their opinion of why I sound that way, or whether it's an occasion for compliment or concern, but I will roll it over and over in my mind, trying to discern what I did to create that impression, what it was they heard.

These strangers don't know it, but they're telling me something about what I'm doing technically. And if I find that what they've described is something that I did not intend to do, it will send up an alarm. Because if it doesn't correspond with what I thought I was doing, that's a signal that I'm doing something wrong.

I think every artist does that, to a greater or lesser extent; I doubt that their fans understand how significant even a casual comment can become in the analytical process of an artist. The fans have no idea they've put an alarm in your head.

The difference with Rosa Ponselle was that I could have absolute trust in her comments. She could not only hear it, she knew what to do about it. She could find the little tiny tendencies that have a way of developing into habits. I didn't have a Madame Kimball like Leontyne. So Rosa temporarily filled that role for me.

I can't do her technique justice in a short space, but it had to do with the body being in good balance, good posture that relates to good tone. It approached the whole body and not just the vocal cords. The first thing Rosa did for me was to point out, "What you have done is to confine your voice from the neck up, approaching it as an intellectual exercise as well as a physical one." As a result, she said, I had pulled the voice into check with such tight control that when I wanted to open up it wasn't there in its full, natural force. The spirit was willing, but I'd weakened the flesh: I'd removed the full strength of the body as the source of the voice.

Her approach was to stand me up in the middle of the floor and say, "Just drop your hands and look at me and say 'Mama Mia!' out loud. With your body, with your body. 'Mama Mia! Mama Mia!'" She showed me what she meant.

"If you were singing," she said, "you'd pitch it up here" and she pinched out a constrained "Mama Mia" for me — "You're not using your whole body, it has to be your whole body that it comes through."

She was right, of course. I had been doing the vocal literature — the lieder, the chansons — and all these things that required coloring but not big sound. Seeking perfection of interpretation in my work with Yves Tinayre, I had narrowed myself down and focused my technique so completely that I had tamed the spontaneous tendency to open up and sing it out. I had to relearn that naturalness.

Like most good teachers, Rosa was drawing out old truths, not inventing new ones. Her approach echoed some of what I'd learned when I first started out at the age of sixteen. I'd been taught that the throat must be free, that the breathing must be absolutely correct, that there should be no strain in singing, that the tone should flow from the diaphragm.

But then my training had continued with Arthur Craft at Eastman and with Yves Tinayre, who both reinforced the concept of focusing the tone and using the diaphragm, not the upper apparatus, as the basis of that focus. And that's when I became so good at using the diaphragm to focus the tone that I lost the full effectiveness of the diaphragm as the great engine of all my sound. Focus had become constriction. Working with Rosa I restored the balance.

Such fine-tuning is a life-long process; no musical artist is ever finished. I went to see Rosa, off and on, for five or six summers. I always benefitted from having her hear what I was doing, diagnosing the details I would have otherwise missed. Her approach worked wonders, and as a result I entered into a whole new phase of music.

Through Rosa I met her associate, Igor Chichagov, who when he wasn't with Rosa at Villa Pace gave classes in New York. We became friends. He would often meet me at the station in Baltimore and drive me out to Villa Pace. I'd spend the whole afternoon with Rosa, usually with Chichagov present, and then he'd drive me back to the station for the New York train.

Even at their peak, my visits to Villa Pace were never more than once a week. In between times, at Rosa's urging, I'd work with Chichagov in his New York studio. Frequently, when I was working with him, he would use one of Rosa's expressions — about the timbre, perhaps, or the "darkness" — in connection with the piece we were studying. In that working context I would suddenly understand what Rosa had been talking about. Sometimes it might be completely different from the quality I had thought she intended. So, between the two of them, I got much more than the sum of their individual instruction.

Chichagov and I worked on literature, and specifically on a whole new line of music. It was with him that I got started on the Russians. For some time I'd felt I was ready for that new musical literature, and now here was Chichagov, made to order: a Russian, a vocalist, a pianist, a coach. We started working on

Musorgsky's *Boris Godunov* and *Songs of Death* and an aria from Tchaikovsky's *Eugene Onegin*.

As with everything that I tackled, I studied the language first. I had done that with all the other musical languages — French, Italian, German. But before I'd had a chance to get around to Russian, I had my Town Hall debut and my career took off. I never had the time or opportunity to go back.

Now, because of my enforced attention to my vocal problems, I found I had the time to do it right. And I had the opportunity, in the person of Igor Chichagov. I took advantage of it.

Before we did any music he taught me the Cyrillic alphabet, the pronunciation, and how the language works. Then I began to accumulate a vocabulary. By the time I was ready to work with the music, I was able to work directly from the Cyrillic literature, which Chichagov had taught me to parse and comprehend.

Some years before, Otto Herz had taught me enough Hungarian that I could pronounce it and do some Hungarian folk music. He taught me that Hungarian is the only language in the world that is completely phonetic; the accent is always the same, with no exceptions. If you know the formula for pronunciation, Otto said, you can pick up a Hungarian newspaper and read it out loud — without understanding a word of it — and anyone who speaks Hungarian will comprehend you perfectly. Otto taught me to do that in Hungarian, so the idea wasn't a novel one, now that I first approached the Russian librettos.

I didn't expect to be able to become a U.N. translator, but I did want to be able to understand the nuances of each syllable I sang, so it was important that I achieve a basic understanding of Russian vocabulary and syntax. I haven't kept active in Russian, and I would have to relearn most of what I once did easily. Fortunately, back when I could do it quickly, I went through most of my music and transcribed the words phonetically. But from time to time I'll need to work with a Cyrillic piece that I had neglected to transcribe, and I'll have to parse out word by word, even letter by letter a verse that I once wrote and read with instant recognition. It's as though another mind had once done my thinking for me, and I'll have to labor intensely just to get to the point where I can pronounce and make sense of material I once sight-read.

During the period that I was working with Rosa Ponselle and Igor Chichagov, I stopped my vocal work with Yves Tinayre. But I renewed my association with Peter Herman Adler. By this time he had become music director for the Baltimore Symphony Orchestra, and he wanted me to perform music from *Boris Godunov* with him.

By that time in my life I was ready for such a role. In the theater, the role of King Lear is rarely effective in the hands of a young actor. Similarly, there are opera roles that require a certain amount of life experience. It had never occurred to me to try *Boris Godunov* earlier; now it fit me like a glove.

To jump forward in time to make a point, I ultimately made a recording of the role with Peter Herman Adler. When it was premiered on a local radio station, I'm told, the switchboard lit up with calls from people who wanted to know the new Russian singer who had performed with the Baltimore. When the station manager told them it was William Warfield, the callers thought he was being flip with them.

Rosa Ponselle had one quaintly endearing custom that was inflexible: every afternoon that I was at Villa Pace, after we had worked together and as I was about to leave, she would sit down and insist that I sing her a spiritual. She wasn't listening with an ear to critique. She was floating with the music, her eyes closed, usually coming to the verge of tears before I'd finished the song.

I first worked with Rosa in the summer of 1959. Four years later I was still making the occasional pilgrimage, to further refine my voice. Though my visits tapered off, Rosa lived and worked another twenty productive years and came to see me perform whenever I was in the Baltimore area.

When I was asked to sing at her funeral on a May afternoon in 1981, I had no question about which piece I'd do. This was her favorite:

Heaven is one beautiful place, I know.
And if you want to get to heaven on time,
You surely got to plumb that line.
There's crying here, there's crying there,
there's a tear wherever I go.
But there ain't no crying over there,
where the tears no longer flow,
Oh, Heaven is one beautiful place I know.

Rosa helped me through a difficult time. By the time the *Porgy and Bess* rehearsals began on Broadway in late April 1961, I was ready. I had been looking forward to this for months.

One of my emotions — the teenager's glee I referred to — was a sense of vindication. I had always had the feeling that I was due my own production of this opera in New York, someday.

That certainty was probably what helped me to write off the Breen-Davis business without too much bitterness. "That's all right," I can remember thinking, "that's okay, it's just not my time yet." I managed to be philosophical about the thought that every dog has his day. That one just wasn't mine. Now it had come.

Some people might well have wondered whether I had lost my mind, whether it made any professional sense at all, whether I really needed this risk at this point in my career. Breen and Davis's *Porgy and Bess* had been such a showbiz industry, involving so many people at so many levels, that there were bound to be cliques out there who would like nothing better than for a new production to fail. Ella Gerber, with the blessing of the Heyward and Gershwin estates, was still staging her twenty-pound version of the script, in venues as distant as New Zealand. There was a dramaturgical subculture that kept track of which *Porgy* productions tended to be more "theater" and which tended to be more "opera." Especially since Dalrymple was planning to restore the recitatives and otherwise depart from the authorized Gerber version of the Breen production, wasn't I putting myself in the middle of a fray I didn't need?

The always lively politics of theater might have intruded into the picture, bringing the "*Porgy* establishment" in to comment through newspaper articles, perhaps even to write reviews. Anything less than raves from the critics could hurt me at this stage of my career.

Did any of these intelligent considerations crowd into my head as I contemplated this offer? No way. Lord, I thought, if there were ever a role that I wanted to do in New York, this was it— if for no other reason than to show Davis and Breen how wrong they'd been when they prevented a Warfield/Price production on Broadway. Wild horses couldn't have kept me off that stage. As opening day approached, I was ecstatic.

Rehearsals were scheduled for only three weeks. The show was booked for a limited run, so the entire experience would be very compact. Robert McFerrin was my alternate as *Porgy*. My Bess was Leesa Foster, who had been in the Breen production, as had quite a few of our players. The back-up Bess was the mezzo-soprano from the Met, Barbara Conrad.

By the time opening night came around I was pretty comfortable in the role. I don't remember being worried what the critics were going to say. I had never gotten into that habit.

I was a great one for entertaining the company, and as I recall I had everyone up at my house on 87th Street. On opening night I called Lulu and she came up from Vandam to prepare the food. It was a great house for those kinds of occasions — we'd have people all over the place, some upstairs playing gin rummy, others eating or drinking champagne, others out in the garden. If it were a typical opening for me — and to my best recollection it was — I would have gone to bed before the reviews were published. As I say, I never have been one for going to Sardi's and waiting up for the reviews.

So I probably heard the reviews, rather than saw them with my own eyes — Larney probably called me to read them to me. But I certainly enjoyed what they had to say:

"The rapture and jubilation that George Gershwin poured into *Porgy and Bess* were at full tide at the City Center last night," wrote Howard Taubman in the *New York Times*. "Mr. Warfield is a superb Porgy. His playing has dignity and humility, and his singing has the kind of nuance, control, and potency that one rarely encounters in the Broadway theatre."

Judith Crist, in the *New York Herald Tribune*, wrote, "We are twice blessed by the City Center this time. Its Light Opera Company has brought *Porgy and Bess* back after an eight-year hiatus and all the musical glories of the Gershwin masterpiece are ours to revel in again. And it has brought us a great Porgy in William Warfield, who is making his New York debut in the role that had won him many honors abroad.

"Mr. Warfield is more than a fine baritone," she continued. "He is a fine actor and his portrait of the crippled beggar of Catfish Row is brilliant in its blending of tenderness and strength, in its pathos and compassion. His is a performance beyond compare . . . an unforgettable Porgy."

We did the production again in a 1964 revival and took it to the World's Fair that year. But the high point for me was that long-delayed 1961 New York debut of my *Porgy*.

That red-letter year   was a particularly lively one for Larney. Leontyne was still under his management (and would continue with him through 1962). In January 1961 she finally had her Met debut as Leonora in *Il Trovatore*, and was greeted with a forty-two-minute ovation, a record for the Metropolitan Opera.

And the year I did *Porgy* at the World's Fair was also busy — because in 1964 Larney was setting up what amounted to a *Porgy and Bess* sinecure for me, with an old friend from Camp Ritchie.

Chapter Thirteen

A MUSICAL LIFE

Marcel Prawy was the director of the Volksoper in Vienna. That was one place where no one was likely to be confused about whether *Porgy and Bess* was an opera or a musical. They simply didn't care about that particular distinction.

In the mid-1960s, Marcel Prawy was having great success bringing in musicals for Viennese audiences. In the broadest sense he considered shows like *Kiss Me Kate* and *West Side Story* to be American "folk operas." Sometimes he'd present them in the original English, sometimes in German translation. He had seen me in the 1952 *Porgy* when Breen took the show to Vienna, and had conceived a desire to present it himself some day. Not long after we did the Jean Dalrymple production — the 1961 version revived for the 1964 World's Fair—Prawy decided it was time to add *Porgy* to his permanent repertoire.

One more piece of evidence that we live in a small world: Prawy, Larney, and I had crossed tracks once before. During my war years, he was one of the refugees who had come through Camp Ritchie for military intelligence training. The three of us had been fast friends. Since the war Prawy had earned his U.S. citizenship, and had become completely fluent in his new language while retaining all his skills in German. In time he'd developed a career as a producer and finally emerged as the Volksoper director.

Prawy was an accomplished writer in both German and English, so much so that he personally did the translations of many of the American musicals presented by the Volksoper. His approach was to acquire the rights, engage a noted director and a few leading actors from the United States or from European engagements where they might be playing, and then fill the minor roles, the corps de ballet, and the orchestra with local talent. For this new *Porgy*, his director would be Nathaniel Merrill from the Metropolitan Opera.

Prawy's production had nothing to do with Ella Gerber's version. I'm not sure how he made his arrangements with the Heyward and Gershwin estates, but when he acquired the rights he passed over the "improvements" Gerber had accumulated, choosing instead to present something closer to the original. Where Dalrymple had removed Gerber's accretions, but stopped short of restoring all the recitatives in her City Center version, Prawy went the rest of the way. Some critics believe that the Vienna production, which we opened in 1965, was the direct progenitor of the revival of the full opera finally presented by the Met twenty years later. That is, some consider that Prawy's production was the one that began a general trend back toward the original intentions of the authors.

Certainly Prawy proved that it would work as a standard repertoire item. I went to Vienna to perform it for him every season from 1965 until 1974, when I began teaching at the University of Illinois. And he taught audiences and critics alike how important those recitatives are to the full emotional impact of the work.

Often the recitatives illuminate the dialogue, or set up songs, in ways that were never possible in straight dialogue. Bess's beautiful "I Loves You Porgy" flows musically as well as emotionally from a poignant line Porgy delivers. When the line is spoken rather than sung, it's an effective set-up; but when it is sung, it's a powerful piece of music that sweeps you up with a breathtaking rush into that climactic song.

For nearly a decade Vienna was like a second home to me. Although I didn't keep a residence there year round, Prawy put me up in a furnished apartment for three months at a time, and it was always in the same block of apartments if not the same actual flat. So I had a neighborhood, a home address on Neustift Gasse, neighbors who looked for me to arrive each year.

Most seasons I was there in the spring, but now and then Prawy would schedule *Porgy* in the fall. In 1971 Prawy added a new item to the Volksoper repertoire — a German-language version of *Show Boat*. (He did the translation himself, and he had me switch from German to English for "Old Man River.") All in all, there was no month of the year that I didn't have some experience of Vienna.

The schedule was very civilized. I arrived in plenty of time to take rehearsals in stride. I performed every second or third night, and in the meantime went to see opera at the Staatsoper or walked over to the Staatstheater for a play.

That was a golden era for American artists in Vienna. At the height of the season we were almost a separate artists' colony there. In that quaintly gilded European capital I was able to go to the theater and see dozens of American singers and musicians and actors, some of them quite renowned, whom I'd never had a chance to see in New York City. There were some years when I had more continuous time in one place in Vienna than I ever managed to get in any U.S. city.

On the nights when I went to the opera or the theater, afterwards I'd often meet whomever was performing at the Hotel Sacher — the famous home of the Sacher Torte — right across the street from the Staatsoper. It was rather expensive but they served a terrific broiled brisket of beef with horseradish sauce, another of their famous specialties.

On nights when friends came to see me perform, we'd go to a cafe called Falstaff. The food was good, the atmosphere was restrained *gemütlichkeit*, and it was conveniently located. It was a gathering place for the performers and for the public, too, who would come to rub elbows with the stars.

But most nights I'd be holding court at Neustift Gasse. A typical example was the night I met André Watts, whom I'd never seen in the States. I visited him backstage, and when we'd finished the small talk I asked, "How's your day tomorrow?" He had a little time before his next engagement. "Come on over," I told him. "I'll make up some old fashioned fried chicken." He brought the beer — it's hard to improve on Viennese beer — and I took care of the rest.

We didn't dine alone. By that time I was used to whipping up a meal for ten or twenty at a time. One of the hazards of touring, for some palates, is that the local cooking can raise more questions than it answers. Especially for the younger kids, the dancers and singers with the corps, they can be surrounded by some of the world's finest cuisine and all they know is that it's (a) unpronounceable and (b) not a Big Mac, Coke, and fries.

I'm not of that taste, but I sympathize with them. And I've always enjoyed an old-fashioned home-cooked meal myself. So it soon became a watchword that when you didn't want to deal with *wienerschnitzel* you should come on over to Uncle Bill's. I had learned where to find the Viennese equivalent of ham hocks and greens, and fish to fry and potatoes for potato salad. We'd have a down-home feast. My apartment was a place where you could let down your guard. Most performers would prefer that to sitting around a cafe.

I don't know exactly how I became Uncle Bill, but it started in Vienna. I must have seemed avuncular, in my ancient late forties, to the twenty-year-olds who were always hanging out at my place. I suppose I was old enough to be looked up to, yet nonparental enough to fall generally into the category of a favorite uncle. In any case, the label stuck.

Prawy presented the American folk-rock musical *Hair* one year. There was a girl in that company who hung around my place with the other kids. Her name was Donna Gaines, and I completely adored her. She was always bubbling with energy and always just dying to do your horoscope for you — she was serious about astrology, knew it backwards and forwards. She continually amazed me with her ability to look at a person and ask him a couple of questions and then tell him all about himself based on her sense of the astral arrangements. I never heard anyone say that she missed on a single hunch.

A few years later on the streets of New York I ran into one of my friends from those Vienna days. "Isn't it wonderful what happened to little Donna Gaines?" she said, and I must have beamed in response — I had wondered how she might be doing. "How is Donna?" I asked, "what's she up to?" My friend motioned to the huge poster that bedecked the bus stop where we were standing, just about every city bus, and billboards all over town — Donna Gaines had become Donna Summer.

When I went to the awards ceremony in 1984 to pick up my Grammy for *Lincoln Portrait*, I was looking forward to the special pleasure of running into Donna, who I knew would be there receiving her own award. She was with a group of friends, agents, and record moguls, dressed to the nines, very much the lady. I tapped her on the shoulder and she turned to look, then

spun around with a shriek, all that beautifully coiffed hair flying
— "Uncle Bill!"

To this day I consider Vienna a second home. I like Paris,
I like London, but in Vienna I get a feeling for the people, the
country, the culture. Could it be, in part, a response to the
beautiful musical legacy of the German-speaking people? Perhaps. But there's something more immediate that I respond to
there. For instance, the spontaneity of the Nashmarkt, about
three blocks from where I lived, where I did all my grocery
shopping. Big bins full of fresh vegetables, fresh meats, smoked
meats, fresh fish alive in big tanks — one of the few places that I
ever went where they keep them all in tanks and you point at
what you want and they pick it out alive for you — all together
alongside stalls where you can buy household utensils, pantry
staples, hardware.

The people at the Nashmarkt were always happy to give
you advice. I discovered various ways of making ham hocks and
cabbage — *gereuchte stolze*, smoked ham hock the same as ours
except that it goes a little further up the leg. I could have them
chop that up into smaller slices and then get some *kohl* — green
cabbage — and then cook it all up for the kids, or sometimes for
my Viennese friends, who would beg me for the recipe. I started
one Viennese family making corn bread one year, and when I
came back the following year he boasted, almost accurately, "My
corn bread is now better than yours, Herr Warfield!"

Maybe there's a distant echo of my earliest family life in
those good feelings I always get in Vienna. Come to think of it,
the Nashmarkt does remind me of Saturday shopping in Rochester, back in those days before styrofoam and Saran Wrap, back
when we'd pick out the produce, even the poultry, from coops
and bins. Somehow Vienna — at least the Vienna of my experience — has managed to blend both the elegance of its fine arts and
the funky immediacy of its daily functions into a smoothly
consistent culture. It's a quality of life that perhaps evokes those
uncomplicated days of my youth, when I'd go down to the
butcher with my dad or chop cabbage with my mom.

My mother died in 1964, my father in 1966.

* * * *

Throughout the sixties and into the seventies I continued with the tours and recitals that Columbia Artists and Larney were setting up for me. Nelly Walter, who had been André Mertens's assistant, took over my personal concert direction after Mertens passed away.

That was also a period of miscellaneous honorifics, each of them individually more meaningful to me, perhaps, than to the reader of this narrative. I had never completed the work for my master's degree in music, at Eastman. Beginning in 1972, I leap-frogged that degree and started collecting honorary doctorates: the first was a Doctor of Laws from the University of Arkansas, where I had been born. Over time I would receive similar degrees — in music, and in humane letters, for the most part — from Eastern Illinois, Millikin University, Wilson College, Boston University, Lafayette College, and my own Eastman School of Music at the University of Rochester.

My programs continued to evolve. One typical program from the late sixties opened with Bach's "Good Fellows Be Merry" from the *Peasant Cantata*, Handel's "Oh Sleep, Why Dost Thou Leave Me" from *Semele*, and Monteverdi's *Psalm CL*, which Yves Tinayre had transcribed from a rare German anthology dating from the seventeenth century. Then I did a Brahms group: "Verrat," "In Waldeseinamkeit," "Wie Froh und Frisch," "Ruhe, Süssliebchen," and "Verzweiflung." That was followed by Prince Gremin's aria from Tchaikovsky's *Eugene Onegin*, and Dello Joio's "The Creed of Pierre Cauchon" from *The Trial at Rouen*. After the intermission I did Ibert's "Chansons de Don Quichotte" straight through, and then closed with traditional tunes: "Passing by Yarmouth Fair" by Peter Warlock, "Childhood Memories," a Langston Hughes poem set to music by Elie Siegmeister, and Margaret Bonds's arrangements of "Didn't It Rain" and "Hold On."

I also took on new works, some of them projects like the film I narrated for Orson Welles, a documentary on the Belgian Congo; some of them pieces that I had long wanted to do but had postponed, like Mendelssohn's *Elijah* with the New York Oratorio Society. In 1969 I sang in recital for the convocation of the National Association of Negro Musicians. I remember that particularly because Marian Anderson was in attendance.

She was in the audience again in 1975, for my Carnegie Hall recital to commemorate the twenty-fifth anniversary of my Town

Hall debut, perhaps even in the same seat where she had been for my original Carnegie Hall performance. The commemoration was a good time, but it's the original Carnegie Hall performance that I'll never forget.

It was a stellar event. All my heroes were there: Roland Hayes, Marian Anderson, Leontyne, Hall Johnson, hundreds of invited guests. And when I walked out onto the stage it suddenly hit me. I looked up to the boxes and there they all were, gathered together in one place as if in a dream, all looking my way and waiting for me.

It was the first time in my life that I was nervous. I had about the world's worst case of stage fright. Hall Johnson? I was singing some of his arrangements. Marian Anderson? I had been in awe of her since my teens. Roland Hayes? I was going to sing "He Never Said a Mumblin' Word" for Roland Hayes?

A little voice might have whispered in my ear at that moment, "Bill Warfield, are you crazy?" As I began the first song, suddenly, I was so winded that I almost couldn't breathe. My only recourse was to stop trying to force myself to breathe deeply, and to start quietly — very quietly, so that the song itself could take over. By the time I finished that first song I had conquered the fear, but I don't remember a thing about the song, or how I got through it. I do remember that, when I finished, Carnegie Hall was rocked with thunderous applause, and I thought, "Thank God, I'm home free now."

To continue this digression, I felt that same crushing stage fright one other time in my life. I was doing a recital at the University of Illinois, some time in my second year there. My first recital there, when I came to the campus in 1974, had been a pleasant experience, and this was certain to be even more so. I was well known on campus by now and had nothing to prove to anyone. I had loaded the program with difficult material, things that a subscriber audience in New York might find too unrelieved, much less a more general audience in Champaign, Illinois — Schumann's *Liederkreise* in the first half and *Dichterliebe* in the second. The hall was sold out, and a large number of university and other dignitaries were assembling for the occasion.

I suspect that I took it all so much for granted that I skimped on my psychological preparation. Whatever the reason, I breezed through the receptions and the elegant dinner before the performance, and at the appointed hour I walked out onto the stage ready to sing — and at that moment I was stricken by that terrifying anxiety: How can anybody measure up to the fanfare and the folderol that has preceded this event? What have I got myself into? How am I ever going to get through this complex literature here tonight?

Once again, it was a matter of opening my mouth and starting slowly. Rather than take a deep breath as the base for my initial projection, I found it helpful to use only a shallow breath at first, which forced a gentler treatment of the whole instrument. As we all know, there's nothing so reassuring at a moment of panic as someone who's deliberate, calm and unflustered. That's true whether it's a parent leaning over a panicky child, or whether you do it for yourself, in one of those rare moments of adult panic such as I was experiencing.

I was already ensconced at the University of Illinois when I made my last trip to perform in Vienna. That was in 1976, as the narrator for Aaron Copland's *Lincoln Portrait* with Leonard Bernstein. On that Bicentennial tour I spent a lot of time with social obligations. Our schedule was dense with receptions and dinners hosted by lord mayors and diplomatic consuls and such. My time wasn't my own, and I was in a hotel suite instead of my little place over on Neustift Gasse. It wasn't the same.

That summer tour was with the New York Philharmonic, Bernstein conducting. We did the *Lincoln Portrait* in French in Paris and in German in Vienna. Then we performed it at the Albert Hall in London, and that presentation was telecast live.

I always had a close affinity with the *Lincoln Portrait*. The first time I did it, Aaron Copland himself conducted, and I could see how he had contrived the music and the dialogue into a perfect fit. In rehearsal we came to the very last moments, with the trumpet solo underscoring the closing phrases of the Gettysburg Address. At the final notes I fit the final words — 'That government of the people, by the people, for the people, shall not perish from ... the ... earth!" — right where they seemed to make the most musical sense. Copland looked up from his score, his arms still busy at work bringing the piece to its finale, and I could hear the surprise in the remark he threw my way. "My God," he said, "that's the first time that's ever been done right!"

I always got along well with conductors. I had a pronounced advantage because of my musical training. Whoever it might be, the minute we started work I could see the conductor's recognition and relief: "Ah, I'm working with a musician." That made possible a good deal of shorthand in our communication. And of course there was a mutuality of respect.

The rapport and respect that I was able to establish with conductors contributed to my own creativity, because when they saw that as a singer I was really able to be a collaborator and not just a necessary evil, they gave me the room I needed to try things that I wanted to try. They understood that my experimentation was coming from a musical impulse, and not just some whim, or personal idiosyncracy, or showing off.

I had that relationship with a number of the great conductors of my day. Aaron Copland, of course, and, while we worked together, Leonard Bernstein.

And Bruno Walter even more so. He was like a master teacher. When we recorded the Mozart *Requiem*, it was with Imgard Seefried, Leopold Simonean, Jenny Tourel, and me. I was the newcomer. What Walter wanted to do was mold together a quartet that was cohesive, that matched, that was aware of what the others were doing, and that was an extension of the music in a unified way, rather than each singing separate solos. By preparing us so thoroughly, drilling us as an organic unit, Walter was able to trust that what he had created would do what he wanted. The night of that performance, he did the least work of any conductor I've ever seen. He just looked us over, gave an indication, and the whole performance came out, broadened within the framework he had established. It was a stupendous musical experience.

In the course of this wonderful experience, Bruno Walter gave me the supreme compliment as a musician. We were in our second or third session, in the middle of the "Benedictus que venite in nomine domini," as I recall, and somebody knocked on the door to say, "Maestro, there is a call from Berlin." Maestro Walter glanced my way and said, "Oh, excuse me, Mr. Warfield, would you rehearse them please," and left. I probably looked as stunned as I felt: I had so much respect for the man, and I knew he had respect for me as a singer. But I had no idea that in the few days we had worked together he had gained so much respect for me as a musician.

We performed in Carnegie Hall before an audience, and then recorded the work in studio.

I had a similar experience with Otto Klemperer. We were doing the aria from Bach's *St. Matthew Passion*, "Mache dich mein Herze rein" (make clean my heart). I had done this with great success in New York with Arthur Mendel, a noted musicologist and Bach authority. He had published a *St. Matthew Passion* which includes a thick section on what purists will accept, where arpeggios can be used, what trills are allowed, all the permissible embellishments considered to be in keeping with the original. He is a complete scholar of the subject. So when I worked with him he had embellished the aria with things that are allowable.

Klemperer, too, was an avid Bach purist, and even more rigid. If it couldn't be proved that Bach did it there, you didn't do it, period, even if the musicologists might find a loophole. So on the first day of rehearsal with Klemperer, I began to sing, "Mache dich mein Herze rein," and at the appropriate point I put the approved embellishment. I heard a tap-tap-tap from the conductor's baton.

Politely but firmly the great Klemperer spoke. "Mr. Warfield," he said, "there is no trill there." And I realized what I was in for.

Oh, my God, I thought, scratching my memory: Which are the ones that are in the original and which are the ones I got from Arthur Mendel? It wouldn't do to confront Klemperer's authority with Mendel's — regardless of their relative merits, which were each incomparable, Klemperer was my conductor.

I decided to play it safe, and not give the score any spin whatever. We got to the next line, and again I heard the tap-tap-tap. "Mr. Warfield," he said, "*there* you can put the trill."

"Maestro," I said, "can we get together afterwards and go over the score?"

"Very good, Mr. Warfield," he said, and so we did, note by note. We were the greatest friends after that, because we were kindred spirits. Though his mother tongue was German and mine English, musically we spoke the same language. And we had a mutual respect. I realized that whether I was right or wrong in some abstract sense, in the immediate practical sense as long as he was my conductor I was in his bailiwick, and I conceded everything to him without reservation. Once that was clear, there were no barriers to our communication. He saw he need not brace himself for artistic bargaining on my part, and in the close working relationship that resulted I could probably have talked him into the very trills and arpeggios that earlier he had been scrupulous to eliminate, assuming that I could demonstrate a valid reason for them.

That's the definition of mutual respect. And I found this is true, with Bernstein, with Ormandy, with Munch — each has what he feels he's bringing to the work, his own signature, his greatness. Once you zero in on that and become a part of it instead of fighting it, the collaboration begins.

Chapter Fourteen

THE TRADITION CONTINUES

All throughout my professional career, I always knew that when the time was ripe I'd want to take what I'd learned and plow it back into the field from which I'd taken so much. I knew I'd be a teacher.

I was already teaching, in a sense. Often when I'd come into a community to perform in recital, particularly when the sponsor was a conservatory or a school of music, I would be asked to conduct a master class as well. Usually, when time permitted, I'd be happy to do that.

In music, a master class is an opportunity for aspirants and students to get the attention of a master — hence the name — for personal evaluation and a little coaching. Each young musician will play or sing for a few minutes, and then receive advice for a few more; and then it's the next musician's turn. Depending on how many students attend (often with their own teachers), hearing each others' analyses as well as their own, the whole thing can last three hours or more. I got pretty effective at the process.

The idea is to give personal, individual attention to the young artist in front of you, and at the same time impart wisdom, or at least a smidgen of new information, to all the others who are waiting their turn. Obviously you can't do a complete diagnosis or make a complete prescription from a single hearing. But you can quickly focus in on one or two salient points, and then discuss them in terms which are general enough to benefit everyone in the room. Over the course of a master class, if you're skillful at it, you can teach a complete lesson through these sequential snippets of discussion.

During the course of my performing career I had received several invitations to become a professor, and though some of them were intriguing none was quite right. Either I was head over heels in my touring schedule and unable to imagine a time when I'd be free enough to make a commitment to students, or I was about to embark on another major project like the Bicentennial tour of *Lincoln Portrait*.

But the offer from the University of Illinois was different. In the first place, it was conveyed initially by one of my accompanists, John Wustman, who was himself teaching there. His personal endorsement impressed me more than the formal proposals I'd received elsewhere. It was working for him, this business of teaching and yet maintaining a performing career. And he spoke highly of the creative environment on the campus in Champaign-Urbana, Illinois.

In the second place, when the offer was formally extended I was left with the clear understanding that I would not only be permitted but actively encouraged to continue my performing. (This actually is not unusual, especially in the performing arts; the school benefits as much as the artist from his continuing investment in the career field.)

Thirdly, when I finally saw the campus and met the people I'd be working with, I was won over. I could see that I would be settling into a cultural and intellectual community that would be as stimulating as the New York circles where I'd been based, without the hassles of urban life. My New York apartment had been burglarized twice in recent years — once I came back from a tour and found that every single piece of furniture in the apartment had been removed — and though I still believe New York City is the greatest city in the world, I had reached the point where the pizzazz wasn't worth the paranoia.

On top of all that, I remember thinking one morning as I was waking up in my beloved Vienna, my knees "all aching and wracked with pain," that the day was not far off when it might not be possible to get down in that little cart and spend the evening on those poor old knees. By 1973, the notion that I'd some day devote myself to teaching became an active question: Isn't it about time? The University of Illinois offer came at just that moment.

The clincher was that the offer was for a full professorship, no intermediate period as assistant or associate, and automatically tenured after one year. I was assured that a professorship in the graduate college would shortly follow (as in fact it did) though that would require the usual procedure of recommendations and vetting by a doctorate committee.

I was also assured that I could continue my performing career and was given the permission to arrange my schedule to accommodate both teaching at the University, and performing abroad. I was also expected to perform at the University and did, in fact, give a recital during my first semester. I met Robert Ray at that time, who accompanied me in this first recital, which was the beginning of a most rewarding collaboration. He has been a dear friend and accompanist for the past 17 years. Anyone who progresses from an active life in a profession to the teaching of that profession will tell you that a teacher spends as much time learning about the subject as he does teaching it. Especially if you continue to practice the profession parallel to your work in the classroom, the one experience feeds the other and the two continually run full circle.

In my first year at Illinois the most important lesson I learned was how to pace myself. A good singing teacher is using his voice all day, and many's the evening when I'd return home hoarse, with nothing left. I would never have been able to teach a day's classes, for example, and then fulfill a singing engagement that night, or even the next day. It took some time to be able to judge accurately just where my limits were, and to stay within them, especially on days when I'd become too enthusiastic about my students' progress to pay attention to my own voice.

I also learned the futility of expecting instant results from my students. Teachers, like directors and conductors — and students, too — need to remember that 75 percent or more of the process of education takes place on a level below the conscious. Things take time to sink in. Ideas are registered, but they're not confirmed immediately, they're not locked into the larger framework of a student's experience; and until they are, they are wandering facts and not elements of personal awareness or knowledge. Sometimes it's simply a matter of time, sometimes it's more complex— a matter of interrelating the information with other ideas and experiences. A good teacher, I figured out, is sensitive to that, and doesn't rush the process. Just because a student isn't giving you back what you thought you so clearly asked for, doesn't mean that the learning isn't going on beneath the surface.

This can be deceptive for a teacher, as I learned, because often a student can *do* what you want instantly, before it's really assimilated. But the development takes longer. A teacher can be mistaken about the student's level of development and move too quickly to the next step.

Some of this I already knew, or suspected. After all, I'd been a student all my life, I had given master classes, and I'd thought about becoming a teacher. That was one factor in my hesitation to commit myself: I knew that a good teacher has to provide continuity of training. Otherwise the lag time in a student's development will result in piecemeal smatterings of information and advice, without real education. I had to be ready to make a personal investment.

I also learned the wisdom of the old truism—if it ain't broke, don't fix it. They say a good theater director is like the man on the aircraft carrier who flags down the planes that are trying to land. If they're drifting to the right, he waves them to the left. If they're drifting to the left, he waves them to the right. If they're too high, or too low, he waves them down or waves them higher. But if they're coming in just right, he stands there, he does nothing. A good teacher has something in common with that. Except that in such cases, when the student is doing fine and coming along nicely, there's still a need to convey the theory of the process. There will come a time in every singer's life when things will go wrong or need attention, and without an awareness of the theory the singer won't know where to begin. That was another set of factors that I learned to keep in balance.

I learned most of my lessons from my students, but I did a lot of reading too. Hundreds of books, some of them real classics, have been written on the theory and practice of both singing and the teaching of singing. The relationship and relative priorities of diction, of phrasing, of breath control, of vocal dynamics, as well as practical advice on warming up, and exercises, and pacing — every teacher has his own approach, and yet there's a common ground in all the approaches. Some of the old timers would use a lighted candle and have the student sing into the flame, studying the splutter to evaluate the enunciation, or the diction, or the breath control. Some employ what is almost a form of massage, to emphasize the role of the diaphragm. The techniques are better studied in one of those texts than in these few notes. I must have read them all. But the kids taught me most of what I ever learned.

And of all the lessons I learned, the greatest surprise was the excitement of a student's achievement. I had heard the clichés but never really understood the reality of the joy, when a promising student transforms all your efforts at communication into a finished product that is so uniquely his own and yet so unmistakably indebted to your instruction. It's a parental pride, a quiet pleasure, but it's as good a feeling as I ever got from a concert hall ovation.

Making your impression on the talent of tomorrow can be a tricky business, though. Sometimes you press things that you didn't realize were in the pattern. That's why teaching is such a learning experience: You're forced to take a hard look at yourself.

That fact takes many expressions. For example, I remember the preparation for one recital where a student, at the climax of a line — "The goblet in my hand!" — waved his arms as boldly and broadly as any swashbuckler. Given the usual refinement of the piece, it was a decidedly undesirable effect, to put it mildly, almost a parody of the song. But it turned out that I had so frequently used my arms to emphasize the bold accent required in the *singing* at that point, he had misunderstood my gestures and copied them exactly.

Another kind of example: In my first year I would frequently fill in as classroom accompanist, playing music that I knew so well from twenty-five years of performance. I played with all the piano embellishments that I'd always used. I learned my lesson at the expense of one young lady when she was making the final preparations for her recital. With the recital date just around the corner the regular accompanist was called in. But he hadn't played more than two bars, when I saw my student looking wildly at me across the studio. He wasn't playing the piece right! But of course he was, he was playing it exactly as it was written. I was the one who had confused her by giving the piece a bit of myself, and it was a thoroughly disconcerting experience for her to relearn her work.

Here's another category of inadvertent "contribution" to the learning process, with a reverse spin: One morning I was working with a student and accompanist and I heard them both hit a particular phrase that I knew was incorrect — both in the music and in the lyric. I interrupted them: "That's wrong," I told them. They looked confused, so I walked across the studio to point out the error. Looking at the music, I was dumbstruck. Here was a piece of Schubert, or Loewe, or Fauré, that I had sung perhaps three hundred times in the last decade. And every single time I'd sung it incorrectly — and now I was about to pass that same error along to a new generation!

After that, as you can imagine, if I heard an error sung or played, I would sidle on over to the keyboard and peek over the pianist's shoulder before I'd open my mouth. I mentioned this incident to John Wustman (currently Pavarotti's accompanist and a pianist who has accompanied all the greats of his generation at one time or another). He made me feel better when he told me that every one of them had their own set of errors or "improvements" in any number of librettos and scores. Savvy accompanists and conductors usually work around these individualities rather than attempt to straighten things out.

One highlight of my early days at the University of Illinois was our student production of *Porgy and Bess*. I've done concert versions since, but our 1976 presentation, followed by a 1977 tour to the festival at Lake George, New York, was the last time I did the role in costume, on my knees.

It had not yet been done at the Metropolitan Opera — that fully staged operatic event didn't take place until 1985. And it had but rarely been done anywhere. I prevailed on the Heyward and Gershwin estates to get the rights, lined up the head of the university's theater department David Lloyd as director, and got the casting and rehearsal process started before I left with Leonard Bernstein for the Bicentennial tour.

When I got back the rehearsals were in progress, and we had the help of the entire university to pull it off — Paul Vermel's orchestra, Robert Ray's chorus, Pat Knowles's dance department, costumes from the theater department. We had the benefit of my experience, most recently in the Vienna version, and did it without Ella Gerber's contributions.

It was a big success, in Champaign and in Lake George. To this day, those who saw it will swear that it was done with full scenery. In fact, though we had all the costumery of Catfish Row, it was performed on a starkly functional set of platforms; the scenery and even many props were the product of pantomime and audience imagination.

The most important consequence of our production, I believe, is that it opened up the opera's availability to other colleges and universities. The rights had always been tricky, but the success of our production at Illinois, I'm told, reassured the Heyward and Gershwin estates that their interests wouldn't suffer. Since 1976 there have been a number of college productions across the U.S.

From the outset, the University of Illinois meant more to me than the sum of its educational parts. In a very real sense I'd come full circle to the bosom of an extended family. To this day, the community of Champaign has become to me in my retirement what Rochester was to me as a student. And once again, as in Rochester, the Warfield house is the center of a lively and diverse family life.

I'm not sure when my "Uncle Bill" persona made the transfer from Vienna to Champaign — I think it was the result of the publicity written at the time I started at the University. In any case, the same natural process was operating in both places. In 1976 there were fewer African-American students going to school at the University of Illinois, and fewer African-American professors teaching them, than there are today. I was one of the first black professors in the School of Music, and the first black students to earn their doctorates in voice were students of mine. So there was an ethnic attractor involved.

But beyond that, for students away from home for the first time, I think I must have been comparatively hospitable. The real world of the performing arts, which I was bringing with me onto the campus, is an open, socially fluid environment; and I've never been one to stand on ceremony anyway. Especially in those early days I must have appeared much more approachable than the average professor. And especially for black students, who had never been so far away from their brothers and sisters (and who were starved for home cooking), my place became a home away from home.

Today the crowd is racially mixed, boys and girls from everywhere, a number of them not even associated with the School of Music.

As in Vienna, from the beginning this home life centered around the kitchen stove. My expertise and enjoyment of preparing meals for large numbers of hungry youngsters was put to good use.

Whoever first called me "Uncle Bill," it soon became my alias around the house. There was never any suggestion of insufficient decorum — I was still Professor Warfield in the classroom. In the matter of propriety in forms of address, there was an even subtler distinction, self-enforced by my students. One day at the beginning of the term, one of the new students darted into the kitchen to ask me for something, and began his sentence, "Bill, would it be all right —"

I don't remember what he was asking; I nodded and went on with my cooking, and then perked up when I suddenly realized I was listening to a silence from the front room. I eavesdropped and heard the new boy being quietly lectured. "Look," he was told by one of the regulars. "When you're his guest here, you may call him 'Uncle Bill.' If you choose, you may call him 'Professor Warfield.' But he is *never* 'Bill.'"

They have proven to be self-organized in other ways as well. Somehow they coalesce in work groups whenever the lawn needs cutting or there's shopping to be done. I'm never without some kind of help for all those daily and weekly tasks, and yet it's as loosely informal as if we were indeed an extended family. They've always been sensitive to reasonable limits on my time, too. I've never had to clear everyone out when I needed the rest of the evening to myself. After a meal, and the kitchen chores that follow, they tend to move on to their other activities — some to the library, some to the bars — and no one ever needs an extra hint.

I flourished in the university environment, moving on to chair the voice department, expanding my teaching schedule, even as I continued to give performances across the country. Since my formal retirement in 1990 I've continued as a visiting professor within the Illinois university system, most recently at Eastern Illinois. And I've continued to appear on stage.

In the months that this book was in preparation, for example: In January 1991 I was scheduled to do *Lincoln Portrait* in

Tuscaloosa, Alabama; to narrate *New Morning for the World* in Springfield, Illinois; and then to tape classical and traditional songs for Chicago television.

In February I repeated *Lincoln Portrait* in three different cities, performed with the Pro Musica in Columbus, Indiana, and appeared as guest soloist in Orlando, Florida.

In March I sang at the Chicago Theater, did a *Messiah* for the United Methodist Church in Chicago (an annual tradition for me), and met with a planning conference for the new black American composers symposium scheduled for 1992.

In April I went to New York to participate in the memorial concert for Aaron Copland at Alice Tully Hall in Lincoln Center, I performed at Penn State, at Fermilab in Batavia, Illinois, at Bowling Green, Kentucky, and with the Evansville, Indiana, Symphony. I narrated a jazz version of *Porgy and Bess* with the James Cullen Jazz Band, and a *Peter and the Wolf* in Danville, Illinois. In May I opened the new steamboat casino for the state of Iowa, performed lieder, opera, oratorio, and *Porgy* excerpts in joint recital with Robert McFerrin in St. Louis, did my duties as a Lyric Opera Center board member and as a judge at the May Whittaker Vocal Competition at the Music Educators National Convention, chaired the National Music Council Awards luncheon, and performed as guest soloist at Oak Brook, Illinois.

And so forth . . . The schedule continues all the way into 1993 — performances, conferences, competitions — and the way things are going, I'm sometimes tempted to call this book "Volume I". I suppose that would be pushing my luck, but where there's music, there's life, and where there's life, there's hope, and I'm hopeful enough to admit that I'm still looking forward to a lot of both.

* * * *

I'm looking backward too, and taking stock. Recalling these life memories, and sharing them with you, has been in itself one of the memorable experiences of my career.

Over and over again, as I review the events of my life, I'm reminded that there have been recurring themes subtly directing my course — like waves that rise and fall but always push me forward. Very early in my career I learned to trust that these waves wouldn't steer me wrong. In little ways (the sudden appearance of a tax refund I'd forgotten about) as well as the big ways (my good fortune in making connections with Larney, and later with Walter Carr) I developed a friendly sense of the cosmos. The world was not inherently evil and filled with malice; rather, it was essentially beneficent and would reward good with good.

That is not to say that I expected all things to come my way. I consider myself very lucky, but "luck" is more than chance: It's preparation plus opportunity. And sometimes you have to go out of your way to make the opportunity happen as my father did, when he and my mother wrenched their family out of economic and educational stagnation and gave them a new life in Rochester.

One of the significant themes of my life has been the importance of family. When my parents created that environment for me, they provided a strong spiritual foundation that gave me the courage to expose myself to challenge and take chances. Beginning with that loving circle at home, the theme of family has remained a constant ever since. Early on, I learned that a family is a network of special relationships, mutual dependencies, and varying degrees of love — the whole range, from love of your puppy to love of your parents.

And I also learned that families can take all kinds of forms. I found a family in the theater companies and the film crews I worked with, and each time that family feeling did much to foster my artistic development. Some of the richest moments of my life were among my Vienna family that congregated in my flat on Neustift Gasse. I found a family even at Camp Ritchie, and what could have been a sterile ordeal was in fact a time of fertile growth.

I found a family in my campus life — first as a student and now as a professor. School has always meant more than education to me, as important as education is. School has also meant fellowship, social learning, and enlightened opportunities for real creativity. Just as I would have been culturally impoverished were it not for the arts-in-education that we kids took for granted, I would have been socially impoverished were it not for the extended family of campus life.

And of course there's my natural family — my brothers and their wives and children, my cousins and uncles and aunts, and all those folks who come together every Christmastime in Rochester to celebrate our lives together: Aunt Lillie; Aunt Ida Mae; brothers Robert, Vern, and Thaddeus, with their families; and my deceased brother Murphy's family, headed now by his widow Ernestine.

There's something almost miraculous in the fact that you can make a family out of the barest ingredients. Single parents create that same holy glow of family, even in hardship conditions all the time. Even if you didn't grow up in a "perfect" family, you never forfeit the right to create your own later. I believe that anyone who is fortunate, as I was, to be raised in the bosom of a loving family is going to have a life long advantage. "Luck" will tend to come his way.

There's another theme that has given shape to my life, and that's improvisation. For someone who had a traditional family upbringing and a solid education in a standard curriculum, I have spent a remarkable amount of my time inventing myself and my career.

That's because there was no definite career field for me, at any point along the way. Thank God for my heroes, people who, like me, also had to invent themselves professionally, people like Roland Hayes and Marian Anderson. Because there wasn't a definite course for a black classical singer to follow, I never had a groove to fall into. Which is another way of saying I was never afraid to try anything, on the grounds that it might be a distraction from my "true" course. My course wasn't true. In the long run, that may have been a blessing; otherwise I certainly would never have enjoyed the adventures I did.

Opera wasn't ready for me, or any black male. Hollywood was still wrestling with its own soul, and not ready to open up to African-American themes. Broadway, and the theater in general, was still struggling with the same issues. As I progressed along my career ladder I found a few rungs missing, and sometimes had to look for a foothold in the most improbable places.

But it never occured to me to give up. What kept me going, I now realize, was that even though I often had no clear idea of how to get there, I always had a clear idea of where I was ultimately headed. I had the example of my heroes: they had proved it could be done. And I had the incentive of my art: I always knew that beyond the nightclubs and the films and the Broadway shows, my destiny lay in the sublime realm of classical music. So I usually found those other footholds where the rungs were missing — and I learned how to jump!

In that way, a high school competition became a college scholarship, in a field which showed little practical promise. Then a wartime military posting became an education in pop music and a whole new set of show-biz contacts. That led to an entire year of theater touring across the country and to more contacts, more education. My G.I. Bill paid for classical training with some of the accomplished masters, while my nightclubbing led to a Town Hall debut. Then I pirouetted from an Australian tour into a big film contract . . . and so on. Giving up the security of earning my master's degree, as it turned out, ultimately did more for my teaching career than if I'd passed up the theater tour and finished my studies. At any point it would have been difficult to explain how I was advancing my career — but at every point I was.

That reveals yet another recurring theme: the importance of the interconnections in the traditions of the arts. In a time of accelerating change and universal innovation, it's important to remember that some traditions have been unbroken from the time of their origins. The worlds of opera and ballet, for example, can trace their entire professional development back through just a few generations; we can even list the individuals responsible for passing the tradition along, one to another.

In classical music the time line stretches further back; but it's still possible to name the people, from one era to the next, who overlapped and worked directly with the generation that followed, and passed the heritage one step further. For that reason, there is no clear separation between the arts as performance and the arts in education. A caring artist is always looking for an opportunity to pass it on to those who are coming along after. Teaching becomes a form of repaying the debt to your tradition.

That's one of the remarkable qualities of great art, and what makes it significant beyond the applause of its audiences: that it's passed on directly, from an elderly master to an eager young novice, from hand to hand, voice to voice, heart to heart. No mass production in this business. It's a direct laying-on of hands, a musical version of apostolic succession.

One set of artistic traditions that was robbed of its history by the inhuman institution of slavery, but which was just as dependent — even more so — on direct transmission from one artist to another. The heritage of African-American music, which has completely transformed the popular culture in my own lifetime (and in an electronic age is becoming ever more vibrant in its influences at every level), can be traced through individuals only a few generations back. But musicologists can establish its roots in the oldest traditions. More importantly, the cultural vitality and energy of this culture has infused the European musical heritage with rich new qualities, and has created contemporary forms that can be dazzling.

By performing the music of both traditions, and by performing music which is a fusion of the two, I have experienced in music what philosophers and preachers sometimes speak of in hushed tones: a reverence for the ultimate harmonies of the family of humankind.

And that leads me to the greatest theme I find returning again and again in the currents of my life, one that ties all the others together. That's the significance of faith in my life.

I don't intend to preach, because I have no way of presuming that my faith is better than the next person's. But I can testify that my faith has led me through the valley of the shadow of death, and across chasms too wide to walk — where a leap of faith was necessary to get me to the other side.

I say this not because without faith I'd be without hope. Rather, because without faith I'd be without purpose. It's that awareness of purpose that has gotten me through the hard times. The miracle is that it has even made those hard times, in retrospect, seem like "the good old days." It is my good fortune to be able to pay this homage to my family and friends, my art, my heritage, and my faith — all the treasures that I will always take with me, wherever the road may lead.